ARCTIC PREDATOR

ARCTIC
PREDATOR

The Crimes of Edward Horne
Against Children in Canada's North

KATHLEEN LIPPA

DUNDURN
PRESS

Publisher: Meghan Macdonald | Acquiring editor: Julia Kim & Kwame Scott Fraser |
Editor: Kwame Scott Fraser
Cover designer: Laura Boyle
Cover image: classroom: istock/skynesher ice: Unsplash/ModCatShop
Map: Julie Witmer

Library and Archives Canada Cataloguing in Publication

Title: Arctic predator : the crimes of Edward Horne against children in Canada's North / Kathleen Lippa.
Names: Lippa, Kathleen, author.
Description: Includes bibliographical references and index.
Identifiers: Canadiana (print) 20240474074 | Canadiana (ebook) 20240481089 | ISBN 9781459754805 (softcover) | ISBN 9781459754812 (PDF) | ISBN 9781459754829 (EPUB)
Subjects: LCSH: Horne, Edward (Teacher) | LCSH: Inuit children—Crimes against—Northwest Territories. | LCSH: Child sexual abuse by teachers—Northwest Territories. | LCSH: Generational trauma—Northwest Territories. | LCSH: Child molesters—Northwest Territories—Biography.
Classification: LCC HV6570.4.C3 L56 2025 | DDC 362.76089/971207192—dc23

We acknowledge the support of the Canada Council for the Arts and the Ontario Arts Council for our publishing program. We also acknowledge the financial support of the Government of Ontario, through the Ontario Book Publishing Tax Credit and Ontario Creates, and the Government of Canada.

Care has been taken to trace the ownership of copyright material used in this book. The author and the publisher welcome any information enabling them to rectify any references or credits in subsequent editions.

The publisher is not responsible for websites or their content unless they are owned by the publisher.

Printed and bound in Canada.

Dundurn Press
1382 Queen Street East
Toronto, Ontario, Canada M4L 1C9
dundurn.com, @dundurnpress

For the children of the North

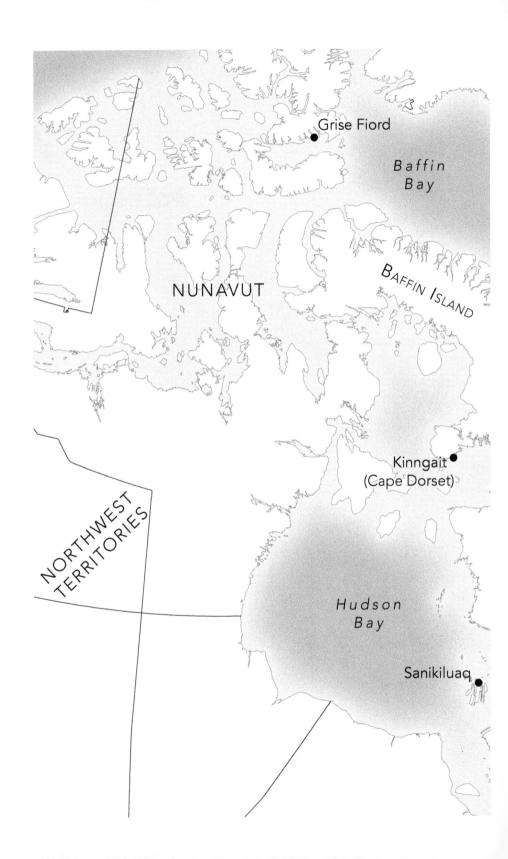

Grise Fiord

*Baffin
Bay*

B<small>AFFIN</small> I<small>SLAND</small>

NUNAVUT

Kinngait
(Cape Dorset)

NORTHWEST
TERRITORIES

*Hudson
Bay*

Sanikiluaq

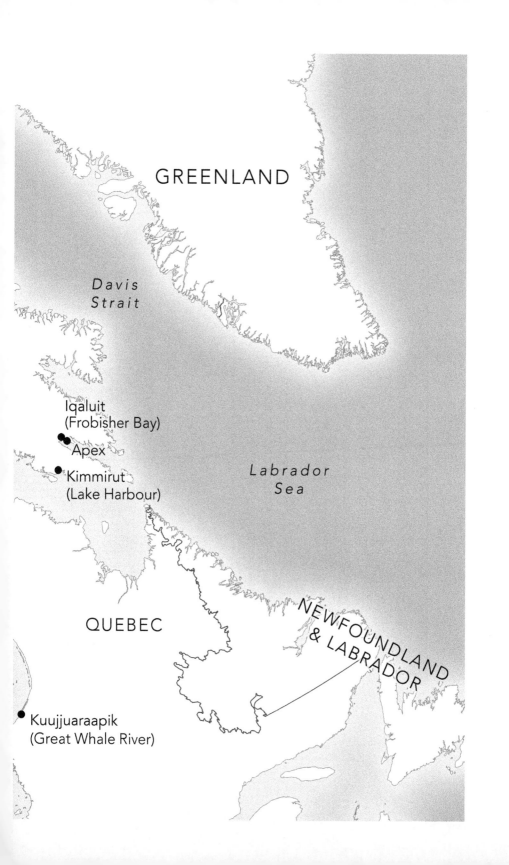

GREENLAND

*Davis
Strait*

Iqaluit
(Frobisher Bay)

Apex

Kimmirut
(Lake Harbour)

*Labrador
Sea*

QUEBEC

NEWFOUNDLAND
& LABRADOR

Kuujjuaraapik
(Great Whale River)

Contents

Cape Dorset, January 23, 2003

A FIRE RAGED IN THE METAL DUMP, YET NO SIRENS BLARED. Townsfolk in sealskin boots and women in fur-lined parkas with babies on their backs made their way up the hill to where firefighters had purposely set one of the community's old school buildings ablaze.

Four hundred people, roughly a third of the community's population, huddled near the flames, a reprieve from the cold in the -20°C temperature. Some people in the crowd were crying. Others picked up rocks and hurled them into the flames, yelling at the disintegrating structure as if it were the living embodiment of the name they shouted — Ed Horne.

Twenty years was a long time to live with the anger. Horne had left their community in 1983, but the emotions his name engendered were still raw.

As the schoolhouse and its secrets burned that night, a young reporter named Christine Kay was at her desk in Iqaluit working the phones. She called hamlet offices in the territory each week, hearing news and gossip that could be spun into features for her newspaper. This was the best a reporter with no travel budget could do. To actually visit a community beyond Iqaluit required an expensive plane ride. The phone was an economical way in. Christine was curious about the fire she was hearing about in Cape Dorset, but she could eke out only a small story for *News/North*, which appeared on February 3. The headline was "Piece of Past Up in Flames." She reported that the burning was part of Cape Dorset's settlement in a civil lawsuit against the governments of Nunavut and the Northwest Territories. The small structure, one of two portable units — free-standing classrooms not attached to the main school — was no longer in use. A year before this symbolic act was carried out, a multimillion-dollar settlement had been made between the two territorial governments, who were the employers of Ed Horne, and dozens of young men — once boys — who had been sexually abused by the disgraced teacher.

Tuugaaq*[a] initially attended the burning but left before the building was razed to the ground.

"I did see people throwing rocks, but I wasn't compelled to do anything because that wasn't where I had the experience with Ed Horne. The older one where we first encountered him is still standing," he said, many years later, explaining that a construction company was currently using that building. "There were two portable schools. The one that was burned down was from later, it was for the younger guys. To me it was like, Why don't they burn the one where it all started?"

---

a. True names of Ed Horne victims are protected by a publication ban. Pseudonyms are indicated by asterisks and do not in any way resemble true names of Ed Horne victims.

Introduction

THERE ARE PHOTOGRAPHS CRUCIAL TO THIS STORY THAT I HAVE never seen. I don't know where they are, or if they still exist. They were developed from a roll of film discovered inside an old school piano in an Arctic community in 1985.

No one should ever see these images. But I wanted to verify their existence because they led directly to the arrest of one of Canada's worst criminals — Edward Thornton Horne.

The photos were reportedly of boys in Thailand, or the Philippines, or Greenland, or the very community in which the film was found. The police officer who first saw the images knew at once that the photographer was a pedophile.

The discovery of the images coincided with an investigation by social workers into sexual abuse involving schoolchildren. No one realized at the time that the teacher and principal of the school, Mr. Horne, abused boys in the community — and that there were victims in other communities who'd been suffering in silence since the early 1970s.

• • •

Iqaluit, Nunavut — I sat in a newspaper office inside the Tumiit Plaza, a building located at the city's "four corners," an iconic spot in the Eastern Arctic where a restaurant called the Kamotiq looked very much like a papier mâché *iglu* when I first saw it.

I didn't know much about "the East," as that part of the North was called. It was May of 2003, and I had just arrived in Iqaluit from Yellowknife to write for *Nunavut News/North*, a newspaper owned by the visionary entrepreneur and newspaper man Jack "Sig" Sigvaldason. The paper in Iqaluit was just one in a chain of papers Sig owned that had reporters covering the North from Inuvik through Yellowknife, Hay River, Rankin Inlet, and Iqaluit. The workload was daunting — we were required to submit at least a dozen stories and photos to head office in Yellowknife for publication every week. We were a people-focused paper, often meaning soft, feel-good stories, but stories that were nonetheless important to people living in the North. *Nunatsiaq News*, our competition, was more centred on what I called "government stories" that critically analyzed the new Nunavut government and the organizations created to serve Inuit.

I was outside most days, stopping people in the street and asking them questions for our weekly "Street Beat" feature that included the person's photo, which I took with my camera. Right from the beginning of my time in Nunavut, locals would speak to me in Inuktitut, assuming I was Inuit, or "half." Being five foot three, with dark hair and facial features inherited from my father's side (long-ago ancestors from the Silk Road made their way to Abruzzo, Italy, where my father was born) gave me a certain look that over the years has appeared to some people to be Indigenous. In Nunavut, my look made me approachable, and this attribute would work to my advantage later, when I arrived in small communities to ask people delicate questions.

My co-worker at *News/North* was Christine Kay, the journalist whose story about the burning school portable in Cape Dorset had caught my attention and would eventually change my life. We wrote widely about Nunavut, from hockey games to housing woes. Nothing ever took hold of me the way the Ed Horne story did.

The crime beat on a newspaper generally did not interest me. I'd won a national award for arts reporting at my first full-time newspaper job in St.

John's, Newfoundland, and when I headed North, I looked forward to all the Inuit art stories I would write. I planned to go to Cape Dorset as soon as possible to report on the carvings and prints being produced there. But the article Kay had written about the people of Cape Dorset watching an old school building burn in a sort of cleansing ceremony took hold of me. Maybe the story reminded me of the Mount Cashel scandal in St. John's, where I grew up. Kay's story mentioned a schoolteacher whose abuse of boys had occurred inside the portable building the people of Dorset burned. Feeling that this was a major story Canadians should know about, I spent the next several years trying to grasp the magnitude of Ed Horne's crimes in Cape Dorset — and elsewhere.

· · ·

During my first year in Iqaluit, a police officer sat down at a table near me in a popular bar called the Chartroom Lounge and, breathing out a big sigh, said, "Just got back from Kimmirut. Angry little town, full of Horne victims." There was a sense that local people knew what "Horne victims" meant. I didn't then. (I would later visit Kimmirut several times. While there are some angry men there, some of whom were abused by Horne, for the most part I encountered generous, kind folks living in a breathtaking Arctic community of about four hundred people.)

I heard things about Horne beyond the crimes that drew me in. He was a brilliant teacher. He spoke many languages, including Inuktitut. He married an Inuk. He had children, one of whom became a police officer. He was Indigenous himself — Mohawk. He had friends in the highest offices in education and travelled the world extensively on his time off.

Everywhere I travelled in the North in my early years there, I heard tragic stories about men who'd been sexually abused by Horne when they were kids. Many suicides of males in the South Baffin region of the newly created territory of Nunavut were blamed on him. And over time Horne had become mythologized. The name Ed Horne alone conjured up the image of a monster hiding inside his role as a teacher. But when I started researching the story, I realized no one really knew what happened at all. The actual scale of the crimes was unknown. Newspaper articles that ever mentioned a Horne criminal case (including one I wrote once) were not in-depth and contained errors. Files relevant to Horne were not easy to access. Only victims knew what happened. And even then, there was a haunting silence — those men, once boys, were desperate to forget what Horne had done to them.

The criminal himself was a mystery. No journalist had ever managed to get more than a few words out of him.[1] Where was he? What happened to him? Was he a free man? No one knew.

Horne's crimes were never covered extensively in any media, except in superficial reports in the northern Canadian press — this, despite the fact he faced two court cases and served two prison sentences. There was also a major civil case that resulted in millions of dollars in compensation for his victims. Another criminal case involving four men and another civil case would follow.

I knew the story needed to be told — for the record, for history, and for the victims to have a sense of closure — even for children to understand their fathers a little better. I also knew that given the shocking subject matter, delving deeply into the Horne story might destroy me emotionally. After conducting interviews and gathering preliminary information, I put the Horne story aside for several years.

But the voices of friends in the North who first told me about the crimes stayed with me. I picked up the story again when I discovered an article in *Inuit Art Quarterly* about a Cape Dorset artist who had drawn images of Horne abuse.[2] With the help of the co-op manager in Cape Dorset, I contacted the artist by phone in 2020. The completion of this book is due in large part to the courage of that artist and of many other people in Cape Dorset, Kimmirut, Sanikiluaq, Iqaluit, and Apex who wanted this story told, and wanted me to tell it.

All quotes and information in this book come directly from interviews I conducted, northern media reports, and from court records, some of which were made available to me through an unsealing order. I have done face-to-face interviews with victims and their relatives. I interviewed police and judges, lawyers and bureaucrats, including former education department officials who had never spoken to a journalist about the Horne case. In fact, most of the interviews were with people who had never spoken to a journalist about the story before, including Ed Horne himself.

. . .

June 14, 2022 — Ed Horne appeared to be asleep when I arrived at the coffee shop at Yonge and Wellesley, in Toronto. I'd wanted to meet him for many years, and finally I was able to do it after numerous chats over Facebook Messenger. (A source alerted me to Horne's presence on Facebook, and I first contacted him via Messenger.) The book was mostly completed by the time I met him. This was mainly a courtesy meeting — a meeting to show him that I was real and I meant business.

He was sitting alone at a table for two — holding his cellphone as it rested in his lap. I knew it was him as soon as I walked in. I'd seen photos of him as a teenager in newspaper clippings from British Columbia, where he grew up. I'd seen him in person once, in May 2005, in an Iqaluit courtroom, head bowed, facing new criminal sex charges. This man before me was 78 years old, wearing light-coloured denim jeans, a fluorescent green-yellow vest with a couple of rainbow pins on it that stated a solidarity with the Pride movement, and a weathered baseball cap.

He came across as nonthreatening. Perhaps it was his stooped back or his somewhat shy demeanour. I was aware Horne suffered from serious hearing loss, so I made a point of speaking clearly and at a decent volume. He once had a deep, authoritative voice, but the tone was now diminished. He made eye contact when we talked — a departure from his usual style throughout his life of not looking directly at people. I didn't think I'd be able to eat or drink a coffee with him given all I knew about his disgusting crimes, but much to my surprise I was comfortable sitting at a very small table with him for over an hour. The fact that Horne didn't give off an overpowering creepiness — at least not to me that day — was notable. Perhaps, I thought afterward, it is this ability he has to create such feelings of normalcy that enabled him to abuse so many children and get away with it for so long.

. . .

I have thought deeply since meeting Horne about why he agreed to be interviewed for this book. I have concluded that he has a desire to be known. He wanted to be an actor in his youth. He still wishes he could act or direct plays. Ultimately, he wants some sort of connection to the North, a place that is close to his heart to this day, in spite of his heinous crimes there. In many ways I represented a northern connection. He asked me about people in the North we both know. Unmistakably, he was most animated when he was talking about teaching in the North.

. . .

From his arrival in the Eastern Arctic in 1971 until his arrest in 1985, Edward Horne's predations on boys would leave a trail of destruction in Canada's North. This book is the first full examination of what happened — the crimes, the mistakes, the lies, and the fallout from the abuse.

There have been other outsiders who lived and worked in Canada's North and abused northern children. A social worker named Kevin Clarke Amyot molested boys in Sanikiluaq in the years 1984–86; seven men alleged they were sexually abused by teacher James MacDiarmid in Pond Inlet in 1969, a tragic situation the anthropologist Hugh Brody later wrote about in his highly regarded book *The People's Land* (without naming MacDiarmid). And Maurice Cloughley was a schoolteacher, world traveller, and artist who abused girls in remote Inuit communities between 1974 and 1979. Following his 1996 trial, where he pleaded guilty to nine charges, he was sentenced to ten years in prison for sexual assaults, forced sexual contact, and forcing students to pose nude for photographs. But in the memories of northerners, Horne has remained the worst of them all, having attained mythical status because of the number of communities affected, rumours about how many victims there were, the enormous compensation payouts victims later received, and Horne's reported professional achievements while he lived in the North.

Sexual abuse of the vulnerable exists to some extent in all societies, and Inuit society is no exception. With the breakdown in traditional roles created by the movement from traditional camps into organized communities, sexual abuse among Inuit also increased without the participation of outsiders.

It is not known precisely how many boys Horne molested, but there is enough evidence to make the claim that his crimes embody one of the worst cases of institutionalized sexual abuse perpetrated by one man in Canadian history.

· · ·

In the 1950s and '60s, most Inuit had moved from the traditional camps where their ancestors had lived into communities that had generally grown up around longstanding trading posts. By the 1970s, that transition was largely complete. Schools and formal education were new to most Inuit in the Baffin Region at the time. But parents quickly became aware that the ability to speak English was just as necessary to their children's survival as hunting and fishing skills. As a result, teachers emerged as an important bridge from the intense world of survival to a world where any kind of job or lifestyle was potentially within reach. Trust in the schoolteacher as the key to that progress was absolute.

The 1970s were an exciting period in the history of the Northwest Territories (N.W.T.). During the previous decade, the administration of the western part of the territory — its government — had moved north from far-off Ottawa to Yellowknife, north of the 60th parallel — often considered the demarcation of the true "North" — on the shores of Great Slave Lake. In 1970, control over the Eastern Arctic also shifted to Yellowknife. Political change was in the air. The Inuit had begun to organize and would shortly begin the research and lobbying that would lead, some years later, to a split in the vast northern territory and the creation of Nunavut, a largely Inuit jurisdiction in the east. The Baffin Region — an administrative area dominated by Baffin Island itself — was the easternmost part of the N.W.T.

In 1973, Inuit Tapirisat of Canada began a study of Inuit land use and occupancy, which would demonstrate the extent of Inuit aboriginal title in the Arctic. By 1976, Inuit Tapirisat was proposing the creation of a separate Nunavut territory as part of a comprehensive settlement of Inuit land claims in the N.W.T. Heady times dominated by big issues draw the offbeat and the eccentric, and they were arriving in droves in the new North, many armed with teaching certificates or law degrees.

Ed Horne was one of those who came as a teacher. Settling the Nunavut land claim, redrawing the boundaries for a new electoral constituency to give Inuit their own voice in the federal parliament, and then drawing another boundary to set the parameters of a new territory and setting the groundwork for that territory — all this was unfolding during the Ed Horne era. The officials in charge of these changes had a lot on their minds. A dedicated teacher who learned Inuktitut and spent all his free time with students was to be praised, not questioned.

The education model, based initially on a southern non-Indigenous curriculum imported from Alberta and blatantly geared to the assimilation of young Inuit into non-Inuit society, was ever-so-slowly changing as Inuit became involved in its development. The administration, ever cautious, encouraged the formation of local education committees. In their early days they were advisory in nature, busying themselves with administering cocoa and vitamin biscuit programs, or the cultural inclusion programs in which Elders came into the school periodically to recount legends and traditional stories. But occasionally the committees took an interest in the curriculum itself. Over time, pedagogical common sense dictated that the focus could not remain exclusively on the teaching of English and that the use of the Inuktitut language had to become an integral part of school life. The training of Inuit teachers and the use of Indigenous knowledge to design and deliver the curriculum became a goal. In such an environment, no one thought it strange when Ed Horne, who married an Inuk in the first northern community in which he taught, and who learned to understand Inuktitut, had his classroom full of boys in the evenings, even after a full day of regular teaching duties. If anything, he was greatly admired for having such dedication to the children and such loyalty from them in those changing times.

Some former education officials still laud Horne's impressive achievement in designing computer fonts in syllabics — the unique writing system used by most Inuit in Nunavut and in northern Quebec — for early personal computers, and for his supposed work in translating certain portions of the

Bible into Inuktitut. Stories like these, coupled with the shock of his crimes, created the myth of Ed Horne.

. . .

Throughout this book, I use the word "victim" when describing the men who were once vulnerable children in the midst of Edward Horne. My use of the word victim, rather than survivor, is intentional. The men who spoke to me, and whose testimony appears in this book, were victims of Horne's predations, and this book is a journalistic examination of what occurred. The men are survivors today, but they were victims when the crimes were being committed. I wrote the story with that in mind.

Clarity is needed for the names of the communities in this story, and for some of the terminology used.

The Belcher Islands are today home of Sanikiluaq — the name of the only permanent community in the island group, which was part of the administrative Keewatin Region; only much later was it transferred to the Baffin Region. Great Whale River, in northern Quebec, is now called Kuujjuaraapik. The Inuit-occupied area of northern Quebec is now generally referred to as Nunavik.

Cape Dorset has been called Kinngait ("mountains") since 2020. Grise Fiord is still officially Grise Fiord, the most northern community in Canada, although Inuit call it Aujuittuq ("the place that never thaws"). Lake Harbour changed its name to Kimmirut ("resembles a heel") in 1996. Apex is still Apex, a satellite community of Iqaluit ("place of many fish"), which was called Frobisher Bay until 1987. In this book, I use the name in use at the time of the events until approximately the time of any name change.

The territory of Nunavut, formed by dividing the N.W.T. in two, came into being officially on April 1, 1999, and includes all the communities central to this book, except Great Whale River.

Inuit is a plural noun referring to the people once known as Eskimos; the singular form is Inuk. Inuktitut or Inuktut is the language of Inuit, still very much alive and thriving today in Nunavut. The Inuktitut word *qallunaat* is used in the book to refer to non-Inuit (singular is *qallunaaq*).

There are sections in this book where some of the sexual attacks perpetrated by Edward Horne on Inuit children are described. True names of victims are protected by a publication ban. I have used pseudonyms and by combining victims' stories and changing personal details have obscured the identities of victims whose voices you hear in this story. A pseudonym does not in any way correspond with the real person's name. At the first use of each pseudonym, I have marked the name with an asterisk.

PART ONE

Frobisher Bay, October 1985

BERT ROSE LIKED TO BE THE FIRST TO KNOW EVERYTHING THAT was going on in town, but this time it would be different. He remembers he was sitting in his living room after supper on October 12, enjoying a cup of coffee, when he got the phone call. His boss, Ken MacRury, regional director of the government of the N.W.T. for the Baffin Region, was on the line telling him that Ed Horne had been arrested for child molestation, and that police officers would be arriving any minute to serve Rose with a search warrant for the primary school in Apex — a village just a few kilometres south of Frobisher Bay where Horne taught and also lived with his wife and their three small boys. Like many jurisdictions, the N.W.T. did not have its own police force, and so the officers were members of the storied Royal Canadian Mounted Police (RCMP).[1]

Two officers were soon at the Roses' door. Bert's wife, Joanne, heard their voices on the porch and came out to see what they wanted with her husband. She saw him scanning a search warrant related to Horne, his old friend. Thinking about that night years later, Joanne said that she had always considered Horne a strange man, but so were lots of people who came to the North to work. The Arctic was full of characters, people who were "different" from your average Canadian or, at least, people who got different as each dark winter progressed. Horne definitely fit into that category in Joanne's mind. And it wasn't even winter yet.

Whenever Horne visited the Roses for coffee, it was teacher talk between Bert and Ed. Often Horne would be abuzz about some new piece of technology he'd discovered, like the large disc music player he'd recently purchased. If you saw him on the street, sometimes he'd be wearing headphones and would just walk right past you, probably absorbed in a new language he was learning.

Horne had been around the North for a long time and because of his language skills, particularly the work he'd done promoting Inuktitut use in the classroom, was one of the most respected teachers in the territory. Now he was charged with sexually assaulting boys. And there was more: the police told Rose that they had reason to believe there were commercially produced pornographic videotapes hidden in the school in Apex, specifically VHS tapes of *Debbie Does Dallas* and *Deep Throat*.

Bert was stunned. As the officers headed out to their vehicle that October night, he stood on his porch for a moment wondering, *How could this be?*

Joanne was equally dismayed. "I have a pretty good radar for people," she remembered thinking at the time. "How could I have been so wrong?"

Shortly before Horne's arrest, Bert Rose, whose career in education had by then spanned twenty years, had accepted a substantial new position as superintendent of education for the Baffin Region within the territorial government. The operation of schools was among his responsibilities. Rose had plenty of issues to worry about in several areas, including a crooked government employee — whom he later fired — who had formed an illegal partnership to run a catering service, which the employee, conveniently, was also responsible for supervising at the student residence connected to the high school. That was headache enough. The last person Rose thought would be causing trouble on his watch was the trusted Ed Horne.

With the couple's two children, Tony and Tina, off playing quietly in their bedrooms, Bert looked calmly at Joanne, then threw a jacket on — no need for a parka since the temperature was just slightly below zero that night — and headed outside to his vehicle, following the police to Apex through gently falling snow.

Apex had an edge-of-the-world feel to it as Rose's vehicle rumbled down the hill into the village that night. The great expanse of Frobisher Bay stretched dramatically out toward the Atlantic Ocean, the gloom of the grey sky offset by the colour of the houses dotting the landscape.

Nanook School had always been thought of as such a joyful place, the ideal small community school. It was one of the little "Butler" buildings — a pre-engineered metal structure popular in the North in the 1950s — in the community; it was historically significant as the first school built in Apex. But now it was shrouded in intrigue as the police officers and Bert Rose pulled up in front. *What could be at the school?* Rose thought. Was Ed Horne, the North's star teacher, really a child molester?

There were four classrooms in the school plus a gym area, workrooms for teachers, and stock and supply rooms. Nanook also had false ceilings that the police searched extensively for evidence linking Horne to the child abuse they were investigating.

The next stop was Horne's house, located almost next to the school. The house was one half of the old nursing station, another historic building that had been renovated into a duplex. Other officers had already arrested Ed Horne there and hauled him away to a police holding cell. Now a team of officers was combing through rooms in the house. When Rose walked in, he saw Jeannie, Horne's Inuit wife, sitting alone on the living room sofa. Rose knew at least one of the Hornes' three boys was also in the house.

Any attempt at conversation with Jeannie was awkward at the best of times. She was hampered by a serious hearing impairment and would generally communicate only in Inuktitut, a language Rose didn't speak. The sound of police pulling open drawers and sifting through them in the bedroom down the hall broke the chilly silence. Rose remembered thinking, *I wonder what will happen to Jeannie and the boys?* At the time, the couple's three children were all under the age of seven. In the end, no conversation took place. The strained silence dragged on until midnight, when police were finally ready to leave. Rose was eager to speak to Horne, even though it would be through the bars of a jail cell. With a subtle nod to Jeannie, he left with the officers and headed to RCMP headquarters where Horne was being held for the night.

A guard was standing next to a little wooden desk, almost like a teacher's small desk, when Rose entered the detachment. To the left, there was a steel door where the "drunk tank" was — a big, nine-by-nine concrete room. Across a three-foot space, there was a door on the left and a door on the right and corridors that led to the cells. Each cell was separated from the adjoining one by a brick wall, painted grey. Each cell had two metal bunks, each with a thin mattress. Horne was locked inside a cell.

"So, we've got these bars between us," Rose recalled. "There was no 'visitors area.' It was very uncomfortable. Ed sat on the floor inside the cell and I sat on the floor outside the cell. And without any prompting he looked at me and said, 'It's all true.'"

Bert Rose has had years to reflect on the drama that unfolded once Horne's predations on children became known. More than once he mused, "He was one of the greatest teachers I ever saw." He shook his head in disbelief when he remembered that just a few weeks before Horne was arrested, there had been a teacher's meeting about, among other things, sexual predation in the schools. Rose recalls Horne being there, taking it all in. "That's how profound the betrayal was for me," he said. "I just didn't see it."

In October 1985, Const. Brian Morrison of the RCMP filed the following report after the arrest of Edward Horne in Frobisher Bay:

> We are dealing with a sexual assault of young boys aged eight to 14. At this point, there are 11 charges and we expect more. We estimate from the charges so far, there are between 100 and 200 assaults. We are not dealing with casual petting, although Mr. Horne would like us to believe this. He has done almost everything sexually possible with these boys — anal intercourse, oral sex, mutual masturbation. Mr. Horne has apparently used his position to intimidate the boys and the effects on some of them have been devastating. There are some indications he has been violent with the boys — last year, he picked up a boy, squeezed him until he passed out, then threw him in a snowbank. He has forcefully undressed some of them. At this time, most people in the community are

not aware of the degree or seriousness of the assault —
this includes his wife.[2]

. . .

I met Brian Morrison over the telephone. An Ed Horne victim from
Kimmirut whom I interviewed over the course of many years mentioned
that the officer's wife was one of the best schoolteachers he ever had in his
community. He even admitted he had a crush on her as she was so pretty
and good-natured. I tracked down the police officer who arrested Ed Horne
by way of finding Donna. When I reached Brian, he was intrigued by the
project immediately, and he seemed to have a brain like a steel trap for
details on the Horne case. Getting RCMP files relevant to this story was
almost impossible, so the Mountie's memories carried significant weight for
me. Brian Morrison retired from the RCMP in 1997 and left tough times on
the job behind him. But he never forgot the Horne case. We spoke at length
over the course of several months.

"I was always pissed off [the Horne case] was never, ever reported in
southern Canada. I don't ever remember getting a call from southern
Canada," he told me. "The fact that Ed Horne was a school principal,
a man in a position of authority and trust, and he would be using that
position to search out more victims, I had a really difficult time because I
had a newborn son, and I was a young father, and I was familiar with a lot
of the details about what he was doing to the boys, and I was just pissed
right off."

Morrison became the lead investigator when Horne was taken into custody in 1985 because he was on duty when the arrest warrant was issued —
his job title at the time was general detachment investigator.

Before Morrison arrived in the North, he had never investigated
such a complex sexual assault case. His hometown is Campbellton, New
Brunswick, and he joined the force on January 29, 1974. His first posting
was in Stephenville, Newfoundland, then in Goose Bay, Deer Lake, and
Burgeo, all in the same province. During his RCMP training, he shared a
trailer with a young police officer named Oz Fudge, later immortalized as

the top cop in the city of Gander in the highly acclaimed Broadway musical *Come from Away.* Morrison laughs thinking about Fudge being famous now, considering that the buddy he remembers with fondness had one serious flaw: he really didn't like arresting people.

In the summer of 1985, the Arctic posting Morrison had been hoping for opened up. He was relieved that Donna, the woman he had married in Newfoundland, was just as excited about the assignment as he was. Brian and Donna first met at the Irving Big Stop gas bar and restaurant in Deer Lake in the days when she was working as a waitress while attending university. The two hit it off instantly — their future adventures in Inuit settlements in the Arctic not even dreamed of then. The couple married in 1980 and moved to Frobisher Bay in July 1985. They had their boy, Adam, with them, and Donna was pregnant with their second child. Complications arose with Donna's pregnancy, and after talking to her doctor she decided to return to Newfoundland to have the baby. Shannon was born on August 7, 1985, and just nine days later Donna and her little girl boarded a flight back to their Arctic home.

Donna — a schoolteacher with a degree from Memorial University of Newfoundland — was happy to stay home with the kids for their first year in town while Brian adjusted to life policing in Frobisher Bay. Donna would later teach grade 2 at Nakasuk School.

The Morrisons were instantly enchanted by the Arctic. The landscape of Baffin Island and the friendliness of the people can be pleasantly familiar to Newfoundlanders, as are the hunting and fishing just a snowmobile or four-wheeler ride away. The couple sensed a freedom they'd been seeking all their lives. But Frobisher Bay was also a troubled town. Alcohol abuse was rampant. And when alcohol wasn't available, other substances, such as gas and spray paint, were inhaled, and items such as mouthwash, aftershave — even shoe polish — were consumed by local addicts.

"It was not uncommon to have two or three suicides a week, and knife fights. It was a crazy time. We had a bad gas-sniffing problem. I look at photographs of Iqaluit today and it is nothing like when I was there. We had people frozen to death on the side of the road after a storm."

Postings to Arctic Bay, Nanisivik, and, later, Lake Harbour gave Morrison chances to hunt, fish, and ride his snowmobile with friends. Those communities had their share of problems too, but they paled in comparison with those of Frobisher Bay in 1985.

"There was one night a guy came to the door when I wasn't home, and Donna answered. He was pretty intoxicated. He was trying to get in. I was called and arrested him and put him in the tank. And I made sure she never, ever left the door unlocked after that. She couldn't figure out why I was so upset that this guy was trying to get into the house. I said to her, 'Donna, you just don't understand how things are here. It's not like Newfoundland.'"

Non-Inuit officers policing in the Arctic — and there are few officers who are Inuit — often felt the crushing difficulty of their position. Relations between RCMP and Inuit have a long history, complicated by the push and pull between language and miscommunication, traditional Inuit ways, and the authority police exert. One of the ways Morrison made inroads with people early in his northern career was through hunting and fishing. By the time he was posted to Lake Harbour, he had been in the Arctic long enough to have acquired "permanent residency." This was important to him as it allowed him to hunt.

Two years in the Arctic and permanent residency meant that he and his wife were entitled to ten caribou per year. That was the limit, but they never filled it — they shot what they needed and if someone came to town for a visit, Morrison would take them out hunting and they would often leave with caribou meat.

The Morrisons supplemented their store purchases of food with wild game during their two years in Lake Harbour. When Morrison wasn't policing the hamlet, he spent many days on a snowmobile hunting caribou, willow ptarmigan, Arctic hare, and ducks, and fishing cod and Arctic char.

In the fall of 1985, when Horne was arrested, Morrison was the second-most senior constable at the RCMP detachment in Frobisher Bay. About fifteen officers were working there at that time, in the midst of what would become a massive, multiyear investigation into child sexual abuse. The investigation would highlight the challenges the RCMP officers faced in the isolated detachments, with language and cultural barriers limiting what the local people could and would say to the police.

. . .

Tuugaaq* was seventeen years old and attending high school in Frobisher Bay when Ed Horne was arrested in 1985. He didn't hear about the arrest. Like his peers from the smaller Baffin Island communities who moved to Frobisher Bay to complete high school, Tuugaaq, who was from Cape Dorset, was embracing teenage life. A strong-looking kid with broad shoulders and a brush cut, he was a tough guy in many ways. But there were things about him no one knew, and he preferred it that way.

"I wore a mask. For a long time," he told me. "I didn't tell anyone what happened between me and Ed Horne. That was how I survived."

Tuugaaq was unaware of Horne's arrest as it unfolded. But he recalls that shortly before the arrest he saw Horne shopping in Arctic Ventures, one of Frobisher Bay's general stores.

Arctic Ventures wasn't just a store in those days, it was a meeting place too — vibrant and eccentric, from the orange-gold coloured siding covering the outside of the building, to the unorganized shelves crammed with an eclectic assortment of goods. You entered the store through thick, plastic freezer strips — the owner had an idea that if they worked to keep heat outside a freezer, they should also work to keep heat inside a store. The ceiling was covered in tinfoil — a material the owner believed reflected heat back into the building, thus making it a bit warmer. (The ownership of the building changed that same year, and the decor shortly thereafter.) Shelves seemed to be everywhere and anything could be on any shelf. It was extremely cluttered. But there were so many aisles, and such a mélange of merchandise stacked willy-nilly on every shelf, that it was an easy place to duck out of sight of someone you did not want to run into. That is the predicament Tuugaaq found himself in. He just wanted to buy a few snacks and get out of there before Horne saw him. But he couldn't move at first. He was disoriented because the moment he saw Horne everything started to move in slow motion. Breathing deeply, he forced air into his lungs and was able to muster enough energy to dash out the door, run down the wooden steps of the store, and head back on a brisk, twenty-minute walk to the student residence where he was living at the time — safe, at least for a while.

His schoolmates at Gordon Robertson Education Centre — known to everyone by its acronym GREC — told Tuugaaq that he acted strangely sometimes. "I was an introvert. I had friends. I had a couple of girlfriends. But the whole community in the residence there thought I was a weirdo. A freak or something, I don't know. I was pretty shy actually. I was pretty shy of other guys in the shower. I tried to make sure nobody was taking a shower and then I would go there and shower. At the high school there used to be a lunchtime sports program. And I was in basketball. A lot of guys were noticing that I wouldn't shower with any of the other boys. And I was all sweaty and all that. I waited for everybody to finish. And then I went in."

His gym teacher and some of his peers at the high school could make him feel small and embarrassed, teasing him about his reluctance to shower with other boys. One day he was showering alone after a particularly gruelling and sweaty basketball practice when he realized the gym teacher had come in briefly and looked at him, promptly returning to join the rest of the boys out in the gym to announce, "Yup, he's a guy! He's just like us!" Tuugaaq didn't think this was funny. What his gym teacher and classmates didn't know was that Ed Horne used to watch boys shower at the school in Cape Dorset. Horne was accused of sexually abusing many boys in school showers, as well as at his home and in the portable school. Tuugaaq was one of those victims.

The school shower in Cape Dorset was not the only place Horne found a way to intimidate and abuse boys. Tuugaaq remembers a darkroom attached to the school where, while he was helping Horne develop photos, Horne abused him.

No amount of alcohol or gas sniffing has erased images in Tuugaaq's mind of the times when Horne dressed him and other boys up in costumes. Tuugaaq believes the clothing must have come from Horne's wife, or the school's lost and found. Less mundane items, like the wedding dress and high heels Horne made him wear, came from Horne's own stash, Tuugaaq suspects. It is not unthinkable that Horne would have collected such items ostensibly for use in school plays, given his extensive background and interest in theatre.[3] The more sinister use of such props was something only his victims would know about. A few victims reported that Horne snapped photos of boys wearing costumes, as well as in their underwear.

Alcohol has been a problem for Tuugaaq since his wild teen years in Frobisher Bay trying to escape the memories of sexual abuse at the hands of Horne. He said he has come close to death more than a dozen times under the influence of alcohol, walking outside and passing out in the freezing Arctic night. Although he made strides to improve his life, taking college courses and working for the Inuit Broadcasting Corporation — an Indigenous television and film production company — he also spent too many nights curled up on the floor of the drunk tank in Frobisher Bay. There was a time when he was drinking so heavily and getting thrown into "the tank" so often that when the new RCMP building was being constructed in Iqaluit, he made a bet with friends that he would be the first person to spend a night in the brand new tank.

The world of parenthood was not one he embraced easily. A few years ago, when his partner announced they would be adopting a girl and a boy, at first he didn't want any part of it. But he quickly warmed to being a father and is especially close to his son. "He's my guy and I love him to death. I call him my dad."

This seemingly odd statement of paternity is not at all unusual in the Inuit world. A child is named shortly after birth, given a name by which they are known and which is registered with the authorities. This is the name the world knows them by. They may also have a nickname. But then there are the honorary names. An honorary name can be given at or shortly after birth, usually to remember the name of a recently deceased person and usually, but not always, a relative. A person may have more than one honorary name. These names are not written anywhere in officialdom, but they are known within the community. People within the family and the community call the child by the relationship that the honoured deceased was to them, notwithstanding the fact that they may also bear a biological relationship to the child. The Inuktitut word for "son" is *irniq*. But Tuugaaq doesn't call his son "irniq." Instead, he calls him *ataata* — "dad." When the boy was a newborn and crying nonstop, he was instantly calmed when Tuugaaq began calling him ataata. This naming system is virtually impenetrable to outsiders.

Sanikiluaq, 1971–74

FROM *TEACH IN CANADA'S ARCTIC*, A NORTHWEST TERRITORIES booklet from 1970:

An increasing awareness among Canadians of their northern hinterland has been reflected in the recent large increases in the number of enquiries about teaching careers in the north. From this large number of applicants, it has been possible to select from across Canada and beyond a competent and experienced staff for the schools in the Northwest Territories. Some of the attributes that a northern teacher must possess in order to succeed are: good health, both mental and physical, to withstand the rigours of the long hard Arctic winter and the loneliness of an isolated settlement, and flexibility and self-reliance sufficient to overcome or live with temporary and sometimes long-lasting inconveniences, such as frozen water lines and inoperable furnaces in the school or home, delays in the arrival of clothes, food stuffs, school supplies and any number of such frustrations during the course of the year; the ability to live with and enjoy a society and mode of existence totally different from that in most communities in southern Canada.

There is no place in the north for the teacher who is interested only in above average academically oriented students. Opportunities for a high degree of subject specialization are limited.[1]

. . .

An application letter from Edward Horne to teach kindergarten and primary school in Sanikiluaq, N.W.T., was received by Gerard Mulders on May 24, 1971. The straight-talking chief of school services, known for his abrupt style of communicating, had an important job hiring teachers for a place like Sanikiluaq that only recently had a school provided, since the 1960s.

On paper, Horne appeared to be an ideal candidate. He had described himself as part Native, and he had been teaching at remote schools in British Columbia for some years. Mulders spoke to Horne by telephone, informing him that if he accepted the job there was a six-week Inuit language course at the University of Saskatoon that would be of great benefit to him working as a teacher in that part of the territory. This language opportunity appealed enormously to Horne.

Mulders gave Horne a brief overview of the location, telling him that his house probably wouldn't be ready to move into on his arrival and he would have to share accommodation with another person for a time. He also spoke of the isolation of Sanikiluaq, a new settlement that had been established just a year earlier, when people moved in from their traditional camps.

After taking the six-week Inuktitut course in Saskatoon, Horne arrived at Sanikiluaq on Friday, August 13, 1971.

The unrelenting winds left the community's Canadian flag badly tattered and frayed. There wasn't even an official airstrip in the early 1970s. A pilot would need good reason then to be going to Sanikiluaq, like delivering food or medical supplies. Planes came and went about every six weeks, depending on the weather. Sometimes it was much longer between planes.

About two hundred people lived in and around the settlement at that time. The Inuit of Sanikiluaq were friendly; most were short in stature, with skin tones ranging from almost black to golden brown, reflecting their ancestors' sporadic contact with outsiders: a few Hudson's Bay Company men from places like Scotland in recent years, and the Cree from northern Quebec from time immemorial.[2]

The treeless land of the region stretched out to jagged, black rocks on the shoreline, and small flowering plants covered the tundra in summer. In a land full of lakes, there was a particularly lovely one, called Emikotailuk[3] — named for the bird, the Arctic tern — hugging the community on the west side.

Inuit fished for Arctic char and hunted seals, polar bears, and the Arctic eider duck for meat in fall and winter. Eider duck down is still harvested in summer when people travel to nesting areas and collect the soft feathers from the abandoned nests.

Ivigak or lyme grasses were used — and still are — to make woven baskets, the grass growing where moss and lichen live. This delicate-looking yet extremely hardy grass is seen along raised beaches, too, some appearing in big clumps near houses along the gravel roads. Along the shores of Coats Bay, or toward the channels from Hudson Bay into the main harbour, swaths of this rugged Arctic grass spread across the land, the wind blowing through it as the sea rolls by.

* * *

When Horne arrived, none of the homes in the village had telephones. There was a radio phone in the community, used for emergencies, connecting the caller to Quebec. The majority of the tiny population of Sanikiluaq was Inuit, or Eskimo as they were called then. The language was Inuktitut. For the most part, no one over the age of twenty-five could speak English. The children were learning, but their command of English was basic.

Even today a trip to Sanikiluaq is difficult: often scuttled by weather and seldom taken by a direct route. The cost of flying there remains expensive. In 1971, the likely route from southern Canada to the islands would have been a flight from Montreal (Dorval) to Great Whale River/Kuujjuaraapik and then, from there, likely chartering a Twin Otter to the Belchers, or it would have been from Montreal or Toronto to Timmins, Ontario, changing planes to a smaller aircraft to Moosonee and to an even smaller one for the "milk run," stopping at small communities along the east coast of James Bay.

When the school first opened in the community, some parents didn't care whether their child attended school or not, especially if the child was a boy and preferred hunting and was needed to help his family. But for the most part, Inuit were eager and attentive students in the early 1970s.

Sanikiluaq was not unique in having a new school. The formal education system in the Eastern Arctic began at different times in different communities. By the early 1970s, all communities had schools, although few went beyond grade 7.

GREC was the only "residential" school in the Eastern Arctic and took students from grade 7 through to high school completion. Breaking from the tradition of residential schools being operated by a church on behalf of a government, it had no religious affiliation, and students from the outlying communities went only if they wanted to. But Inuit parents in the small settlements were often nervous about sending their adolescent children to this school in Frobisher Bay (with its live-in residence a kilometre away), because the town had a reputation for drunkenness and debauchery. The school's enrollment numbers reflected that displeasure as the number of students dwindled year by year.

Often a classroom, except in a major centre like Frobisher Bay, had no qallunaat students — classes were usually entirely Inuit. While the government of the day often professed the praiseworthy intention of including Indigenous languages in the classroom — Inuktitut in the case of the Eastern Arctic — the reality remained that non-Inuit teachers seldom acquired fluency in the language and were able to teach only in English. The plan was the acculturation of Inuit children. In what may have seemed to be a counterintuitive approach at the time, but was indeed a wise idea, Inuktitut was seen as a means to that end, a way of easing the children into the formal educational environment in a way that made them feel comfortable and at home. One way of bringing more Inuktitut into the classrooms was the use of classroom assistants — Inuktitut-speaking Inuit who had a reasonable command of English.

Many of the students were the first members of their families to ever attend school, especially if their family had only recently moved into the settlement from a more remote camp. Such a student, even if in their teens, was invariably placed in a class with younger students who were already used to school and were expected to work at a first-grade level until they had achieved some mastery of English. This could be demeaning and damage a student's self-image. The system even had a name for the circumstance, a name that didn't sugar-coat it and was as demeaning as the situation it described; that name was "age-grade retardation." Many students, if they picked up English quickly, breezed through the formal requirements of arithmetic and other subjects and achieved higher grade levels rather quickly. The use of classroom assistants facilitated this advancement.

The education division of the federal Department of Northern Affairs and National Resources was quick to support the use of classroom assistants because they saw that northern teachers, especially those teaching the primary grades, needed help.

Suitable young Inuit adults who worked as classroom assistants, some of them still in their teens, did not deal only with issues of language. In many cases, the classroom assistant would act as interpreter during parent-teacher discussions and be instrumental in interpreting the school philosophy to the community.

Among the more routine duties of a classroom assistant were preparing and distributing working materials, supervising seat work, routine marking, and washroom supervision before lunch when students washed their hands and after lunch when they brushed their teeth. All of this allowed the regular teacher to focus on teaching.

. . .

Edward Horne was greeted at the Sanikiluaq airport upon his arrival that August day in 1971 by Don McCoy, with whom he was expected to live for the next few months until his own house was made ready. A drive through the community would have shown the newcomer the stark realities of the new settlement: there was a nursing station, an Anglican church, a co-op store, a Hudson's Bay post, the school, staff houses for the qallunaat, as well as a collection of Inuit housing of various styles. There was no consistent RCMP presence until the late 1970s.

Three portable buildings, roughly attached, made up what was then the school. Houses in the community weren't numbered, and only the nursing station, McCoy's house, and a few other homes had running water.

The principal of the school at the time was a tall, Black Caribbean man named Allan Clovis. His wife, Joanne, was the other teacher at the school, along with an Inuk classroom assistant named Jeannie Iqaluk, in charge of teaching the children syllabics and carrying out the other duties that went along with the job.

As was common in small schools, Horne taught all subjects to his grades, with English as the language of instruction. Using the knowledge of Inuktitut he had gained in the summer course in Saskatoon, and by studying the local dialect, he made tentative steps at incorporating the local language into his classroom — preparing material in Inuktitut syllabics for wall displays, for example — with Jeannie Iqaluk's assistance.

During his years in the community, Horne, with the help of his students, compiled a rudimentary but nonetheless impressive Inuktitut-English dictionary, written in his distinctly calligraphic style, with fine illustrations by Lyall Hallum, who was then the school principal.

But Horne recalled that his attempts at speaking Inuktitut in the early days were ridiculed by the people in town who were proud of their unique dialect. Out hunting with local people, he was offered more food after having eaten a substantial portion and replied "Kaanngitunga," which means "I am not hungry." The people laughed, calling it "baby talk." Soon afterward he heard another person give what he took to be the exact same response and not be criticized. He was told that the person was from Great Whale River and "they all talk in that baby talk over there!"

Throughout his time in the North, Horne would garner immense praise for his knowledge of Inuktitut. But he told me during interviews for this book that his competence in Inuktitut was overstated by the officials he worked with. He described his Inuktitut as "very poor" and said the Department of Education of the day "were pleased enough to have anyone who had any Inuktitut, and exaggerated what I did. At Sanikiluaq many regarded it as an invasion of privacy that I was at least able to understand them."

After one year of teaching, Horne resigned his position, complaining that the curriculum was shapeless and that he was given inadequate direction. Thus began a pattern of complaints against authority that would be a hallmark of his northern teaching career — *he* was good enough, but the "system" was a failure. But instead of moving out of the community, which most government employees did after leaving their job, Horne found work at the local co-op, and in the summer of 1972 he travelled to Ottawa to attend training at the headquarters of the Canadian Arctic Co-operative Federation. The co-op was much more than a small general and grocery store in Sanikiluaq. It was a multifaceted enterprise responsible for services like garbage collection, water delivery, the sale of gas, and the marketing of soapstone carvings. Of his decision to leave teaching at that time, Horne later said, "I was restless. I wanted to accomplish something, I wanted to be an achiever. I saw a community that was wildly dysfunctional and being bled dry by the Hudson's Bay Company. I saw an opportunity to make a difference." He reasoned, "I am teaching six-year-olds. It is not six-year-olds that shape a community, it is adults."

But that wasn't the whole story.[4]

During Horne's first year in Sanikiluaq, Allan Clovis was told that Horne had molested a schoolboy in the settlement. Clovis did not personally witness the molestation, but he reported it to superintendent Gerard Mulders at the regional education office in Rankin Inlet. Mulders was not due to visit Sanikiluaq in April 1972, but he changed his plans because of Clovis's allegations against Horne.

Clovis expressed to Mulders his view that Horne was a danger to the settlement and that the Department of Education had an obligation to get Horne out of the community since they had brought him in. There were no mental health services on the island to cope with the problems sexual abuse would cause. Given a population that had only recently moved in from the land and was unaccustomed to living in a community, Clovis thought that keeping Horne around was simply too much of a risk.

Despite Clovis's pleas, no action was taken.

It is difficult to pinpoint exactly when Horne began abusing boys in Sanikiluaq, but according to police reports, it started soon after he arrived.

One evening in 1971, a young boy of about twelve was visiting the home of the new teacher, Mr. Horne, with a bunch of his friends. The boy's family had come from Great Whale River and had settled into a matchbox house in the community. The boy went to school in the village but was not in Horne's class. Horne asked the visiting boys if they would like to have a shower, and they agreed. Most of the Inuit homes at that time had no running water.

The boy showered with his friends, and after they had towelled off and dressed, they took off quickly. The boy found himself alone in a bedroom with Mr. Horne.

"He took my hands, both of my hands; I couldn't move," the boy later said, describing Horne touching his penis while holding him down with strong arms. "I was lying down on the bed, he was on top of me. I tried to get up, I couldn't move. So I just let him finish what he was doing. After that I ran out and never came back to the house."[5]

The boy was subjected to an even more humiliating sexual assault a few years later by one of the boys who had gone with him to Horne's house that evening. It is possible the boy's friend was also a victim of Horne and was acting out what Horne had done to him. If that were the case, it would not be the last time Horne's predations had a grave impact on children's behaviour in the North. Many boys who were abused by Horne would become abusers themselves.

Horne started his co-op job and was no longer in the school system, no longer working for the government of the N.W.T. Horne would often move on swiftly from one job to the next in the North, obscuring what he had done and making it hard for officials — who changed jobs quite often themselves — to keep tabs on him. It was hardly an isolated event that suspicions about Horne molesting boys were reported but not followed up on, or were blatantly ignored by government officials.

. . .

The daunting, austere landscape of Sanikiluaq captivates most visitors, and Horne was no exception. He spent time alone on the windswept tundra and hunted and fished. He had perhaps at last found a place where he felt at home.

But he would often perceive sexual innuendo all around him. Perhaps in a bid to justify his own actions, he would later recall moments where he felt Sanikiluaq people were sexually permissive, more open and fearless when it came to sex.[6] He described these scenes as examples of how "weird" the community could be: he saw two men holding hands one day walking down the street, early in his time in the settlement. Another time, while with a group of people out camping, he encountered two men, one a teen, the other a little older, who seemed to want to spend extra time together alone. "I asked the older one for a ride back (to the community) and he got very flustered and upset.… I felt like he wanted to be alone with his buddy there. Also, that same person, when we were sleeping in a tent out in the camp, he, in the guise of a playful wrestling match, pulled down my pants and made a couple of grabs." Horne said he didn't overreact to the fellow grabbing him because he had started to believe that was the sort of thing people did in Sanikiluaq. He noted rumours of incest, too, including gossip in the community that a mother and son were a romantic couple and that a man allegedly had several children by his niece.

During his trip back to the islands to start his job at the co-op in the summer of 1972, travelling on a Peterhead boat, Horne claimed he witnessed things that corrupted him — changing him from a man easily shocked into a serial sexual abuser. He said there were nine or ten men on the boat, a woman with a child of about four, and a boy about thirteen years old. The trip of just over one hundred and sixty kilometers took four days due to bad weather. During this longer-than-expected voyage, Horne said the men of the boat were relentlessly pursuing the thirteen-year-old boy sexually. Horne claims he intervened, telling the boy he'd defend him, but the boy told him he could handle himself. Horne also said the woman on board made herself sexually available to him, and the two subsequently had an affair, even though he felt guilty afterward because she was married.

Once he arrived back in the village, Horne said he was propositioned by the new female schoolteacher, who crawled into the tent he was living in one night, eager to have sex with him. He claimed he turned her down.

Horne also said years later that Joanne Clovis had made a pass at him and, perhaps in a bid to discredit Allan Clovis because of information he had about Horne, claimed that the principal was not trusted in the community because he had a roving eye for the women.

There were few organized activities for children in those early days of settlement life. There were no Scouts or Girl Guides, no youth organizations.

"Really there was nowhere that the kids were interested in going, other than their own homes where there was nothing happening," Horne later said. Superintendent Gerard Mulders had given Horne the impression that the school should be the hub of activity in town, the centre of the action. But as far as Horne was concerned, social life in Sanikiluaq was bleak. The only bright spot, he said, was the films that were shown in the school some evenings. And when a film new to town was popular, it was often shown over and over. Horne claimed to have viewed *The Last Wagon* and *Love Me Tender* at least a dozen times.

In most communities in the early days of settlement life, Inuit students liked to visit their teachers at their homes whenever it was convenient. The teachers' houses were often less crowded than their own, and there were usually books and magazines to enjoy. Television was as yet unknown in the settlements, but a teacher would have a radio and sometimes a record player. Students were also likely to be treated to cookies and a soft drink or glass of juice. In those trusting days, adult Inuit never knocked before entering others' homes, either Inuit or qallunaat, for a visit. Children would occasionally knock on a white teacher's door and wait for a response before shyly asking, "Visit?" But other times they would simply enter, often silently. It was not unusual for a teacher, perhaps reading after a meal, to look up and realize he or she had a visitor, a student standing quietly waiting to be acknowledged.

Unfortunately, it was not long after children started visiting Horne at his quarters in the village that he would begin interpreting their friendliness as a signal that they were open to sexual acts. He recalled once seeing two boys in his shower together, and overhearing one of them saying "Caught red-handed!" Horne said he assumed they were fooling around with each other and just ignored them. He'd also seen boys playing around in his home with their shirts off, one boy playfully whipping another with his shirt in a style that seemed "sadomasochistic" to Horne. They may simply have been emulating something they had seen in a movie, but Horne said it made him uncomfortable.

He later claimed that boys used his shower without hesitation and when he lived in a house with a bathtub, were willing to take baths. Later, under interrogation, trying to deflect any suggestion that this was unusual, Horne justified the behaviour by saying that a previous teacher, whom he described as "flamboyant," had encouraged these activities. Yet it was not the aberration that it might seem in hindsight. Teachers' homes generally had a large water tank and a water heater — the type of plumbing teachers would have had in the south — but the facilities in Inuit housing of the time were more rudimentary. Often an Inuit home would have no running water, its meagre supply of water stored in a plastic tank with no way to heat it. Parents, therefore, thought nothing of their children coming home from a visit to the teacher's house scrubbed and clean.

But, in the case of Horne, sexual assaults on boys did occur in these situations. Horne would touch the boys' genitals when he was washing them and towelling them off. One of his victims, Tim,* was the little son of the married woman he had fooled around with on the Peterhead boat. One wonders if Horne's main attraction to this woman was her son.

Tim was severely damaged by Horne's molestation of him. In a police report filed in 1999, the boy, by then a man, told investigators Horne fellated him, among other assaults. The following is an edited excerpt from an interview when Horne was asked about Tim. The investigators were challenging Horne's claim that he had never molested a boy younger than ten years old — a claim later proven to be untrue.[7]

Horne: He hung around a lot, and he just seemed to be the kind of kid that needed affection. And in my sick mind, a lot of the criminal activity I would have identified at the time was offering affection to a child who needed affection ... the affection I never got from my father. And it's very difficult to say things that are as hateful as that.

Lawyer: I will say, before we go any further, that you said many times in your statement that, at that time in your life, you were very sick. You have said that about as frankly, perhaps, as a person can. So, I accept that, and we need not go into it ... perhaps we may later ... but, you said in 1999 and you are saying now, this was a sick desire and that you were sick to act out on it. That's all understood, isn't it?

Horne: I'm not entirely sure what was the sexual component in it. I was not homosexual. I was not, primarily, oriented toward children. I think there were other demons that led me into this. I think it was the need to be close to other human beings. It was the fact that I had been the battered child, and that I was trying to undo my own past through others.

Lawyer: The impetus aside, the way it manifested itself was through sexual acting out with male children?

Horne: Yes, and there is something else that I mention, that I am reluctant to mention because it sounds like I am trying to make an excuse. But I'm not, and even one of the interrogating policemen mentioned this, that Inuit children, at that time — probably still — are very physical. They talk to you — say, if you are sitting on a chair, they will hang onto your shoulder, they will crowd around in a group. And I have mentioned my first reaction to some of the things I saw in Sanikiluaq was horror. I sort of came to enjoy this, the children crowding around.

Lawyer: [Tim], as well — I have only known [Tim] as an adult. Do you believe it would be accurate to describe [Tim] as developmentally delayed?
Horne: Yes.
Lawyer: As well, perhaps, a little socially awkward, and physically, a little gauche, a little awkward, in that respect?
Horne: All this was true when he was a child, too. But I didn't help matters. I felt, when I saw him in the court, I nearly broke down because I felt like this is a shipwreck of a human being, and I don't think he got that way on his own.
Lawyer: Just to finish that thought, he got that way, in large part, you concede, because you sexually molested him?
Horne: I can't say I know that for a fact, but I have to live with this.

Horne said he believed Tim was around ten years old when he abused him. But investigators concluded that he was likely eight, and Horne eventually conceded that they were right.

• • •

In Sanikiluaq, Horne had a relationship with a male in his late teens for a little while, someone older than most of his child victims. The man was never one of Horne's students. At one point, the two had what was described in testimony as interfemoral sex, a simulated sexual act in which a man moves his penis back and forth between another person's thighs. Horne claimed the young man taught him this and that was what unleashed his deviant sexuality. Horne would later retract this statement, saying he did not blame this man for turning him into a criminal child abuser. In any case, the man would apply for compensation during a civil action years later, claiming that much of the sexual activity that went on between him and Horne was not consensual and that he felt victimized by Horne. The government challenged the man's claims, as they would those of a number of other men, due to his age at the time of the alleged sexual assaults and the fact he was never a student of Horne's and may not have ever attended school at all.

. . .

Eric* remembered he was six or seven when Ed Horne began molesting him. He met the teacher at a dinner party with his parents. Horne had invited them over to his place.[8]

The boy lived in a more cohesive family than many of his friends did, but his father was an alcoholic who received bottles of booze in the mail, even though the community was "dry" — alcohol possession was banned. Sometimes, when drunk, his father would beat his mother, leaving her with bruises on her shoulders and face. His father smoked weed and hash too, and although he attempted to hide his drug use from his children, he didn't succeed — Eric found a couple of joints one time hidden in a drawer.

Despite his parents' many flaws, Eric thought of them as hard-working, good people. They never hit their kids; punishment for bad behaviour was grounding, not beatings. The family had food in the house, both country food and store-bought, as well as running water.

At that first dinner party at Horne's house, nothing out of the ordinary occurred. Two days later, Eric and his mom visited Horne and, again, Horne didn't touch him. The third time would be different. He doesn't remember why he ended up alone in Horne's house that day, without his friends or parents, but he did.

Eric remembered Horne giving him cookies and juice. Then, when the boy had finished the snack, Horne began touching the boy's penis underneath his clothes while sitting next to him on the living room sofa. Horne then exposed his own penis and put the boy's hand on it while continuing to touch the boy. Then Horne gave the boy some more cookies and the boy went home.

The boy claimed Horne later raped him:

"He put me to the floor and I was facing to the floor and then he took my pants off and then he started rubbing his penis to my butt crack," he said in a statement years later. "And just about [when] he was done, he put his penis to my ass, but not all the way, but about this big," he said, using his hands to show how far he was penetrated. "I was crying, I couldn't do anything. He was too big, he was too strong."

Horne denied Eric's claims, calling them "absolutely false, and deliberately mendacious."[9] He said the boy never set foot in his house.

. . .

Horne succeeded in keeping his criminal conduct in the community a secret. His reputation as a hard-working, creative, community-minded individual remained intact, at least to most of the community. And so it was that in 1981 the Winnipeg Art Gallery published a slim volume, *Belcher Islands/ Sanikiluaq*, to coincide with a show at the gallery.[10] It featured an essay by Horne, "A Sense of Self, A Sense of Place," based on his experience as the co-op store manager.

"Carving is often thought to be woman's work and it is true that the small birds that are so important to the economy of Sanikiluaq are carved mostly by women," Horne wrote. "I paid them for their carvings and they would wander around our co-op's store and buy boots for the children or skidoo parts, gas or groceries. More likely, they would pocket the money and head for the Hudson's Bay Company store."

He wrote of a new item that appeared in the store much to the delight of some of the Elders: an ashtray that made coughing noises when a cigarette was butted in it. One of the old men in town commented, "The white people have so much imagination, they can make incredible things. What do they want with our wretched hunks of rock when they can make such wonderful things themselves?"

He concluded, "I can't believe there will ever be a time at Sanikiluaq when carving will be less important than it is now. The work of the younger carvers shows that they are no less competent than their parents. They may, in time, find their own themes and techniques, rather than imitate the work of present carvers. Eskimo art is not static, and the art of Sanikiluaq is likely to grow and mature and change into what we cannot now imagine."

Sanikiluaq, 1975–77

WHEN ANTHROPOLOGIST HUGH BRODY AND HIS GIRLFRIEND, Christine Moore, arrived in the settlement to begin their northern adventure in the early 1970s, they fixed up a rundown building that had once been a museum and made it home for a while. At first, the few other outsiders who had settled in the community tried to convince the young couple that qallunaat like themselves should not live this way, in a dilapidated museum, so close to the Inuit. They may, in fact, have been a bit envious of the warm camaraderie the young couple was developing with the locals. In any event, Horne certainly had no qualms about the couple's unique living arrangements. He liked to visit them, dropping by the old museum for tea and conversation, as many of the Inuit did.[1]

At that time, Horne was already spinning a yarn about his ancestry to anyone who would listen and might be impressed. He claimed to be a person of Indigenous or part-Indigenous heritage. Based on the stories Horne told of his youth, Brody believed Horne was of Athapaskan (Dene) ancestry. So, early on, Horne was adopting the persona of a not-quite white man, while enjoying all the perks that came with being non-Inuit at the time.

It wasn't long before Horne's visits began to grate on Brody's nerves. Horne could not or would not hide his competitiveness and what appeared to be an innate hostility. He regularly started arguments with Moore over basic feminist principles, and he would dominate conversation with no regard for other visitors, horrifying his gracious hosts.

Horne would sometimes stop by and suggest a game of chess with Brody, who was fond of the game. This was agreeable for a while, until Horne realized the anthropologist was a better chess player than he was, and Brody learned that Horne was a sore loser.

Annoying Horne further was Brody's adeptness at learning Inuktitut, a language Horne desperately wanted to master. Inuktitut is not an easy language to acquire, and Horne appeared frustrated that his friend was gaining proficiency rapidly. Of course, the anthropologist had a decided advantage in this context, being unburdened by the constraints of a day job and therefore able to maximize his time with Inuit adults.

"He did a lot of work on Inuktitut academically after I knew him," Brody recalled. "When I knew him, he was just beginning. He was so tortured with self-consciousness and fear of failure and all those complicated things that went on in his troubled mind that he wouldn't speak out loud in Inuktitut in front of me. And I didn't hear him talking to anybody in Inuktitut."

Moore thought Horne came across as a know-it-all who didn't like using Inuktitut in their presence. "I suspect that was a fear of being outsmarted," she said.

The visiting between Horne and Brody was one-way. As was the custom with federal day-school teachers, Horne lived in a standard government house that was spacious and comfortable compared to most other dwellings in the community. But there was always a heavy curtain, like a blanket, drawn across his living room window. It seemed uninviting, even ominous, so the anthropologist and his girlfriend never went to visit. Nor did Horne ever invite his friends over. It was just as well; after getting to know Horne, they felt it was better to keep their meetings with him short and chess-related.

Despite their concerns over many aspects of Horne's behaviour, the couple had no inkling of the teacher's sexual predations on the boys of the small community. Many years later they learned of Ed Horne's crimes through the northern news media and friends in the North they kept in touch with.

Behind the scenes, in interviews and conversations Brody had with Inuit adults in Sanikiluaq, he found they were not shy about stating their frustrations and objections to the way qallunaat behaved toward them in many situations. So why did they not say anything about Horne? Brody suspects it was because they didn't know — that the children didn't tell anyone.

The simple fact is that the community was fragile. Inuit, who had been accustomed to living in small family camps dispersed across a vast geography, were now living together in a settlement, sometimes beside neighbours they neither knew well nor trusted. Jobs were scarce, especially for men. Yet hunting, a traditionally male pursuit, was more difficult with a concentrated population, and fur prices were not high. Some found solace in alcohol. Some, especially men whose traditional roles seemed increasingly untenable, turned to violence, often against family members. The majority quietly tried to hold their families together and prepare for an uncertain future.

Regardless of what outsiders may have thought of Horne, the Inuit looked upon him as a white man. And white men (and a few white women) held all the power in the Inuit communities of the 1970s. They controlled commerce, through the Hudson's Bay Company post and the local co-operative store; education, through the non-Inuit teaching staff in the school; and health services, through nurses brought in from outside. Eventually, when a police detachment was built, the officers were white. Non-Inuit controlled access to jobs, welfare, and other services.

Outsiders at the time often commented on the desire of Inuit to please, to give the always-questioning white man the answer that he wanted, or that they thought he wanted. This is rooted in the Inuit concept of *ilira*, explained as "a great fear or awe, such as the awe a strong father inspires in his children, or the fear of the Qallunaat ... held by Inuit."[2] This concept has been much quoted as an explanation for Inuit behaviours in light of the power imbalances of the time. And so it is possible, even likely, that some parents, even if they had suspected Horne of improper behaviour, would not have challenged him, a white man with power. It is likely Horne was able to take advantage of people because they were so easygoing and respectful of white people, Brody later said.

"He was already at Sanikiluaq when I first arrived in August 1971," Horne recalled of Brody. "He was fluent in Inuktitut, far more fluent than I ever became. But he seemed prone to gossip rather than independent investigation of whatever he was supposed to be doing."

Horne said Brody "bad-mouthed people I liked, especially Don McCoy, the settlement manager. Don was a typical colonial manager, but he worked hard and presided ably over the transition to local government. Hugh and I were friends, I supposed, but I didn't trust him."

Notably, when I first made contact with Ed Horne about this book, he suggested I read Brody's book, *The People's Land*, citing it as a good source of information about the Eastern Arctic.

· · ·

After almost two years at the co-operative, Horne was restless again and left the community in 1974 to take a job at another co-op in the High Arctic at Resolute Bay. It was the second-most northerly community in Canada. He lasted there four months. He applied to return to Sanikiluaq to teach, but the education committee, a group of local citizens who functioned in an advisory capacity, rejected his application. Warren Rongve, an education official whom Horne had known at an earlier teaching position in British Columbia, later told Horne that committee members had serious concerns about his mental stability. So Horne headed to Great Whale River, on the nearby Quebec mainland, to teach in September 1974, staying for a full school year. Rongve seemed to have been made aware of Clovis's concern about Horne, but again, it didn't prevent Horne from continuing to work as a teacher. The problem of Horne — if he was perceived as a problem — was passed on to another jurisdiction where, if he acted up, other administrators would have to deal with him.

Horne's past in Great Whale River came back to haunt him in 1999 when he had to face four charges stemming from his year as a teacher there.[3] Horne was accused of groping students who were between six to eight years old. The Crown later did not proceed to any hearing after determining that there were no reasonable prospects of conviction due to a lack of evidence to support the Crown's case.

. . .

Near the end of his stint in Great Whale River, Horne reapplied to return to Sanikiluaq. The local education committee, which had expressed misgivings when Horne had reapplied earlier, was either not consulted this time or was ignored. Allan Clovis's official complaints to Gerard Mulders should have been on file in the regional education office in Rankin Inlet or at headquarters in Yellowknife, perhaps both, but either those files were not consulted or they were disregarded. Allan Clovis had moved on, and a new principal, Bob Gamble, and a new regional superintendent of education, Larry Gilbert — no doubt impressed by the stellar reports of Horne's in-classroom performance — both supported rehiring Horne.

In 1975, Horne returned to Sanikiluaq to teach kindergarten and grade 1. The growth of the school, now called Nuiyak School, in just a few short years surprised Horne. There were four classrooms and a large building used as a recreation centre. In what was becoming a pattern, however, he expressed disappointment in the teaching staff who, in his opinion, were racists who viewed the local people as little more than primitives.

Soon after settling in, Horne, who was then still single, began complaining about his house, firing off a letter to Gilbert describing the dwelling as cold, drafty, and unfit for human habitation. Horne would eventually move to a new house. These moves would complicate matters when investigators later needed to corroborate his victims' descriptions about where they were abused.

But much more serious than a drafty house was Horne's increased sexual contact with young boys in the community and his mental state, which by his own admission — much later, during interrogations — was deteriorating in 1976.

Horne was aware that what he was doing with boys in Sanikiluaq was wrong, and he even consulted a couple of doctors on his condition. A psychologist based in Victoria, B.C., proved to be no help at all — he was apparently more interested in hearing tales from the Arctic than in assessing Horne's mental health. And Horne admitted, "I didn't have the guts to force the issue." He acknowledged at the time that when he was seeking help he was in a contradictory mental state: "I was trying to hide the fact there was a problem, and I was trying to cry out for help."

Horne suffered from hallucinations, especially when tired, and said that he was often psychologically churning with random feelings of anger — ironically, these were problems many of his victims would later report experiencing as well.

Horne had become obsessed over issues in his own childhood — his relationship with his father, in particular, was causing him mental distress.

He had begun to feel that Sanikiluaq was an "unhappy community," and he could not seem to find a meaningful role in it. But the idea that he may have been the root cause of the social ills he was observing had apparently not crossed his mind. When little boys would roam the village and show up unannounced at Horne's home, he treated them "like kings," one victim said. Horne would let the boys do whatever they wanted. Food and games were readily available — an incredible sight for Silas,* whose mother, in previous years, often had to scour the dump for something to eat while carrying her son in an *amautik* on her back. Silas liked the food and games Horne provided, but explained the main reason he went to Horne's home was because his own house, like many homes in the village then, didn't have running water. Horne's house did.

"I heard that students were going there to take showers and baths there, and so I followed them and visited him and I wanted to take a shower then. But I asked him if I can take a shower with my friends there but he insisted that I do it alone," Silas recalled. "He came in while I was taking a shower and started fondling me down in the anus area and the penis area, and I was asking why he was doing that, and then I yelled for one of my — one of the people visiting there — and then he went out and I just pulled my clothes on and went out."

As Silas hastily dressed, he said Horne confronted him, telling him to keep quiet about what had occurred in the washroom, or else.

"I think that when someone tells you he's going to do something bad to you and not to tell anybody else, it gets into your head, especially when you're a small kid," Silas said years later.[4]

. . .

When Rick* was a little boy, his father still went out hunting using a dog team, an ancient way of travel that began to die out in the 1970s in Sanikiluaq and elsewhere in the North as snowmobiles took hold in the Eastern Arctic. He lived a traditional life with his family, enjoying the riches of the land: seal meat, fish, birds — including ducks — clams, and sea urchins.

School was an exciting prospect for Rick, and he attended eagerly, eventually finishing his education in Frobisher Bay. But whatever success he may have had once he was grown, Horne's sexualizing of Rick when he was a boy was devastating.[5] From the first days that Horne set foot in the village, Rick remembers the teacher encouraging boys to come to his house:

"When we were young, before we turned ten, Ed Horne used to persuade us to go to his place to go play table tennis, so we did. We went to his place and played ping-pong as he requested, and then we started sweating and then he asked us to take a bath so he could take pictures of us.... He was fondling with them. They were terrified, they were scared of him."[6] When they weren't being touched and photographed naked, the boys were corralled into helping Horne compile the dictionary he was later praised for.

"We helped him a lot with the words because he had no idea how to speak Inuktitut," Rick said. It was years before he realized how wrong Horne's behaviour was. "They don't want to talk it out in the open," he said of his friends. "It's too shameful to talk about it. They don't want to tell anybody about it, it's very shameful stuff he did to us. It's been very shameful in my brain trying to talk about it and it's difficult how to explain to my kids now what I'm crying about."[7]

The Disappearance of Alec Inuktaluk

THERE ARE MANY STORIES ABOUT ED HORNE'S TIME IN THE North that survivors have shared with people they trust. One of those stories is about two Inuk boys Ed Horne took on a trip to New York City.

During summer vacation in 1976, Horne reportedly took two boys from Sanikiluaq to New York City with him for a few days. One of them was a teenager, Alec Inuktaluk.[1] It had already been determined that Alec, whom Horne later referred to as "excellent," would be his classroom assistant in the new school year. This, in itself, is noteworthy because Horne was often openly critical of teaching assistants.

Some observers thought there was a bond between Horne and Alec, but Calvin,* the other boy on the summer trip, said Horne had a short fuse where Alec was concerned; the two seemed to argue constantly.

Horne allegedly provided the boys with spending money and gave them alcohol to drink, possibly vodka. Calvin said he passed out once and felt sick the next day. He isn't sure what occurred while he was incapacitated but claimed that at one point during the trip Horne gave him a blow job. He also said Horne took the boys out of the hotel one day and abandoned them alone on the streets of New York City. He didn't remember how long they were on the street and had no idea why Horne did it. Perhaps it was to dispel any illusion the boys may have had that they were not totally within Horne's control.

Before returning to Sanikiluaq, Alec went to Rankin Inlet, the then regional administrative centre for the Keewatin Region, to take a course to prepare for the role he would assume as classroom assistant once he was back home. Meanwhile, Calvin and Horne took a trip to Montreal and Vancouver. Eventually, all three returned to Sanikiluaq.

Calvin had contact with Horne going back to when he was eleven years old. In 1972, he was one of the many boys who took a shower at Horne's house, and Horne washed him with soap, rubbing him all over his body, including his penis. Calvin did not think there was anything wrong with that at the time. He did, however, acknowledge that it seemed Horne was always trying to make him feel comfortable — rubbing his legs, his shoulders, and wanting to be close to him.[2]

• • •

Sometime in the late spring of 1977, Horne's government-provided home in Sanikiluaq was vandalized. Alec Inuktaluk was one of the culprits. He had free access to the building where Horne, then still unmarried, lived alone, because he sometimes acted as a caretaker for Horne. Alec's friend Rick, himself a victim of Horne's sexual predations, saw the destruction as it was happening. "One day we heard a loud banging next door to our place," Rick told lawyers years later. "We heard loud banging, so we went to look at what all the commotion was with my sister. We saw through the window a couple of guys tearing down the place, like, taking down the furniture, smashing the walls."[3]

The vandalism to government property was duly reported, and Olaf Christensen, an employee of the government's Department of Public Works — who was scheduled to visit Sanikiluaq on other business — was asked to investigate and report on the condition of the house. Recalling the trip some years later, Christensen told a friend the house was a wreck, with everything smashed — the furniture, the lamps, everything. But for Christensen, there was something even more disturbing about the attack — feces were smeared all over the walls, even on the ceiling. This really affected Christensen. "I have seen houses wrecked by vandals before," he said, "but this was different — this was an act of hate."[4]

Christensen included a description of the damage in his trip report. That report and the destruction it documented presumably lies buried somewhere in government archives, but it lived on in northern legend. It was brought up by lawyers in the second civil case against the governments. At that time, Horne downplayed the extent of the damage, saying nothing had been stolen. But reportedly, as the trashing was underway, Alec removed a disturbing box of photographs from Horne's home. A short time after Horne's house was vandalized, Alec disappeared.

• • •

On October 16, 2005, an Inuk man, whom I will call Michael, sat down and gave an interview to a lawyer in Sanikiluaq in connection with a civil case. During the interview, the man talked about a mystery still haunting his community: Alec's disappearance. Alec had worked for Horne from September 20, 1976, until his resignation, well before the end of the school year, on April 21, 1977.

> **Michael:** He disappeared, he walked away.
> **Lawyer:** He walked away?
> **Michael:** Yes.
> **Lawyer:** When did this happen?
> **Michael:** In 1977.
> **Lawyer:** And how old were you at the time?
> **Michael:** Sixteen.
> **Lawyer:** OK. And what do you mean he walked away?
> **Michael:** He took off to the land.
> **Lawyer:** ... Did he tell you that he was going to hurt himself?
> **Michael:** Only once, but he really never talked about it.
> **Lawyer:** And when did he tell you that?
> **Michael:** Just ... in the morning when he told me about it, I was alone with him. But in the afternoon, he walked away.
> **Lawyer:** He walked away?

Michael: Yes.

Lawyer: And did he tell you why he wanted to go away?

Michael: I don't know. I don't know. He didn't tell me why.

Lawyer: He didn't tell you why?

Michael: No.

Lawyer: Do you think that this had anything to do with Ed Horne?

Michael: He was kind of scared because he was in charge, in charge of the house, and he was kind of scared of Mr. Horne.

Lawyer: Alec was?

Michael: Yes.

Lawyer: And do you think that Alec's disappearance had anything to do with Ed Horne?

Michael: I don't know, maybe. Maybe.[5]

A lifelong resident of Sanikiluaq heard another story from villagers. According to that person, Alec went out hunting with Horne in 1977 and never came back. Years later, Cree hunters found bones on the mainland. The RCMP sent the bones out for examination, hoping they had finally located Alec, but a year later the results came back: not human. Maybe bear.

Const. Brian Morrison, who arrested Horne in 1985, also heard a version of the Alec story, this one from an RCMP officer named Randall Park, stationed in Sanikiluaq in 1987.

"It was one of the stories that popped up through the Horne investigation, interviewing people," Morrison said. "And I remember I called down to Sanikiluaq and asked — can't remember his name — to make some inquiries, and I learned there were a lot of stories about boys who had been assaulted down there. And [the officer in Sanikiluaq] took it as far as he could. He spoke with some of the locals, and the story he relayed to me was that this young boy went missing and Ed Horne was instrumental in initiating a search party to go out and look for him. And they searched for I don't know how long. But at one point Horne said, 'You guys go over there and search over there, I'm going to look over here.' And to me at the time that was extremely suspicious. Why would he send a bunch of searchers in one direction and he went in another direction? So, the question that I had in my mind was, Did he go and make sure that the body would not be found? And I may be wrong. But I always felt that the young fellow was probably murdered."

Even Bert Rose, who had been one of Horne's staunchest supporters, eventually heard a story implicating Horne in Alec's demise.

"The search was organized by Horne," Rose recalled hearing. "How he got the authority to organize the search, I don't know. The community had an opinion on where the search should go. But Ed took them in the opposite direction. There was no success in the search and eventually the boy was presumed to be dead."

The RCMP in Sanikiluaq speculated to Rose that Alec may have been molested by Horne, surmising that the situation was getting out of control and that Alec was going to talk; Horne panicked and had to do something about it, so he killed him.

While some people suggested the young man may have decided in a moment of anguish to end his life, Rose pointed out that suicide in the Eastern Arctic wasn't common before the 1980s. In the years to come, it would be an all-too-familiar end to the tortured lives of many of Horne's victims. In any case, charges were never laid in the disappearance and presumed death of Alec Inuktaluk. "There was no evidence to prove the story," Rose said. "But the RCMP officer was sure Ed had planned the whole thing."

Alec had done the damage in Horne's house because, as his friend Rick explained years later, "He had seen bad pictures of young boys with no clothes on." The pictures were in a box that Alec allegedly stole during the vandalization of Horne's home. "He showed me those naked pictures of young boys," said Rick. "There were too many pictures. I could not recognize them. I could not recognize their faces."[6]

Alec was being sought for questioning into the vandalism when a series of menacing incidents occurred. Hearing that the authorities were looking for Alec, Rick hopped on a snowmobile, taking Alec's girlfriend with him, and headed about ten kilometres out of town, where he knew Alec was living in a tent. "When I went to him, he showed me the box of those naked young people, a box full of it. And then I told him the police is calling out his name and that he should go there, but he didn't want to because he was terrified of Ed Horne."

Rick continued. "After we were at Alec's tent, [Alec's girlfriend and I] headed back home on a snowmobile, and then we saw Ed Horne coming real fast on a snowmobile, and he aimed his shotgun right in my forehead and it was like I was gone, like, I couldn't … It was a terrible feeling.

"When that happened, I had to point where Alec's tent was, because I was afraid he was going to shoot me. And then he went really speeding away to the tent, right away, real fast on his snowmobile."

Rick, who was thirteen or fourteen at the time, hightailed it back to town, leaving Alec on his own at his tent site, explaining that he took off quickly because he was terrified of Horne.

Back in the community, the people who were so eager to question Alec about the raid on Horne's house seemed to have vanished. "It was absolute silence, nobody there to talk to," Rick recalled. Later that evening, Horne returned to the community carrying what looked like the incriminating box of photos and Alec's tent. But there was no sign of Alec.

"[Horne] had a tent and a shoe box that he carried, and then he gave me the tent, Alec's tent," Rick said. "He was all smiles, like, very happy now. First he was really sad when he pointed the gun at me, and now he was all smiles." There was no explanation about the gift of the tent, and Rick didn't ask. "He was just all smiles. 'Here, you can have this tent,'" Rick recalled.

Rick later told a female friend that Horne had pointed his gun at his face, asking for Alec. Much later, when he finally told the authorities about it, they didn't do anything except tell him to consult with a social worker. (There was no RCMP detachment at Sanikiluaq until after 1977.)

Meanwhile, he'd put up Alec's tent near his own home, and it wasn't long before Alec's parents recognized it and asked him about it. He refused to discuss it. Nor did he tell his own parents about the gun and the tent, or about Alec and Horne's troubled relationship.

A month or so later, Rick was out on a hunting trip to Kataapik[7] when he saw Horne pass by on his snowmobile ("I could recognize his big glasses far away") carrying what seemed to be the remains of Alec's Ski-Doo, now crushed. Rick was born and raised in the area, where a channel runs between the northwest tip of Flaherty Island and the islands just to the north. The channel is narrow and currents are swift from the harbour or Coats Bay, following the tide. Seafood harvesting at Kataapik is still a popular activity for many people in town, as the area is walkable from the community. An old campsite on a nearby island has several "box" graves — burial sites boxed in by stones — and all around are Tuniit (Dorset) sites. Because of its natural beauty and history, the site was recently chosen to be a new territorial park. When Rick saw Horne riding across Kataapik that day, he believed Horne was out there trying to dispose of Alec's snowmobile.

When asked why he didn't tell anyone that part of the story at the time, Rick replied with words that exemplify the frustration of Inuit in those years in the face of white authority: "Who do we tell? If the court is on Ed Horne's side, who do you tell? Like, it's the hardest thing to talk about, I didn't know how to explain this. Because if the RCMP is on Ed Horne's side, who are you going to talk to? It's very difficult. I couldn't even talk to Alec's parents because I was frightened of those naked boys, and it's terrible."

There was no RCMP presence in the community. The only time they came in was for investigations or court hearings, Rick recalled.

During the summer of that year, Rick went to every little island in the region looking for Alec's body. "We could not find him," he said. "After all these events, I get — my brain — it gets weak, and I start crying a lot about it. It's been very difficult."

If the loss of his friend wasn't bad enough, Horne wasn't quite finished with Rick yet. According to Rick, the teacher wanted to do him harm and allegedly assaulted him in a darkroom that Horne used to develop photos. During the final week of school before summer break, Rick claimed Horne deliberately splashed photo acid into his right eye. Despite the actions of his quick-thinking sister, who rinsed his eye with water, he said the incident caused permanent eye damage.

Horne later denied Rick's recounting of events, saying, "I am stunned and flabbergasted by many of the allegations, but particularly the one that I pointed a gun at somebody. This puts me in an entirely different league, if that were true. There were police in town at the time. If somebody pointed a gun at me, I would go straight to the police. Instead, he seems to have waited close to 30 years to come up with this story."[8]

. . .

Horne was a suspect in Alec's disappearance and possible murder. He later said he took two polygraph tests connected to the case. Horne was on the island when Alec went missing but claimed to be nowhere near where Alec reportedly was.

"I was at some distance away," Horne later explained. "There were, literally, dozens of people that were closer to the area than I was. I and another person had hiked down to South Camp, because I suspected that Alec might have taken refuge there. He had spoken to me about wanting to live alone with another person ... I mean, live with one other person at South Camp. And I thought that was a good place to look. At that time of year, it was difficult to access South Camp. I and a Hudson Bay clerk hiked down there. The accusation was that I might have found him down there and disposed of him."[9]

Speculation about Horne's involvement in Alec's disappearance continued swirling, at least in the Inuit and law enforcement communities. But surprisingly, the stories had no effect on Horne's career. Education authorities and administration officials either didn't hear the rumblings from the Inuit community and visiting police officers, or they purposely ignored them.

Whatever the truth is about Alec Inuktaluk's final moments, Horne remained working for the Department of Education. As far as officials were concerned, he was one of the most dynamic teachers they had, a treasure to be nurtured, perhaps even protected. A month after Alec's disappearance, Ed Horne got married.

Wedding Bells

IN 1972, HORNE HAD BEEN SCHEDULED TO MOVE INTO THE OLD nursing station in Sanikiluaq, which had been converted into a staff housing unit. But the move was delayed because the visiting Anglican minister, Rev. Caleb Lawrence, his wife, and an Inuit housemaid from Great Whale River were living there temporarily. The Lawrences came periodically and typically stayed for a few months. Their maid was Jeannie Cookie. Horne liked her instantly. During her visits, the two would go on walks together and talk. But marriage was still well in the future.

Jeannie may have been one of the reasons why Horne moved to Great Whale River to teach for a year, in the 1974–75 school year. The romance apparently blossomed there, and that fall Horne asked Jeannie to marry him. She said no. Her family needed her at home a bit longer, she said. But in 1977 she relented, and Reverend Lawrence married the couple on July 7. Jeannie moved to Sanikiluaq to live with her husband.

"She spoke limited English, with a lovely Irish accent that she picked up from the Lawrence family," Horne told me during the writing of this book. "Throughout our courtship Jeannie spoke to me in Inuktitut and I spoke to her in English. This worked, as each spoke his or her best language. People said it was weird to hear us together. She also spoke Cree, and it was a family tradition that she spoke Cree when she was asking for money."

The couple would remain close with Caleb Lawrence and his family. Lawrence was a missionary at Great Whale River from 1965 to 1975 before serving as archdeacon of Arctic Quebec and bishop of the Diocese of Moosonee. He would later be named godfather to the Hornes' first-born son, John Paul Akavak. The bond between the Hornes and the Lawrences was such that Caleb's wife, Maureen, became godmother to the Hornes' second son, James Atsainaq; and Sean Lawrence, the couple's son, was godfather to Ed and Jeannie's youngest boy, Daniel.

Horne recalled that Jeannie's father, Joe, was "a sweet old guy" who died not long after Jeannie and Horne were married. Her mother, Winnie, Horne described as "sharp, domineering, active, I believe, into her eighties. My mother visited them for a month shortly before she died. Joe Jr. visited me and the family when we were living at Red Deer, while I was on parole from my first sentence. As a family it was more or less traditional — a high rate of adoption blurred family lines. I liked them but had little social contact with them."

In the spring of 1978, Kenn Harper, a former teacher who was then working as a municipal affairs officer for the government of the N.W.T., was in Sanikiluaq on government business and went to visit Horne, who was at that time no longer a classroom teacher but, rather, was working in adult education. The two men had first met at a teachers' conference years before and shared a strong interest in Inuktitut. Harper had dropped in briefly for a cup of tea at Horne's house, but Horne suggested they go for a walk and continue their conversation. The landscape of Sanikiluaq was flat so it was easy to see far off in all directions. Harper and Horne became immersed in a discussion of Inuktitut grammar, a topic they could have spent hours on. After a while, Harper glanced back toward the village and saw that someone was following them at a distance, careful to not get too close but never falling very far behind. It was Jeannie. *This is weird*, thought Harper, and he asked Horne if they should perhaps wait for her to catch up. No, replied Horne, offering no explanation for his wife's behaviour. Harper concluded that Jeannie didn't trust her husband but had no idea of any reason for that mistrust.

Harper thought Horne's choice of partner unusual. Horne was outgoing and dynamic with Harper, especially when conversing about language, while

Jeannie seemed standoffish and suspicious. But having a wife who preferred to speak Inuktitut afforded Horne an advantage in his language studies — he learned Inuktitut more quickly after his marriage. When the family moved on to other communities, though, the preponderance of coastal Quebec dialect — similar to that spoken in Sanikiluaq — used in the home may have hampered his attempts to learn other dialects that he considered more "mainstream." Students in southern Baffin communities considered his Quebec dialect strange.

Jeannie was a rather plain-looking, plump woman, yet Horne placed a high value on physical fitness — or was that simply a reason to run exercise classes with male students? Moreover, Jeannie was wary of strangers. Many described her as cantankerous or ornery. She was a devout Anglican and much of her life centred around church events. Appearing to be antisocial, perhaps because of a hearing difficulty, she often left the house when visitors were there to see her husband. To outward appearances, it was an odd marriage. Was this a desperate attempt by Horne to adopt a more normal, a less deviant lifestyle? Was Jeannie his "beard," a cover to allay suspicions about his sexual predations by conveying the appearance of a happy marriage? These questions were never explored during the examinations of Horne's life that eventually resulted from his crimes. In 2021, I asked Horne about his relationship with Jeannie.

"The fact that Jeannie and I both had serious hearing loss was a sort of bond between us," Horne said. "I was twenty-seven when I first arrived at Sanikiluaq, and I wanted to be married. But the girls there were loud, uncouth, and if close to my age, had kids and were promiscuous. Jeannie was twenty-five, quiet, decent, cute, liked, and respected me. It wasn't passion, it was her suitability that attracted me. I loved her, not much at first, more at times and less at other times, now more than before. But I will never forgive her for the deaths of my sons."

The tragedies that were to unfold in Horne's life and the lives of Inuit in the Eastern Arctic would be more than anyone could have ever imagined.

. . .

Sanikiluaq, like Jeannie's home community of Great Whale River, 160 kilometers away on the Quebec coast, was a staunchly Anglican community, at least nominally. But older beliefs were barely hidden below the guise of a devotion to Christianity. In 1941, a series of ritualistic murders rocked the sheltered life of the islands' camps when Peter Sala, "a natural leader," pronounced himself to be God, and Charlie Ouyerack announced that he was Jesus. Soon, nine adults and children would be dead, killed in an outburst of religious fervour caused by a misunderstanding of what their leaders had read in the syllabic Bible brought to them by visiting missionaries who, unfortunately, had not remained to teach the meaning of the words. A trial had ensued and most of the perpetrators were imprisoned and eventually released. But even after that, no resident missionary came to the islands. Religious instruction was left up to local catechists with little or no training and an occasional missionary from the mainland. Age-old beliefs in shamanism were at the root of what has gone down in northern lore as the "Belcher Island Murders." The power of the *angakkuq* — the shaman — was still feared in many families, though they might call themselves Christians.

Horne was likely aware of the power of shamanism and the hold it still had over some Inuit, having lived in communities where such beliefs still lingered. He was curious about religion. In fact, he was a religious chameleon — he professed to be Anglican in Quebec and Baffin Region communities, but in Iqaluit he attended the Roman Catholic church; in later civil investigations, he claimed to have been a follower of Islam even during his early days in the North.

. . .

Jeannie apparently remained unaware of her husband's abuse of boys. In her obliviousness she may have effectively, albeit unknowingly, shielded him from official suspicion. Nonetheless, according to Horne, it was Jeannie who pushed him to get out of Sanikiluaq and move to Cape Dorset, because she wanted to get away from her relatives. Years later, Horne said he had also wanted to leave because he had come to view the community as a sick and unhealthy place and that its weirdness was getting to him. As an example, he recounted a story from his first years in the village when he had given a little boy a piece of the chocolate bar he was eating. The boy had shocked Horne by promptly pulling down his pants, revealing himself. Strange incidents like that, Horne said, became "part of the process by which I came to believe that certain things were silly but okay ... not okay, but I did not recognize the behaviour that I was sliding into was viciously criminal and damaging. I had no conception of that. I had flashes of conscience at times, but they were all too brief."

He sounded as if he was blaming the system for not pointing out the criminality of sexually abusing children. In a statement stunning in its naïveté or its attempt to shift blame and avoid responsibility, he said, "In teacher training there was never any mention of the dangers of getting yourself on a slippery slope that would lead to your actually abusing children. It was not an issue in 1965, I feel. I think it's important to see the difference between what we know now and what we knew then to understand how I slipped into the system."

Horne was, in effect, claiming that he did not know, because no one had ever told him, something that every other teacher was expected to know: that sex between a teacher and student — or any child — was wrong. Horne would go on to describe his awareness of right and wrong when it came to sexual contact with his students as "flickering and intermittent."

No criminal charges were brought against Horne during his time in Sanikiluaq. Those would come twenty-one years after he left the community.

Cape Dorset, 1978–80, 1982–83

ED AND JEANNIE HORNE MOVED TO CAPE DORSET IN 1978. HE claimed the move was Jeannie's idea, but he also said he applied for the Cape Dorset job because the curriculum needed refinement, and he wanted to develop materials for it. He said as well that the Inuit language he was learning in Sanikiluaq was "a backwater dialect," and he wanted to learn a more "mainstream" version of Inuktitut.

Cape Dorset, now called Kinngait, is one of the north's most ruggedly beautiful communities. Situated on the southern point of Dorset Island, one of a group of islands on the south coast of Foxe Peninsula, the "cape" of Cape Dorset is a group of high hills rising over 240 metres above sea level, part of the Kinngait Range. I was told once that if you look off into the hills near Kinngait, and it's a clear enough day, you may see the shape of a naked woman lying on her back. I have seen this formation out there, and I suspect this artistic, sensual way of viewing the land makes everyday life somewhat less harsh.

Kinngait means "high hills or mountains." Ice and snow blanket the land much of the year. Images projected out into the world through films and photographs from this area often feature this gleaming frozen scene, often with Inuit in white parkas travelling by dogsled across it.[1] But Inuit in this region don't travel across the land by dogsled anymore. And the ice and snow melts. For a precious short time in the summer — August and September — little berries spring up, and the rusts and greens of hardy vegetation spread across the land. Arctic mountain avens, which resemble tiny daisies, appear, Arctic cotton grass fringes the marshy areas, and bright red seaweed clings to the shoreline.

There were about seven hundred people in the community when Horne arrived, with forty or so white or non-Inuit residents serving as Hudson's Bay Company staff, nurses, administrators, hotel staff, and teachers. The majority of Inuit in the region can trace their lineage in that place back hundreds of years, with many ties to the neighbouring community of Lake Harbour, as well as ties to northern Quebec. It can seem as if everyone in Kinngait is related, because in one way or another the Inuit of the region are. One of the most difficult parts of researching this story was realizing just how intricately connected the victims were. The close relationships between families through blood or marriage made Horne's crimes in Kinngait that much more sinister and destructive.

Every Eastern Arctic community Horne lived and worked in had deep-rooted social problems. Volumes have been written analyzing the reasons for the social malaise that permeated these small towns, but a simple consensus of opinion was that the discord stemmed from a clash between the cultures of Inuit who had recently moved into the communities and the qallunaat, who had arrived to administer and staff the new institutions.

Horne worked in schools that were located in the communities, often in the very centre, and the children lived with their own families. The Department of Education used a curriculum imported from Alberta but was working to incorporate northern realities into that curriculum. Being an early non-Inuit advocate for Inuktitut in the schools boosted Horne's reputation, at least among the departmental administration, and gave him more clout.

Cape Dorset was in a stronger position than most other Eastern Arctic communities to take advantage of better schooling because of the presence there of another unique and remarkable institution. The West Baffin Eskimo Co-Operative has been acclaimed throughout the world for its success in developing the artistic talents of its members and marketing their creative efforts globally. Starting from humble beginnings in the 1950s, the enterprise grew steadily. Its success as a stonecut print shop and a purveyor of soapstone carvings attracted artists, teachers, and students from throughout the world to study and share techniques, an exchange that exposed the people there — the Kinngammiut — to even more transformative ideas.

But success was a double-edged sword. Copious quantities of money had been flowing into the community through art for years before Horne arrived, but it didn't always result in positive change. For many complex reasons, alcohol and drug abuse, too often resulting in family violence, was already a part of Cape Dorset's reality. By the late 1970s, when Horne arrived, children in a number of families were not getting consistently positive parenting through their formative years.

Many Inuit at that time were still trying to maintain as traditional a life as possible, travelling outside the settled community to hunt and to visit relatives. When children stayed in town with other relatives or friends, Ed Horne led sports-related activities for the boys, and welcomed the boys into his home. In some cases, he became something of a father figure to them. The guilt and shame parents later felt when they realized Horne had abused their children while they were away was overwhelming. Many Inuit who lived through that time would never trust outsiders, especially schoolteachers, the same way again.

• • •

Horne's first two years in Cape Dorset could be viewed — from a teaching standpoint — as his "golden years," with students who were enthusiastic and co-operative. A class vote on favourite TV shows one year revealed two-thirds of the class liked the Canadian Broadcasting Corporation (CBC) investigative journalism program *The Fifth Estate*, with *Hockey Night in Canada* a distant second. This suggested to Horne that the children in Cape Dorset had great potential for learning.

He allowed kids to sit wherever they wanted in his classroom, not necessarily at desks, and he didn't hush up their loud voices when they became excited. They were not even required to attend lessons if they were concentrating on a personal project.

"I know how I hated to be pulled away from something as a kid if I was busy and it was time for the next lesson," Horne said.

One memorable class assignment took place during the Iranian revolution led by the religious and political leader Ayatollah Khomeini. Horne later recalled that his students were aware of the political turmoil unfolding in Iran and were doing mock executions during recess time. Most homes in Cape Dorset had no television at the time, although CBC Radio was almost always on in most Inuit homes, and Horne himself, interested in world affairs, was probably responsible for his students' awareness of the revolution. Horne suggested his students draft a class letter to the ayatollah; it began: "We don't like some of the things we've been hearing about you," and went on to outline the students' displeasure. The letter was then mailed to Iran. Not surprisingly, no answer was ever received.

"They were quite agitated for days after that, that they were going to have white-robed Arabs slinging their swords outside the portable, yelling 'Death to class 8!'" he recalled.

He had also noticed early on that some of the boys in town were gifted with natural physical strength.

"I saw potential in those kids," he later said. "On a weekend afternoon I had the TV in my classroom tuned to a youth athletic competition. They were weightlifting. A group of kids walked in and without any warmup they tossed more weight than the 'champions' on the screen," he told me. "There was huge potential around me at Cape Dorset, but I didn't have the knowledge or training to cultivate it."

In Cape Dorset, Horne found a community that was further along the road of development — some would say to acculturation — than Sanikiluaq had been. Local leadership was more cohesive. Many homes had telephones. Air travel to and from the community was more frequent. The children had more proficiency in English than did the Sanikiluaq students.

The local dialect of Inuktitut was strong, but young people preferred to use English among themselves. Horne, perhaps to counter this trend, claimed this emboldened him to use more Inuktitut in his classroom.

For two years he had a class of about twenty-four students, the third year about twenty.

He said his contact with his students' parents was minimal. This, in itself, is odd behaviour from someone wanting to improve his knowledge of the local language — sooner or later adult conversation is necessary to augment what one learns from children.

Horne taught in Cape Dorset on two separate occasions. When he transferred there in 1978, he remained for two years. He returned in September of 1982 for one more year. The principal of the school during his first stint in Cape Dorset was a man named Frank Gonda; when Horne returned, Gonda had been replaced by Terry Hobday. The education advisory committee was composed of local people — Inuit, most of them the parents of students — but Horne, in a complaint that became all too common, found the committee ineffective. Cape Dorset was within the Baffin Region, and Department of Education officials worked out of Frobisher Bay, from where they supervised and occasionally disciplined teachers, saw to hirings and transfers — there were seldom any firings — and directed the work of education in a far-flung geographic region. Depending on the year, these officials included Bert Rose, Brian Menton, Eric Colbourne, and Peter Grimm.

• • •

Horne liked to look his best when teaching, believing a teacher's appearance in front of a classroom was important in order to command respect from the children. Soon, he was making sure his male students looked well put together, too, supplying them with ties to wear with their own shirts — he devoted little attention to the girls in the class. Later, he acknowledged a sinister force behind his attention to the boys' clothing:

"I wanted them to feel good about themselves, and toward the end of my first year and throughout my second year, I imposed a dress code," Horne said. People in Cape Dorset still remember those little ties the boys wore. They wore their shirts and ties in the morning.

"In the afternoon it tended to get hot and that was uncomfortable, and they took their ties off in the afternoon," Horne later said. "But they felt themselves as being pretty special. I think the fact that my kids were instantly recognizable by the fact that they were dressed up, I think that was important. And I think it also ties in with the abuse I committed, that I think part of my mindset in dressing them up like that was similar to the mindset of a little girl playing with dolls, that I was becoming interested in them physically. And I think the fact that the classroom was, broadly speaking, a place where there was a lot of fun and a lot of high spirits and a lot of adventure led the kids to put up with the abuse that they otherwise would have objected to. I think it was the success of the class that made the criminal activities I imposed on them — I think in their minds, were relatively unimportant. I think the harm ... the hurt came later."[2]

. . .

In his second year in the community, Horne had a class of all boys. This was not normal in the North, but Horne had never been one to do things normally, and his bosses in education did not bat an eye at such a unique development in a Horne-led class.

"I think my class became more predominantly boys because I was taking in students voluntarily that other teachers felt they couldn't handle, who were boys," Horne said.

By 1979, Ed and Jeannie had become parents. Jeannie had a hard time with her pregnancies, two of them having been ectopic. Even though Cape Dorset had satisfactory health care services, Jeannie went to Frobisher Bay's hospital, where many women from the communities were sent for delivery if they were having difficult pregnancies. The Hornes' first child, John Paul Akavak, was born on April 20, 1979. Although Ed didn't accompany her to Frobisher Bay, Jeannie wouldn't be alone — education official Peter Grimm and his wife made sure she was taken care of during the birth of the Hornes' only biological child.

It was after the birth of Akavak, as he was known, that Horne said he began experiencing hallucinations and becoming unhinged — a feeling he described incongruously as "a terrifying happiness," explaining later, "I was obsessed with the idea that I should not have had John [Akavak]."

Horne told investigators later that he never expected to have children — that Jeannie believed she would be unable to bear children. He felt like he wasn't meant to have a son, that he had stolen Akavak somehow, and that punishment was coming. He soon heard a warning. "One night in the school I heard a voice in my ear and it was the Virgin Mary snarling threats at me," he said. He claimed to have reached out to a visiting psychologist in Cape Dorset at the time but was told the psychologist was too busy to help him.

. . .

"I was always a great observer of outsiders," a Kinngait woman named Rosemary* told me. "Even what they wear, what they do. They were always interesting. It seemed that back in the 1980s, Inuit just began to be in the white man's world, therefore they would have said 'Yes' to Ed Horne. He probably observed how he could fool Inuit because Inuit lack English knowledge or education. Therefore, maybe he only did it to Inuit because he knew they were powerless, or had lack of knowledge of how the system really works. So, he manipulated every little area. I never heard Inuit say, 'He's so smart, he's so educated.' He was never really talked about in my young life."[3]

I met Rosemary in 2005, in Cape Dorset, and we formed a bond very quickly through our shared interests in northern history. Rosemary was one of the first people to tell me about the crimes of Ed Horne. Although there was a gap of about fifteen years between our interviews and meetings, Rosemary's stories about how Horne's actions destroyed her family never changed.

Horne was Rosemary's grade 9 English teacher. She felt he was nervous around her. "He would just look down on the floor with chalk in his hand, and he always rolled the chalk with both hands. I was in pain so silently, so secretly. I was so angry inside. He knew I was the best-speaking English student in the class, and he never, ever acknowledged me."

Rosemary remembers Horne walking into the portable classroom one morning back in 1978.

"I would sit straight up, with my arms crossed on my table, and I would always look over to the door, and every time he walked in, even before he stepped in, he would look at my spot right away to see if I'm sitting there. He feared me, I could tell, and I didn't know why. I know he wrote and spoke Inuktitut and I would speak Inuktitut to him — my first language. I made sure he got the message twice. I would say, 'I am not a floor,' and 'Look at me when I'm talking to you,' and 'I am not the chalk.'"

Some students gave Rosemary a hard time about disrespecting Mr. Horne. She didn't care. He frustrated her to no end, especially his insistence on playing the Boney M. hit "Rivers of Babylon" during class. *Nightflight to Venus* had just been released, and Horne — always wanting to be the first with the latest fad — brought the cool new record into class. To this day, Rosemary can't listen to "Rivers of Babylon" without shuddering. "It haunts me forever now," she said.

Boys were the focus of Horne's attention. They suffered in silence, muted by the shock of his assaults on them, while the girls suffered in a different way — by being ignored and not getting the attention they deserved. Rosemary had big dreams. As a child, she thought that she would eventually write a book. At the very least she wished to be acknowledged for her skill in English. But Horne focused exclusively on the boys in her class. Rosemary is still incensed by this, lamenting what was lost, how much she could have thrived with a better teacher.

"My attentiveness, my alertness, my willingness — he never saw that. I had millions of questions. He ignored my schoolwork, and I lost interest in school. Then later at home in the evening, Mum would question my brothers: 'Why do they have to go there, to the school at night? And why do they smell of aftershave? Why shave already?' They answered that they had been weightlifting. They would go straight to their rooms."

It would take time for Ooleepeeka,* her mother, to realize that the man who was always at the school, teaching boys how to shave, leading popular weightlifting classes, surrounded by colourful wall displays, and promoting Inuktitut language use in the curriculum, was the most dangerous person in their community.

• • •

While Horne was ignoring his female students, his principal was often ignoring him.

"He may have been more involved with some teachers than he was with me, but I simply couldn't interest him in what I was doing," Horne later said of Frank Gonda. "I think my main contact with him was my constant complaining about the temperature in that classroom."

A bizarre example illustrates how little oversight there was at the school. Once, when head lice were detected in the community, a woman with no official role with the nursing station (but who clearly wanted one) took it upon herself to go to the school and shear all the boys' heads (girls were spared this indignity) without the permission or knowledge of the parents. According to Horne, what the woman was planning to do was misinterpreted by a number of his students, who wrongly believed the woman was coming to circumcise them, so they nervously avoided her. (The Inuktitut verb "kipi-" means "to cut" or "shear" and is used in the Anglican Bible to describe the circumcision of Jesus.)

"I remember some of the boys had their head shaved to the skin and it was weird," Rosemary recalled. "It was not a planned thing, so kids were really shy about their heads. Eventually they had to take their caps off and they didn't feel comfortable, but of course they were teased. Poor kids. We did not know."

• • •

Horne was up every morning at 6 a.m. in Cape Dorset, jogging around the gym at Peter Pitseolak School for exercise before the day officially began. He believed physical fitness and mental fitness were deeply entwined and claimed this was why he encouraged his students to be physically active. "Chess grandmasters train as athletes," he told me when I asked about his interest in fitness.

A government official who lived in Cape Dorset when Horne did remembers something that struck him as strange at the time. He had to bring Horne a file at the school, and even though it was evening, he walked in and saw a classroom full of boys, all wearing ties, looking like proper schoolboys.

Wow, he thought. *What dedication!* This official also had suspicions about the weightlifting program Horne was running because, as he recalled, Cape Dorset had "fabulous recreation programs. The school there was very progressive." He wonders today why no one in the community questioned a weightlifting program run by Horne, an educator, not a coach.[4]

Horne would later explain that the weightlifting program he operated in the portable school was never an official school program but was primarily for himself, so he could keep in shape. Although he denied he had ever organized an "official" weightlifting class for boys, such classes had indeed begun in the portable school after regular school hours.

In the Portable

LUKE* WAS ONE OF A LEGION OF YOUNGER BOYS WHO HAD BEEN sexually attacked inside the portable school that was burned in the communal fire. Horne was his teacher between the years 1979 and 1983. Years after suffering childhood abuse, he was incarcerated at the Baffin Correctional Centre in Iqaluit for crimes of his own. While there he spoke to a lawyer about his childhood.[1]

Luke recalled that he was playing games with his friends after class one day when Horne pulled him close, then assaulted him.

"I felt bad, you know. When he pulled my pants down and touch my dick," Luke said. "After that, he took me to the washroom. And in that washroom I struggled. I struggled and I struggled and I struggled. Never had sex like this. Or been touched like that. I've never been touched like that. And it hurt, it hurt, and it hurt. As soon as he was done I couldn't stand up right. And couldn't walk around normally."

He doesn't remember how he fled the schoolhouse. But his friends were still playing in the classroom. He never told a soul what happened.

Luke is dead now. As an adult dysfunctional father, he threw his infant son to the floor in a drunken rage; the boy was brain damaged and crippled as a result.

. . .

"I went to Ed Horne's school, that portable school," another victim recalled years later. "It was in the morning before school started. I was in awe, when I first walked in the portable school, of that Atari game that he used to bring to school. One morning I went there to play a game before his students came. That was in the morning. There was only me and Ed Horne. I played that game for about 10 minutes, when Mr. Horne took me by the arm and took me to the corner near his desk and laid me down on my back, unzipped my pants, and he pulled them down. He pulled his pants down. I am still lying there on the floor on my back. I am helpless. And he starts to have intercourse with me. And he didn't stop until he was finished. I am lying there, and I am helpless, and he's doing me. I never experienced anything like that in my whole life. I could hear my heartbeat there going 100 miles an hour. I am crying, and I am thinking he's going to kill me. He's going to kill me if I show myself in the state where I was."[2]

This victim believes school officials knew about Horne's predations:

"I think they all knew what was going on. They just didn't have the guts to do something or say something. Back then when we were kids, in the school, they all knew what was going on. The [Baffin Divisional Board of Education] knew what was going on. Everyone knew. They just didn't have the guts to be the one to point Ed Horne out."

Later in life the man abused drugs and alcohol and struggled to keep a well-paying job. While he admitted his home life as a child was far from perfect, he blames Horne for destroying his life.

"What Ed Horne did to me, it's always going to be in me. It's always going to be in my head, in my heart, be it a thousand miles away, be it if I am alone or whatnot. It's always going to be with me. Whether your mom or dad urges you to forget it, how can you forget it? How can I forget it? How can I make it go away? It can't go away. It can't. I wish it could, but it can't."

. . .

Rosemary was helping with spring cleanup during the 1996–97 school year when she found disturbing images that would be forever etched in her mind. The photos were from the early 1980s when her brothers were so cute and innocent.

The attic was small and hot. No one had gone through the tiny space and given it a good cleaning for years. There were a lot of Inuktitut books up there, and she was carefully retrieving them when one book drew her attention. This one was not in Inuktitut. There was no title on it. It was 8.5 by 11 inches with a homemade-looking cardboard cover. Rosemary recalled:

> When I saw it, it took time for me to react because it was like in the cartoons when they see something and it is a broken line from their eye to the thing — that's exactly how it was for me. I opened it from the middle. And I saw a picture of my late brother right away. I was so shocked. I looked at each and every picture. Underneath them Ed Horne had written captions. Crazy stories. Just crazy. I read every one. I knew it was Ed Horne who had written those stories. I recognized his handwriting right away. My brothers were there. In one of those pictures I saw my other brother — he was so small and scrawny. In that picture he is just wearing his briefs, and he is sitting on top of a fuel tank; it is summer outside, sunny. He was smiling really hard, you can tell because of his eyes. He is feeling the adrenaline rush of being on top of the tank. That was our school, the portable school, and it was the weight room at the same time. Ed Horne obviously had them taking off their pants and their shirts to do weight-lifting or something.[3]

She told her brothers a few years later about finding the photos, and they didn't react. "They became quiet. And I told them, 'I understand.' From that reaction I saw how deep the scar is."

Another picture was so disturbing it took her years to even mention it to her brother. "My brother was wearing a wedding gown. Another boy was wearing a tuxedo. And they were obviously forced to smile." Under the picture Horne had written: 'When these boys grow up, they will marry each other.'"

• • •

Horne victims were prone to depression and angry outbursts. Some drank too much alcohol, sniffed gas, and got high. Others killed themselves — death by hanging was the most common method of suicide. Parents were at a loss to know what to do; they were powerless in the face of what turned into a suicide crisis.

Rosemary's mother, a survivor of sexual abuse herself, realized the only way to stem the tide of dysfunction and death in her community was to speak out against Horne. She knew by 1985 that her sons were Horne victims. When the Crown was seeking witnesses in the first Horne criminal trial, Ooleepeeka flew to Frobisher Bay and gave a statement.

It is hard to imagine today how intimidating it would have been in the 1970s for an Inuk to speak out against a schoolteacher in such a rapidly evolving system. Inuit could feel dominated by the mostly male, qallunaat power structure running things in Frobisher Bay and Yellowknife. Ooleepeeka doubted her proficiency in English, but in fact it was excellent.

Horne would eventually enter a guilty plea, so the case never went to trial. There would be no boys having to take the stand, so families were understandably relieved. But as much as parents and officials tried to protect the victims from any further harm, the true impact of Horne's crimes would emerge over time.

PART TWO

Who Was Ed Horne?

EDWARD HORNE'S LIFE BEGAN FAR FROM THE ARCTIC, IN Waglisla, or Bella Bella, British Columbia, on October 2, 1943. His parents, Walter Hugh Horne and Muriel Bertha Hawkins, were both from Montreal. Walter moved to British Columbia in 1915, but spent time with his future wife in Montreal in the 1940s before the couple settled in the West for good. Walter only had a grade 6 education and worked as a taxi driver in Vancouver, a milkman in B.C.'s interior region, and as a cook in logging camps before he got married. He had been a boxer but retired when his last bout put him in the hospital for a week.

Walter and Muriel were married on August 15, 1942, in All Saints Church, Vancouver.[1] The bride wore a floor-length gown described in the newspaper as "white burnt chiffon" and carried a bouquet of red roses with orange blossoms. Her mother walked her down the aisle.

Walter was serving in the Air Force during the Second World War and was stationed in Bella Bella when Edward was born. The family moved to Langley shortly thereafter, where Walter worked as a cook for Ocean Cement's tugboat division and also began farming. The farm the family lived and worked on had chickens, cows, and goats but was never a big money-making endeavour; that's why Walter had an extra job on the tugboat. Walter purchased the farm from his parents, who were divorced, and

Walter's mother settled next door in a house that was built for her. Walter's mother had been a housewife, born on isolated Anticosti Island in the Gulf of St. Lawrence. Orphaned at age ten, she had been raised in Boston.

Walter and Muriel had two boys, Edward — always called Ted as a boy — and his brother, Terry, who was a year younger, and two foster children, Kathleen and her younger sister, Patsy, who both joined the family in the early 1950s. Kathleen, Horne recalled years later, was resolutely optimistic, and he always enjoyed her "brash, outspoken attitude."[2] Patsy was mentally disabled and reached the point where the family could no longer care for her and had to put her in a care home. She died in her twenties.

The family were politically conservative and members of the Anglican church. In 1977, Muriel received the "Senate Award," given to a Progressive Conservative party supporter for their long and dedicated service to the party in the Langley area. Muriel reportedly thanked the members for their kindness to her and said she felt she was "only doing her duty as a citizen."[3]

Horne says in those days he was clumsy, stubborn, and uncommunicative but a voracious reader, taking *Reader's Digest* to school. He described himself as a "brooding loner," and said he had a "battered" childhood,[4] with a father who was an ex-boxer. Ted claims to have left home at age six, already seeking a life of his own, sleeping in a cow barn, or in the bush.

Horne has said things about his childhood and youth that were, if not outright falsehoods, embellishments of kernels of truth. Ted may have had a difficult relationship with his parents. But he always had a warm bed to go home to at night and parents who, although they may have been old-fashioned and had their share of problems, cared for him.

Ted's foster sister Kathleen was said to have worshipped him. He was the brainy big brother who could be charming when he wanted to be. Girls at school noticed him, and he dated a little, but never had a steady girlfriend.

Younger brother Terry and Ted were not close. When they were little, they were about as different as brothers could be. Ted reached a height of five foot ten, while Terry remained short-statured like their father. Terry was fair-haired, gregarious, robust, and wasn't into reading or intellectual pursuits like Ted. The brothers "despised each other, could not be left in a room together," Horne said.[5] This would change in later years when the two would occasionally meet up for a coffee, or communicate via Facebook Messenger. When this book was being written, the two men were not in contact.

In those early days on the farm, Terry tackled all the jobs that needed doing, whether it was shovelling cow manure or feeding the animals. At the house, there was a set of old boxing gloves, and sometimes the boys would horse around with their father. When Terry got a bit older, he joined a boxing club and got into weightlifting. But Ted wasn't into those activities at all, not even hockey. In the winter, children in the area liked to go skating, but Ted never joined in.

Even at a young age, Ted showed signs of mental illness. He had strange mannerisms and bizarre speech and was generally uncoordinated. He refused to take part in scrub baseball or soccer with his classmates but did well enough in school — though the teachers complained about his behaviour. His mother speculated that Ted misbehaved because school bored him.[6]

Acting on the stage lit a spark in young Ted. At Aldergrove High, a popular counsellor, teacher, and dramatic arts director named Alex Goostrey took a keen interest in him and would sometimes drive him to school and rehearsals. Goostrey lived nearby in Murrayville, so it wasn't out of his way to give Ted a lift. The farm Ted grew up on, like Murrayville, was out in the country, a bit of a distance from the school.

As a teen, he played the lead in a number of high-school theatre productions and seemed gratified by the experience. On June 23, 1959, he was mentioned among the cast who performed scenes from a play called *Teach Me How to Cry*, put on by the Langley St. Andrew's Players in the church hall. His family may have been pleased that young Ted had found a stimulating activity in his spare time, but they were not particularly arts-inclined or curious about stage acting.

Muriel was a member of the Orange Lodge. She encouraged her boys to be engaged with the Anglican church like she was, although her husband never attended. Ted did not like Sunday school or doing chores, either in the house or the barn. This created friction with easygoing Terry, who liked to please his parents.

Horne would later say he was "borderline" abused by his mother, complaining she sometimes accompanied him to the washroom long after such an act was normal for a parent. He said his once-happy parents had grown apart, and he speculated that his mother's disappointing relationship with his father may have led her to reach out to him for a closeness missing in her marital life. Ted felt smothered by her.[7]

To escape from what he perceived as a stifling home life, Horne hitchhiked, rode his bike far and wide, and acted in local theatre productions. These were no doubt enriching experiences, but they also presented situations where a confused young boy could possibly be molested. But Horne told me he was never sexually abused. "I can't remember ever knowing there was such a thing," he said.

One enduring interest in Ted's life was riding a bicycle — a pastime, and even a means of making a living he has relied on occasionally throughout his life. He used to ride his bike everywhere, even into the United States from Langley — a notable ride being to Lynden in Washington State, a thirty-three-kilometre trip. Port Kells, a neighbourhood in Surrey, B.C., was another place Ted liked to go, an eleven-kilometre trip that took about forty minutes of pedalling one way on a good day.

Ted was about twelve years old when his parents took him for a brain scan, or EEG. Over the years he has offered different reasons for this procedure. One was that he'd had a bike accident and was knocked unconscious. Another time he said the scan was prescribed because he'd banged his head after fainting during a blood test. Yet another reason given was that his parents (and perhaps Ted himself) suspected all was not well with young Ted, so he had a couple of appointments with a neurologist.

"I was clearly a troubled child," he said later. "And I should have had more honesty with myself to realize that I was not fit for the challenges I was undertaking." He was alluding to the challenges of teaching in the Arctic.

Horne claimed his mother, just before her death in 1984, told him the neurologist had raised the issue of autism, but that in 1955, when he was examined, autism (or any spectrum disorder) was poorly understood and thus not properly diagnosed and treated. Horne later told me that the EEGs he had "indicated epilepsy, though I didn't have symptoms at the time. I was on medication for three years, which must have been some sort of tranquilizer."

In his first month at university, he went to health services and was prescribed thalidomide, a prescription that was soon withdrawn, perhaps because of the dangers later noted with that drug. Through it all, his feelings of inadequacy persisted. "I was haunted by the feeling that I was deeply repulsive and shouldn't be alive," he said.

Not helping matters was his father, who Horne said was "unforgiving" toward him, convinced young Ted was "dirty" due to his darker complexion. His father would toss him into the washroom and scrub him, "angry that this filthy cowering wretch was his son."[8] To avoid further antagonizing his father, Horne claimed he always wore gloves when he went out on his bicycle to prevent his hands getting darkened by the sun. Horne would later turn that darker complexion to advantage when he claimed in adulthood to be an Indigenous person, a claim that was believed by many.

Ted was a good-looking young man, with black wavy hair, full lips, and a slight overbite. In some photos from that time he looks like a young Anthony Perkins when he smiles. But he always had difficulty meeting a person's eyes; he would have his head slightly turned, his gaze averted, when speaking — a trait most people who knew him would comment on. Perhaps this was an indication of the spectrum disorder the doctor told his mother about.

Ted had a paper route, which of course involved him riding his trusty bicycle to make his deliveries. The paper route ended up paying off for his education in a substantial way. In 1958, when the *Vancouver Sun* and *The Province* merged to form Pacific Press, Ted was one of four *Vancouver Sun* carriers who received a fifty-dollar government bond from the Department of Education for academic excellence. Ted received this award at age fifteen, while he was a student in grade 10 at Aldergrove High School in Langley. Applicants had to have been carriers for at least a year to be eligible for the award, which honoured the memory of former *Sun* vice-president Sam Cromie, who had tragically drowned a year earlier. In a *Vancouver Sun* article on September 15, 1958, "Sun Carriers Awards Aid 4 Bright BC Students," Ted, always precocious, told the reporter he was studying Arabic "because he believes a knowledge of the language will help him to a better understanding of the Middle East situation." He also said he hoped to study psychology.

Near the end of grade 10, Ted told his parents that he was going away for a while. He planned a trip through the United States over to Montreal to visit relatives.

At that time, 1959, the bus fare from Vancouver to Montreal was thirty-eight dollars, and a room at the YMCA in any city was three dollars. Ted was sure that the money he'd saved from his paper route would last forever. But when he got to the United States, he didn't have an easy time getting his Canadian dollars changed, so he spent a few days hungry. A bright light in his memories of this time was his arrival in Chicago, and in Grant Park, on the shore of Lake Michigan, he saw a performance of *Gigi* at an outdoor concert.

He was living almost as an adult but was still a puny, socially awkward child, fifteen years old, often frightened and confused. That all changed in Montreal, the home of many of his relatives whom he barely knew but had heard stories about around his kitchen table back on the farm. Ted liked the offbeat sense of humour of his city relatives. His light-hearted Uncle John secured young Ted a job installing air-conditioning equipment on the roof of a downtown skyscraper, and two weeks at an appliance company as an office gofer, earning what was to him the staggering sum of $125. The gregarious spirit of his uncle impressed young Ted so much that he says twenty years later he named his first-born son, John, after him.

When Ted got back to Langley, energized by his adventures, he skipped a grade in high school. To graduate, 120 credits were required. Ted was apparently earning 150 credits staying up late into the night studying, so by January 1960, he was transferred from a grade 11 to a grade 12 classroom. He became class president and won the award for best actor at the Fraser Valley Drama Festival. He was also editor of the school newspaper, placed well in two public speaking contests, and won a Canada Council scholarship to study Shakespeare. He would later win awards that provided financial aid when he attended the University of British Columbia (UBC). In the graduation class of 1960 at Aldergrove High, he shared the role of valedictorian with a female student. He was a triple award winner that year: the McDonald Cedar Products university scholarship award brought in $250, the Aldergrove Valedictorian Scholarship was worth $100, and he took a

$25 Citizenship Prize awarded by Langley Branch #21 of the Canadian Legion to a veteran's son or daughter in grade 12. Nevertheless, he still had to borrow from his parents to attend university.

With high school behind him, Ted became Ed and entered UBC as a sixteen-year-old liberal arts student in 1960. By November he was listed as a staff member on *The Ubyssey*, the highly regarded student newspaper known for its award-winning writing.

It was around this time that Horne seriously contemplated killing himself. He chose the Lions Gate Bridge in Vancouver, an imposing suspension bridge that crosses Burrard Inlet, as the place where he would end his life. Horne later told me: "I walked to that bridge around midnight thinking I was going to throw myself over the edge. I see now that I was looking for attention, that I hung around the middle of the bridge so that someone would come along and rescue me and talk me out of it. I was seventeen. What bothered me most at the time was that in the previous year or two I had strong sexual feelings for three young men." He said it was "a calamity" to be homosexual in 1960. In later years, under questioning, he would claim not to be homosexual. "This awareness did take me to the brink of suicide at times, and I was not alone in that feeling, in that danger. This faded, especially when I came back from Europe and found better relationships with two or three girlfriends. But the short answer, I was fantasizing an escape from a situation that horrified me, not seriously wanting to end my life." He stood there for half an hour before he turned around and walked away.

He continued seeking out acting roles on the stage, performing as one of the knaves or messengers in a production of *Henry IV, Part One* directed by UBC's arts department. His acting experience would stand him in good stead during the duplicitous life he would lead as an adult.

He took the first three years of a B.A. program, dropped out for a year to travel in Europe, then returned to UBC for one year — the bare minimum for a licence to be a teacher. "I did not graduate because the pay scales were so heavily based on paper credentials that a person could price himself out of the market," he later said, turning his failure to complete a degree into a plus.

In any case, not having a university degree at that time would not affect his ability to secure a teaching position, especially in isolated locations;

teachers were in short supply in the mid-1960s. He would eventually complete a B.A. from UBC in 1980 by taking correspondence courses.

. . .

Horne was drawn to isolated places with small, Indigenous populations. His first teaching job, in 1965, was in Quesnel, B.C., teaching grade 4 in the Quesnel School District. He spent one year there. He believed he did a good job, but later, under interrogation, couldn't remember if he had resigned or been fired. In any case, he admitted that he felt inadequately prepared for the position.

Still with a keen sense of adventure, he moved farther north in B.C., taking on the daunting task of teaching all grades from 1 to 8 in a one-room school in the Fort Nelson School District at Mile 392 on the Alaska Highway. As the school's only teacher, he was the de facto principal as well. This posting also lasted just one year before he went on to teach a grade called "Beginners" at the residential school at Lower Post, just south of the Yukon border. Lower Post was funded by the Canadian government but operated by the Roman Catholic church, and was open from 1951 to 1975. One of the most brutal schools in the sordid history of residential schools in Canada, it was the site of horrendous abuse of Indigenous students, abuse so traumatic that the school was physically demolished in 2021. "Beginners," the class that Horne taught, were generally of grade 1 age, but the term was used because it also included older children who had never been to school before. Horne worked there at the same time as Jerzy George Maczynski, a dormitory supervisor later convicted of twenty-eight sex abuse crimes.

I asked Horne about his time at Lower Post. He said he left after a year and a half because he was appalled at how the students were treated.

"I don't think there was any sexual abuse while I taught there. I am confident there wasn't. I was only dimly aware that sexual abuse of children was a possibility or actually occurred. There was a time when it wasn't on our radar screen. It should have been, but it wasn't."

During his time at Lower Post, Horne claims to have met and begun living with an Indigenous woman. The principal of the school scorned the couple, calling their living arrangement "against God's law." Horne said the woman drank too much and that their relationship was over before he left for his next job, teaching an anthropology course for teachers at UBC in the summer of 1969.[9] But a fragment of the relationship is reflected on the marriage certificate when he wed Jeannie Cookie in 1977 — Horne claimed to be a "widower."

I asked Horne about his marriage in Lower Post, and he said he was never married to the woman. The closest to it, he said, was that the couple was blessed by a "rogue priest" but never registered as married. "I would have lost my job, which at the time I still cared about," he said. "We never lived together. I was living in the school and I don't remember where she lived. I was infatuated with her, but it was difficult to spend time with her. I finally moved away from Lower Post without her because she was a heavy drinker."

When asked to explain what a "rogue priest" was doing at Lower Post, Horne explained the man was one of two priests at Watson Lake and was a "rogue priest" because he was "clearly at odds and he offered to bless us, which was not a normal way to proceed. I had gone to him only for advice. He left the church to work for a private company not long after."

Horne said he ultimately didn't get along with the principal at Lower Post and left in 1969.

After teaching a summer course at UBC in Vancouver, Horne moved on, this time to the Burns Lake District in the central part of the province, two hundred to three hundred kilometres west of Prince George, where he taught grades 1, 2, and 3. This, like other postings, lasted one year. Next came a job he was happier about — librarian at Silverthorne Elementary School in Houston, B.C. He was soon pressed into teaching half-time there, though, and felt he'd been "double-crossed" into having to take on the extra workload. It was a large school with about three hundred students. Cataloguing hundreds of books while attending to his teaching duties was crushing, so again, propelled by restlessness, Horne began scouring the newspapers for job postings. That's where he spotted an ad seeking teachers for the Belcher Islands, soon to be renamed Sanikiluaq, in the Northwest Territories.

• • •

While in Quesnel, his first posting out of university, Horne aligned himself with the Scouting movement, leading "hardy Red Bluff scouts," as the local newspaper called them, on a multiday camping expedition during the winter. The *Quesnel Cariboo Observer* presented an overview of this adventure where a group led by Horne huddled together in subzero temperatures at Beavermouth, fifty kilometres up the Quesnel River. Horne devised the trip as a "toughening up exercise," the article reported, with Horne quoted as saying, "Anybody can camp out in the summer, but you learn a lot about camping in conditions like this."[10]

There were three more camping trips in the works to be led by Horne, and he told the newspaper that, while the locations of these excursions hadn't been decided yet, he and a number of Scouts were doing a lot of "pouring [*sic*] over maps."

Someone brought an apple pie on the journey and it froze in the cold. This lent itself to what was supposed to be a high-spirited photo-op of the group with the pie, with Scoutmaster Horne holding a small woodsman's axe over the pastry, about to chop into it. In retrospect, the image is a most sinister one. The faded old newspaper photo only enhances the creepiness of the scene: Horne emerges out of inky blackness in the tent, holding an axe, looking menacingly at the camera, unsmiling, while all the boys around him look thrilled.

• • •

Horne knew how to keep secrets. When he was in his twenties, he had a son with a woman in the Philippines, conceived while he was on vacation. He told very few people about this boy, now in his fifties and working as a computer technician, because he was worried that Jeannie, known to be a jealous wife, would find out. He also claimed to be worried that the authorities would alert his son to his criminal behaviour.

Later in life, Horne would claim that teaching had never been his life-long dream at all and that while in the North he had approached the CBC about working for them as a journalist. He reportedly filed freelance reports for the CBC out of Grise Fiord in 1980. He claimed to have written a civil service exam while in Cape Dorset and was informed his score on the exam was not high enough to warrant consideration.

"I had initially wanted to be a researcher in blood diseases, but I did poorly on my science courses in university," he said. "But still my thinking was that if I went into teaching for a couple of years I could put away enough money to go back to university and go into something like pharmacy or research in genetics or something like that." This, in fact, has been the dream of many young teachers, to teach for a few years and save enough money to do something else, like travel or go back to school, or change careers. But many never make the break. In Horne's case, was his admission of not wanting to be a teacher mere bravado? Or did he, even then, harbour the knowledge that he should not be in a classroom with young boys?

Bert Rose

THE YOUNG TEACHER STOOD ON A SNOW-COVERED ROAD, LOOK-
ing around at his new hometown of Broughton Island in the High Arctic. It
was 1968. It was cold. The sky was a mix of coal-grey clouds. He remembers
thinking *I've made the biggest mistake of my twenty-four-year old life.* But
once classes started, things began to look brighter.

There were five teachers at the school in all. Rose was teaching grades
3 and 4, and he loved it. The children were generally well-behaved and
eager to learn. In the classroom next door was a tall, outgoing Ontario
native named Kenn Harper. Rose wasn't a language guy. Harper was. In
fact, Harper was so interested in learning the language of the Inuit he
had posted words on the wall over the honey bucket so he could learn
while he relieved himself. The men would remain friends over the next
half-century.

By springtime, when teachers were required to make their intentions for
the following year known, Rose signed on for another year. Always devoted
to his students, he had gradually developed an interest in their community,
their experiences, and the new environment in which he was immersed, so
different from that of his formative years on the Prairies. He was quickly
warming to the Arctic. Despite his initial misgivings about his island home,
Bert and Joanne would spend a total of nine years on Broughton Island.

They had their first child, and they built their own home, a hippie-style geo-desic dome. And to top it off, the Inuit gave him not one but two Inuktitut names — Uluusialuk (big Rose) and Umilialuk (big beard).

. . .

In 1972, a teachers' conference was held in Frobisher Bay. Such conferences were annual events, almost always held in February, generally the coldest month of the Arctic year and the month when, the administration had come to realize, teachers needed a break from the isolated settlements where they had been living since the previous summer. People's nerves were frayed, and petty tensions developed as southern teachers endured and adjusted to the unaccustomed darkness of an Arctic winter. It seemed that as the light returned and the cold perversely increased, teachers needed a change from their stressful realities. It was at that conference that Rose encountered Ed Horne, who was then working in the Belcher Islands. Horne's engaging teaching methods were said to be getting positive results out of kids there. Rose wanted to meet this fellow.

Horne would later claim that teachers were not highly regarded in the Belcher Islands in the early 1970s — that the public did not show them proper deference. Rose recalls that Horne was wearing a suit and tie, quite different from his conference colleagues who trended toward a more relaxed, casual style of dress. But Horne always made a point of dressing smartly — feeling it was an important image to project. Rose and Horne attended many of the same sessions, including one about a new methodology for training and hiring classroom assistants. Horne seemed open to embracing such new and innovative ideas in the classroom.

. . .

After nine years in Broughton, Bert and Joanne Rose moved to Whale Cove, where Bert became principal of a three-room school. There, they had a tele-phone at home for the first time, but you couldn't call outside the commun-ity. Their phone number was "12."

Living in Whale Cove meant the Roses were now in the Keewatin (now Kivalliq) Region, on the western shores of Hudson Bay; with education being administered regionally, they seldom heard a word from many of their teacher friends in the Baffin Region.

After one year, the Roses left and Bert returned to university for one year to add to his qualifications. When they returned to the North in 1979, it was to Fort Franklin (now Deline) on Great Bear Lake in the Mackenzie Valley, where they remained for a year and a half. In 1981 the call came for the Roses to head back east, to Frobisher Bay — Bert had been appointed supervisor of schools for North Baffin. One of the schools he was expected to visit and oversee was the school in Grise Fiord, the most northern community in Canada.

. . .

Horne socialized with Bert and Joanne in the few years when they lived in the same community. Jeannie was rarely in attendance at these gatherings, church or child-rearing obligations cited as reasons for her not joining them. Unlike many northerners, the Roses didn't drink alcohol. This suited Horne fine — he was never into alcohol, quite content with the soda pop or coffee on offer at the Roses. On one visit, Horne kept fiddling with his pop can all evening, preoccupied by it. It had Arabic script on it, among other languages. At the end of the evening he told Bert and Joanne he wanted to take the can home with him. At work the next day, Horne made sure to tell Bert Rose he'd translated the Arabic script on the can.

Horne went to China two summers in a row to study Mandarin during the two-month summer holidays teachers get every year, and he would share stories with the Roses about these trips. Bert recalled that Horne said he was frustrated after the China school experience because he thought he would have progressed better in a beginner's class rather than the more advanced group he found himself in. Around 1983, Horne went on a summer holiday to Peru, where he reportedly studied an Indigenous language and brought back a toy llama for Tony, Bert and Joanne's son.

• • •

In the early 1980s, Rose heard from an education official that Horne had been getting up to some "shenanigans" in Cape Dorset. Some anecdotes centred around antics intended to delight the children in town. One was that Horne had two pairs of glasses. He somehow broke the right lens of one pair and the left lens of the other. One pair was sunglasses, the other clear. So, he combined the two, creating one pair of glasses with two different lenses and went everywhere in the community wearing them, causing some people to laugh and point at him, which was probably his intention. Horne would go to extreme lengths in the classroom to get his students to react and talk. One day, he stood up in front of his students, pulled out a pair of scissors, and cut his tie in half. He often wore mismatched shoes, anything to create intrigue and stories for the children.

But Rose heard more troubling stories that pointed to a hot temper bubbling beneath Horne's carefully constructed persona. One was that he had gone to Montreal for a medical appointment and eventually sought a hotel room at 1:30 a.m. When Horne was told there was no vacancy, he "freaked out" so severely that police were called and he spent the night in a jail cell.

One incident that Rose heard about during Horne's time in Cape Dorset was indeed serious. It involved a boy being choked in the schoolyard. While not admitting to it, Horne did later acknowledge he once grabbed a boy by the arm in that community, leaving three bloody scratch marks. The incident, he said, was investigated by the school committee. Horne was not disciplined for the use of excessive force.

Horne did things that went far beyond normal teaching duties and might be considered the hallmark of an exceptional teacher, such as writing a personal letter to every boy and girl in his class every day, Rose recalled. "And he was posting each letter to them in the mail. Why? So they would get something in the mail. Again, something to talk about." Rose then said, sadly, "It's all part of the mask. Where do you go to do that? You go to the school. You go back to the school at night. So, inside the community you're creating a pattern so that the entire community knows what you're doing. Or, they think they know."

Grise Fiord, 1980–81

HORNE'S FIRST STINT IN CAPE DORSET LASTED TWO YEARS. IN 1980 he asked for a transfer to Grise Fiord, the most northern settlement in the Northwest Territories.

Many adventurers saw a posting to Grise Fiord as the ultimate northern experience — Canada's farthest northern civilian settlement, situated on the southern coast of Ellesmere Island, which stretches northward to within eight hundred kilometres of the North Pole. A Twin Otter was the usual mode of transport, a plane able to take off and land on the community's dangerously short runway and still carry a decent cargo load. Only experienced pilots flew that route. The landing called for flying directly toward a mountain, then making an abrupt turn to put the machine down on the gravel strip.

The population of this outpost usually hovered around one hundred, but the community had a school, nursing station, police detachment, co-op store, and government administration. The location had never been a traditional Inuit camp. In fact, in historical times Inuit didn't live that far north. But in 1953 the federal government relocated a number of Inuit from Port Harrison in northern Quebec to the High Arctic, to Resolute and Grise Fiord, where it was hoped that hunting conditions would be better. They also moved a few families from Pond Inlet to help teach the Quebec Inuit how to live and hunt in the dark of winter. And dark it was. Port Harrison is well below the Arctic Circle and so never loses the sun in winter, but in Grise Fiord the sun sets in October and does not reappear until February. Living there, for Inuit and qallunaat, took considerable adjustment.

For a man who suspected he suffered from depression, or seasonal affective disorder, a move to Grise Fiord would prove a real test of his resilience. In fact, Horne had first applied for a job in Grise as early as 1966, after his year of teaching in Quesnel; wisely, the government usually sent only teachers who already had a few years' teaching experience to such a remote location.

Grise Fiord had eighteen students when Horne arrived, down from twenty-one the year before. One of Bert Rose's first official acts after he accepted the position of supervisor of schools in 1981 was to head to Grise Fiord on an inspection visit in late February. He wanted to see how the man whose abilities he had so admired was faring, and to meet the school principal, Merle Tippett; a classroom assistant named Mary Flaherty; and the janitorial staff. Rose himself had never been that far north. As a man with a private pilot's licence, getting there on a commercial Twin Otter flight fascinated Rose, as did the logistics of maintaining a settlement so far north.

It was — as one would expect — freezing cold in Grise when Rose arrived. The sun had only recently begun to peek above the southern horizon for a short but increasing period each day, but it was dark most of the time. Horne took Rose on a tour of the community, which involved stops at the nursing and police stations. The community tour delighted Rose, but he kept looking down with dismay at Horne's choice of footwear: Horne wasn't wearing boots — only duffle socks, the thick high socks that Inuit wear inside sealskin kamiks or a pair of rubber boots. "The snow is hard and it won't stick to your socks anyways," Rose reasoned, "so I guess he didn't bother with boots." Horne didn't seem to think there was anything unusual about this, but Rose thought it was peculiar. But again, it was the North. It attracted offbeat people then, as it does today. Horne was just one of those guys Rose had come to expect would be eccentric, and he looked past it.

Horne wouldn't have been Horne if he was satisfied with his position. In his previous postings, he had clashed with authority or his colleagues. So it should have been no surprise that as Horne chatted with Rose about how things were going at the school, he made it abundantly clear that he didn't like Mary, the young Inuit teaching assistant. "In retrospect, it's because he couldn't get away with anything," said Rose. "Mary was always there. She was always in the environment of the school." It is perhaps a testament to Mary's diligence and constant guarding presence that Horne did not have his way with boys in Grise Fiord like he did in other communities.

Mary went on to work as an Inuktitut language instructor at a school in Iqaluit. Recently she recalled that she was pregnant when she was working with Horne in Grise Fiord.[1] Because she was expecting, she wasn't moving about quickly at that time and, yes, she was usually in the school, assisting the children with Inuktitut language learning. She loved leading Inuktitut lessons for the children and still does to this day. Horne, while praised by the non-Inuit officials for being such a shining star in Inuktitut, didn't impress Mary one bit. She was fresh out of school and remembers that Horne was unfriendly to her. But if Horne didn't like her, the feeling was mutual. She remembers Horne always had his head down, and she doesn't ever recall him talking to her — never making small talk, never asking how her pregnancy was going, asking how she was feeling, or being helpful to her in any way.

She says she can't assess Horne's strength in Inuktitut because he never once so much as gave her an "Ullaakkut" (Good morning) or "Qanuippit?" (How are you?) the entire year. She would see Horne walking briskly to and from the school, often wearing odd footwear, very possibly duffle socks. Was he odd? Absolutely, she confirms. But she had no idea he was a child molester.

The population of Grise Fiord was ninety people at that time, so being invisible was impossible. In other places in the North, Horne knew how to become invisible, how to move from his house to the school without people seeing him. In Sanikiluaq and Cape Dorset he was able to spin his dedication to teaching and late nights at the school into the sexual abuse of boys without generally arousing suspicion. "People got used to seeing him there with the kids at night," Rose said of those communities, pointing out that in Grise Fiord such secretive activity was almost impossible.

Horne claimed he never molested anyone while in the community but did admit that he had attempted to molest one of his Grise Fiord students while on an exchange trip to Greenland.

During Horne's year in Grise Fiord, there was a visit between Grise and the community of Qaanaaq, Greenland, even farther north. A group of people from Qaanaaq flew over to Grise to spend a week there, and among them was a Danish teacher named Hans Engelund Kristiansen, who was also the editor of the monthly local newspaper, called *Hainang*. His wife, Arine, also a teacher, was a Greenlander who acted as translator for the newspaper. Hans Engelund spent a week in Grise Fiord while Kenn Harper, the former N.W.T. schoolteacher who knew Ed Horne, happened to be living in Qaanaaq. Harper told Hans before the trip to Grise Fiord that he would encounter a "very intense" schoolteacher there named Ed Horne. When Hans returned from his trip, he told Harper that, indeed, he had met Horne, who was greatly involved with his students, including after-school programs. Hans found Horne to be more than intense; as he put it plainly, he found him "bizarre." Hans also got the impression — why is unclear — that Horne was homophobic. Hans assumed that Horne had a sense of humour — an assumption that was probably wrong — so to play a joke on him Hans prepared a fake edition of the newspaper when he arrived back home in Qaanaaq. It was actually a previous edition of the paper, which may have been ten or twelve pages but with a fake cover replacing the original. Hans was a talented photographer and a sharp manipulator of photos long before Photoshop. He had taken pictures of Horne in Grise Fiord and used one of them on his phony newspaper cover, manipulated to show Horne wearing a dress. Hans thought this was hilarious and assumed Horne would find it funny too. On the next charter flight back to Grise, Hans sent his "newspaper" to Horne as a gift. But rather than laughing at the creative cover poking fun at him, Horne was irate. A few weeks later, he sent a blistering note to Hans excoriating him for his meanness and insensitivity.

Horne's reaction is curious. If the stories of Horne dressing up boys in women's clothing in Cape Dorset are accurate, it looks like Horne could dish out humiliation to his students but couldn't take it himself. He could photograph boys in various stages of undress, make them wear high heels and a wedding dress costume, as one traumatized boy never forgot, but when it came to himself, Horne didn't want any part of it.

. . .

After just a year in the community, Horne applied for a transfer to Iqaluit to work on Inuktitut curriculum development.

"I was absolutely fed up with the fact that I had been lied to about the level of funding that would be available for Inuit language projects," Horne later said to me about requesting the transfer. "I had been over to Greenland a couple of times and seen what they were able to accomplish."

According to Horne, the year he and his students visited Greenland, the country had published over two hundred titles in Kalaallisut, the Inuit language of the country, for use in schools, while the N.W.T. had done two or three. His request for a transfer was approved by education official Eric Colbourne. Colbourne was the new regional superintendent, committed to working with the education advisory committees and getting more Inuktitut learning materials produced.

Nakasuk School, 1981–82

COMPLAINING BITTERLY TO GOVERNMENT OFFICIALS ABOUT THE lack of funding for Inuit-language material, Horne moved into what many would consider a plum job doing consulting work for the Department of Education, ostensibly to advance that cause. His office was in Nakasuk School in Frobisher Bay.

Nakasuk School had always stood out because of its design: it resembles a space-age iglu — all white with no discernable windows visible on the outside — one of three similar buildings, two of them schools, a strange choice of architecture that blocks out natural light and a view of the landscape.

Horne's job was language development in a swiftly evolving curriculum.

He went to significant lengths to try to get English-Inuktitut translations done, including ones for a book of Japanese legends and for *Tom Sawyer*. The number of people who could do such translations was limited, and ultimately, despite good intentions, *Tom Sawyer* was never finished. Printing was still a cumbersome process in those days, and publishing in syllabics was a daunting prospect but one Horne was up for.

There were other pioneer developers of syllabic fonts for the ubiquitous Macintosh computers, but Horne was best known for doing this in the N.W.T. He was responsible for three typefaces called Iqaluit, Nunavut, and Kimmirut, incorporated into the MacTitut package at the time.

Horne later downplayed the significance of his work. "A company in Yellowknife was trying to cash in," he told me. "They sold a font that had to be part of the operating system of the computer. And they were charging, I think, a thousand dollars to install Inuktitut on one computer. I simply wrote ordinary fonts that anyone could install free in any computer, and I gave them to anyone who wanted them with permission to install them anywhere. It was new technology and quite easy to use. My work attracted attention because it was practical and easy to use. But within two or three years, laser fonts were developed and replaced my work."

In a number of exchanges I had with Horne, he clarified his Inuktitut ability — he was not an expert in Inuktitut, as was generally believed.

"Sadly, people had their own reasons for overstating my work. Yes, I uncovered vocabulary that younger people didn't have. My work in Inuktitut in the classroom was entirely in teaching the writing system, in implementing the system approved by Inuit Tapirisat; I did this within the Anglican church too. I never freely spoke Inuit. It's hard to convey to you now what a mess written Inuktitut was at the time."

But education was unmistakably evolving in the North in the 1970s. There was movement to lessen the centralization of all administration and put more authority into the hands of people at the community level, so the Baffin Regional Council was formed. It had no legislative authority, only an advisory mandate, but still, it showed that people were interested in advancing the cause of local administration of their own affairs. That desire extended to control over education as well. Eventually a regional board, the Baffin Divisional Board of Education, was created.

At this stage in his career, Horne was poised to move quickly up the education ladder in the territory. But the most heinous crime he would ever admit to, a crime that carried a 14-year jail term at the time, would occur right inside the very school he was so proud to be working in.

Horne would sometimes bring his son, Akavak, then age two, with him to his office at Nakasuk School. A boy named Sam* liked to stay after school and tidy up classrooms. One day, Horne asked Sam to watch his son while Horne completed school tasks. Sam, ten years old at the time, agreed. Another day, Sam visited Horne in his office, but little Akavak wasn't there.

Horne asked Sam to follow him, so he did, perhaps thinking he would take him to see Akavak. But Horne had other ideas.

With Sam following closely, Horne made his way to the gymnasium dressing room where there were bathrooms and showers. Once there, Horne took off his own clothes and started having a shower. He told Sam to wait for him and they carried on a conversation while Horne showered. After a few minutes of this, with the shower still running, Horne approached Sam and told him to strip. The child obeyed. The boy did not want to take off his underwear, so Horne removed them himself. Then he told Sam to go in the shower where Horne proceeded to wash the boy with soap. Sam remembers just standing there and that his heart was beating fast. He wanted to leave, but every time he tried getting out of the shower Horne put his hand on his shoulder, stopping him.

Horne then fondled the boy's penis. He told Sam to lie down on his stomach, which he did. Then the boy felt Horne's body positioned over his. Horne then penetrated the child's anus with his penis. Sam tried to keep his muscles clenched and his legs together hoping to prevent Horne from continuing, but it didn't work and he could feel the pain as Horne was penetrating him. Sam said of the attack, "I thought it ripped and felt like it was bleeding inside and my stomach was in pain." He remembers that he tried to get up to leave but he could not move.

Sam suddenly heard a noise in the dressing room. It appeared someone had come in. Horne stopped and covered the boy's head. When the unknown person left, Horne got off the boy. Sam got up and eventually dried and dressed himself. Horne took the boy to the gymnasium exit and left him there. Sam couldn't walk fast because his anus and stomach were hurting. He somehow got home but does not remember how. It was not until he was in his twenties that he told a girlfriend he'd been raped by Horne, and in 1997 he told his parents.

Horne later disagreed with the boy's recollection of events. He admitted that he sodomized him twice — the other time was at Horne's house. But Horne's criminal defence lawyer at the time had told him to "shut up about that." In Horne's mind, the boy's complicity in the sex act was "very real."

. . .

Horne's sexual assaults during his year in Frobisher Bay were never brought to the attention of authorities, either in government or the police, at the time. But, following an established pattern, Horne was unhappy in his position. The complaints were the same — there was never enough support, the department wasn't fully committed to change, he was the only one dedicated to seeing an increase in the use of Inuktitut in the classroom. It was time to move on.

He asked to be returned to the scene of some of his horrific crimes — a transfer back to Cape Dorset as a classroom teacher. With no blemishes on his official record, the request was granted. Horne returned to Cape Dorset for another year.[1] But he was no happier there than he had been anywhere, and it was always someone else's fault. In 1983, after only one year in Dorset, a year in which his sexual depravity continued, he asked for another transfer, this time to Lake Harbour, a small community on the south coast of Baffin Island, east of Cape Dorset. As usual, his request was granted.

"He Killed My Brother"

WHEN HORNE ASKED FOR THE TRANSFER TO CAPE DORSET, there was no challenge to the request and no questions asked about why Horne, who had spent only a year in each of his last two postings, wanted to move again. And at the end of one year back in Cape Dorset, he requested yet another move, this time to the principalship of the school in the small community of Lake Harbour, south of Frobisher Bay on the shores of Hudson Strait. That request, too, was granted. Horne was steadily moving up the education ladder. But even in the tight-knit, traditional Inuit community of Lake Harbour, Horne would continue to abuse boys, with violence that in hindsight appeared to be escalating.

While in Lake Harbour, Horne allegedly choked a schoolboy until he passed out. It was similar to an allegation made against Horne earlier in Cape Dorset, but this time the incident was reported to officials in Frobisher Bay. The problem was, it was Horne himself who reported the choking. At the regional office in Frobisher Bay, the report landed on the desk of Brian Menton, assistant superintendent of schools responsible for Lake Harbour. There is no evidence that any action was taken by Menton to deal with the incident. There was no written report. There was no follow-up. The fact the violent incident is known at all is a result of community gossip, RCMP memories of the event, and a report done by an education consultant named Kevin Van Camp after Horne's arrest.

Horne later said of his crimes: "The broad pattern of my victims is that they were kids that were pretty well adrift, that they were not close to their families, that they were hanging around outsiders just because of a void in their lives and that they were unhappy and I hate to say it, vulnerable."

• • •

The year was 1984. Although Horne was considered one of the North's best teachers by education officials, for weeks eleven-year-old Jonathan* and his friends wrote "I hate Mr. Horne" all over Lake Harbour in black marker and pen and, using their fingers, in the dry dirt on unwashed vehicles. They had seen dark sides of Mr. Horne. For one thing, Horne was too touchy-feely and they didn't like it. He would give the boys bear hugs. Other times he would pick a boy up, with the boy's feet dangling over the snow, and rub his scruffy facial stubble on their cheeks "for fun," one victim told me, shuddering at the memory.[1]

Horne didn't socialize with adults in Lake Harbour, either Inuit or qallunaat, focusing instead on school events. Jeannie rarely went anywhere other than church services. Their three children — the oldest was then four years old — played with other kids, although many townsfolk laughed to themselves about the youngest Horne boy, Danny, who was often seen on what to them resembled a leash. It was actually a kind of harness Jeannie used to control the rambunctious child.

Akavak, the Hornes' oldest boy, made friends in the village but was regarded as a bit strange; one year during a child's birthday party, he walked straight in and immediately handed the birthday boy cash. The boy, taken aback by the gesture, stashed the money out of sight of the other partygoers, and continued on with the games. The Horne family spoke an Inuktitut dialect from northern Quebec, which Horne's students found unfamiliar but understandable. Horne impressed them with his knowledge of the language, as it was rare for a qallunaat teacher to learn any Inuktitut at all.

The Hornes may have seemed like a happy family when they arrived in Lake Harbour, but all was not well. Jeannie, apparently unaware of her husband's abuse of students, also seemed oblivious to the important position he occupied within the education hierarchy. She was dismissive of his abilities and apparent accomplishments. When I interviewed Horne about Lake Harbour, he told me Jeannie was bewildered when she realized he'd been named principal. "She wondered how the Department of Education could hire such a loser."

After school, late at night, early mornings before school started, or when his wife was out of town, Horne spent a lot of time with his male students. But not until an unrelated attack by local boys on a little girl was reported did the true story of what Horne was doing with boys in town — and, ultimately, what Horne had been doing to boys throughout his time in the North — emerge.

• • •

In Lake Harbour, as in Cape Dorset, Horne was often preoccupied with the boys' physical fitness. Teacher Maureen Doherty was suspicious of Horne for being overly interested in their muscle development during the 1984–85 school year. Horne answered questions about his habit of measuring boys' muscles during questioning in 2007. This is an edited portion of that interview.[2]

> **Lawyer:** [Maureen Doherty] had seen you measuring the boys' muscles … It's what we call … us, as the plaintiffs' lawyer … your measuring routine, "You do the weights, now I'll measure your muscles."
> **Horne:** They weren't doing weights unless they were 14 years or older. But they were doing vigorous physical exercise.
> **Lawyer:** And you would measure them to see their development?
> **Horne:** Yes, and they were … what I found was dramatic, the regular attenders, the hard workers, the physical improvement was dramatic.

Lawyer: You would measure their muscle development?

Horne: Yes.

Lawyer: With a tape or something?

Horne: Tape measure.

Lawyer: You would put the tape measure around upper thighs, correct?

Horne: Chest and waist was what I was most interested in, and upper arms.

Lawyer: Thighs as well, correct?

Horne: I don't remember this, but it's plausible.

Lawyer: Yes, because we heard the other side ... you were the phys ed teacher holding after hours sessions. There's the good Ed Horne at work here. But then we had the sex abuser Ed Horne. So measuring muscles gives you a chance to move up the thigh, doesn't it?

Horne: This is one of the things that, at the time, I would have been able to provide a very good rationale for what I was doing ... looking back on it now, I have to admit that this looks very, very bad ... certainly looks very bad to me, now.

Lawyer: You are now recognizing, really, this gave you reason to touch them, because that excited you?

Horne: I wouldn't say it excited me, but I am saying it's something ... you certainly have to be worried about my motives in doing it, because I am, right now, worried about what were my motives in doing it. There are so many cases here where ... like the fact that I ran them hard in the gym program. I can provide a perfectly good justification for it. But in the background there is this ... boy, this sure created a lot of opportunity for me to enjoy their company.

Lawyer: More than enjoy their company. Touch them, get them to pull down their shorts, measuring upper thighs, touching their body, "Oh, let me see your muscle." Because you could play it off, say, "Oh, gee, I was just measuring them," correct?

Horne: You are absolutely right.

Lawyer: And it was, somewhat, grooming, getting them used to your touch, because there's a progression, isn't there?

Horne: I can't say, right now, that this was part of a progression, part of a grooming process. I can't say that.

Lawyer: What was it? You are recognizing there, now, that this wasn't just muscles. This had the sexual side to it, as well, or the predatory side …

Horne: Which I would not have acknowledged, at the time.

Lawyer: No, but today, you do acknowledge this fed Ed, the predator?

Horne: I think, even if I hadn't been the predator, I would have been doing some of these things. I would have been running them hard in the gym. I would have been monitoring their muscle development, even if I hadn't been a predator. Because many of these things worked.

Lawyer: But it's hard to even look back because you were the predator, right?

Horne: Of course, it's hard to look back, and of course, I was a predator.

• • •

Jeremy,* who later spoke out against Horne, grew up hunting with his father in a house full of brothers. His mother carved and his father worked at regular jobs in the community. His parents did not drink alcohol. Food was readily available in their home, which was warmed by a fuel stove. Jeremy was sexually abused from a young age, starting with a woman who visited and took advantage of him, straddling him one night, making him penetrate her. When he got a bit older, a teenage girl abused him as well, as did a male acquaintance and an employee at one of the local stores. Jeremy never reported any of the sexual abuse. He just kept it all inside and continued going to school, trying to get an education, knowing in his heart he would probably leave the community eventually and move to a city. But then Ed Horne came to his community and was his teacher.

The following is taken from testimony Jeremy provided regarding Horne in Lake Harbour:

"Mr. Horne used to come to our class to take over for our teacher for one period. He taught Inuktitut, the syllabics and the Roman orthography and all that. One day, in the portable school, he measured my body parts starting from my arms, my chest and down to my private parts, in the supply room, after school hours. All the kids were hanging around there so I was hanging around there, too. Bunch of kids. All the kids in Kimmirut. All the boys, actually."[3]

Horne was the only teacher that was staying at the school after hours, Jeremy said. Notably, Horne let the boys use razors (or an item that mimicked a razor), to pretend to shave their faces, Jeremy said — the same activity boys in Cape Dorset described having done with Horne.

After recalling with great anguish how he felt when Horne took him into the supply room and assaulted him, Jeremy said, "He killed my brother. That's how I see it when [my brother] committed suicide, looking back. He committed suicide, but the way I look at it, Ed Horne killed him."

Jeremy's brother was a Horne victim too.

· · ·

Maureen Doherty was still a relatively new teacher, but she knew one thing for sure: there was something very wrong with the new principal. The Dohertys would spend four years in Lake Harbour. In 1984 Maureen taught grades 3 and 4, and during that time she witnessed numerous incidents involving Horne and boys that seemed alarming to her.

One incident occurred in October 1984, around Halloween, when she had been teaching Horne's class while he was away at a conference. Scrawled across his chalkboard in the classroom were all kinds of sexually themed words, including "transsexual." He was also believed to have shown pornographic material to the children (and one of the complainants later listed the names of the people that saw it). Horne later claimed it was all a big misunderstanding as the film was a David Suzuki documentary. Horne consistently denied ever showing boys porn,[4] but reports from various sources said otherwise. There were statements given to the RCMP from the boys in Lake Harbour that Horne had a copy of *Debbie Does Dallas*. He did admit to owning a copy of the erotic historical drama *Caligula*, however, saying, "I had no idea how bad a movie it was. But it's a movie that I never let fall into the hands of the kids."

It bothered Maureen that Horne seemed to favour the boys over the girls in the school and that he could be hostile in his remarks about females. She recalled a disturbing story about one young girl in the school who had been abused in another community. When the teachers were discussing her situation, Horne was totally dismissive of the child and her needs, remarking, "She flashes her twat at anyone." When investigators questioned Horne about this, he denied it.

Bryon Doherty said that after Horne's first year in the community, teachers had escalating concerns about various aspects of Horne's behaviour. According to Bryon, Horne had "no social skills, whatsoever" — an observation that has been made against Horne many times over the decades — and that he was "shifty, manipulative and controlling."[5]

Horne kept all the keys to the school, deciding when it was locked or unlocked. This may have been standard practice for a school principal in a small community, but other teachers felt Horne's control of the keys was obsessive and limited their access to their classrooms.

Throughout the school year, Maureen saw Horne become increasingly erratic; she said he was "a madman." She felt threatened and intimidated by him. When Horne later heard this report, he said: "It severely undermines what I regard as being the bright spots in the past. It seems to me that even the bright spots weren't there."[6]

Maureen also told investigators that the suspicion of sexual abuse was first mentioned to her by staff member Peesee Pitsiulak with specific reference to an ongoing relationship Horne was having with a boy who later filed charges in the first criminal case against him. Pitsiulak encountered the red-faced boy she suspected Horne had abused exiting the school feeling what she sensed was shame. That night, Pitsiulak had gone to the school to look for something, and she went to Horne's office but found it locked. As she began using a key to open the door, she heard Horne yell from inside, "Wait!" "I felt this was strange," Pitsiulak later told police. A few minutes later the boy emerged from the office and walked away without saying anything.

Pitsiulak also witnessed Horne wrestling with boys in the evening. Horne disputed this:

"Obviously, a wrestling match between me and any of these individuals would have been pretty one-sided," he later said. "I was an adult in good shape. They were in their mid-teens. I am remembering that I would sometimes wrestle with two or three opponents against me. But I can't say when, where."

Pitsiulak also noticed that Horne would be in the shower room with the boys when they were taking showers. "I felt he made them take a lot of showers," she said.[7]

. . .

Parents were noticing Horne's odd behaviour too, and they went on community radio, complaining that the school was open too late at night and that the boys were there all the time. It's not known if these complaints reached the regional office in Frobisher Bay but, at any rate, no action was taken. There was another boy Pitsiulak suspected was being abused by Horne and she reported it to Frobisher Bay officials, saying, "It was not just a teacher's pet situation."[8] But nothing was done about that report either.

Female teachers were particularly concerned about Horne's treatment of his youngest son, Danny, whom he occasionally brought to school. According to a report filed with the RCMP around the time of Horne's arrest, a teacher observed Danny, who was then about two years old, left alone in the teachers' staff room for a few hours. The child appeared to be extremely frightened and afraid to move.

Bryon Doherty was also worried about Horne's relationship with Danny. He, too, remembered the child being left in the staff room and the look of fear in the child's eyes when Horne returned. Bryon approached education officials Fiona O'Donahue and Jeanette Ireland, both teacher consultants based in Frobisher Bay, about Horne's behaviour in the school, but all concerns were brushed off with comments like "Ed is so great" and "You are lucky to have him."[9]

"I have acknowledged that I deceived those people," Horne later said.[10]

The heat was rising in Lake Harbour, although Horne later claimed he was unaware of it.

A new teacher on staff, Ivan Gallant, who had replaced Maureen Doherty during her maternity leave, was extremely wary of Horne and reported one incident to the RCMP. He later made the following report to investigators:

"In my classroom, I faced boys who absolutely hated the girls. They threatened them and hit them … the boys fought back often and were quite aggressive to me. It came to the point where one boy attacked me…. This boy I had witnessed in a fight with Mr. Horne in April. This fight was one of the strange incidents that led me to speak to the RCMP."[11]

The Piano

A PIANO ARRIVED AT THE RCMP STAFF HOUSE IN LAKE HARBOUR in 1985. It had previously been shuttled between the school and the teacher's house, but now it found a new home as a gift to Const. Jim Raeburn and his wife, Joanne, from the school principal, Ed Horne.

The RCMP staff house, attached to the police building itself, was only a kilometre away from Aqiqqiq ("ptarmigan") School, so it wasn't difficult for a couple of strong men with a truck to make the delivery. Once the piano was set up in the house, Raeburn may have tried to play the piano and noticed that the tuning was off. Then he noticed the top of the piano was nailed shut. Prying it open, he saw that the strings and hammers looked fine, but something caught his eye, glinting on the soundboard. It was a roll of film. He thought there might be historical photos of the town or the school on the roll, so he called the RCMP's lab and told them he was sending the film out to be developed as soon as possible.

According to one of his colleagues at the time, Raeburn was a laid-back man. Nothing fazed him. But when the photos came back, he was alarmed. The roll contained pictures of scantily clad boys.

Plenty of erroneous stories have circulated in the North over the years about what was discovered inside the Lake Harbour piano and led to Horne's arrest. One was that a list of victims was found, another was that actual photographs were found featuring naked or half-dressed Inuit boys, or northern boys experimenting with gym equipment. The judge in the first criminal trial would agree that the images found by Constable Raeburn belonged to Horne and that they were the "paraphernalia" of a pedophile.[1]

Jonathan remembers being asked to go over to Constable Raeburn's house and describe what he knew about the piano. Before he left home to go answer the officer's questions, Jonathan's mother was in the kitchen, no doubt sensing her boy's anxiety. His mother was a formidable figure, an Elder who had endured much hardship in her life; she crouched down, put her hands on his shoulders, looked into his eyes, and said, "Just tell them the truth."[2]

One of Jonathan's favourite cousins went with him, and he recalls that they clinked away on the keyboard, probably making a racket. Constable Raeburn asked the boys questions about Horne, and if they had ever seen him put a roll of film inside the piano. Jonathan doesn't remember what he said, but he had no knowledge of the film. His most vivid memory from the officer's home that day was trying to play the piano with his cousin.

• • •

This is the story Ed Horne told me about the roll of film:

> I had translated a gym manual from Greenland, from Danish to English, hoped the education department would publish it. I took photos of one person, older, probably not a student, illustrating some of the exercises. The piano was in the school library, already an anachronism with newer technology then used for any music in the school, but it was an item of value and teachers were trying to keep kids off it. I don't remember how we became aware of Constable Raeburn's interest in the piano, but with permission, we were pleased to be rid of it. I also took pictures, possibly of the same person, showing the use of a piece of exercise equipment called a Bullworker, but I think those were

developed. I regret that you say the roll of film was "hidden." At the time I saw nothing wrong with the photos and never suspected they would be regarded as anything but what I intended them to be. I don't know how they ended up in the piano.[3]

. . .

At around the same time that the roll of film was discovered inside the piano, in the spring of 1985, disturbing reports from Lake Harbour reached the offices of the Department of Social Services in Frobisher Bay. The roll of film had already alerted police to the fact that Horne was likely a pedophile, but that information had not yet been shared outside the detachment. But then a seven-year-old girl was raped and nearly killed by three boys between the ages of fourteen and sixteen in the community. She was transported by medevac to a hospital in Frobisher Bay as the nursing station in Lake Harbour was not equipped to handle such a case. Social workers in Frobisher Bay were alerted and soon arrived in Lake Harbour. During a therapy session, one of the boys said something to the effect of "Well, if the teacher can do it, why can't we?"

"What teacher?" a social worker asked. One of the boys broke down and eventually said he committed the offence because he felt stigmatized as a homosexual. Further questioning revealed he felt this way because he had been sexually assaulted by the principal of the school, Mr. Horne.[4]

In fact, there had been a rash of sexual assaults by boys on girls in Lake Harbour in 1984 and 1985. The RCMP and social workers began interviewing parents and children about the possible root causes of the uncharacteristic child-on-child sexual abuse now ravaging the village. The finding was catastrophic: the children of Lake Harbour had been acting out with other children what Mr. Horne had done to them. The police and social workers were stunned. They began to quietly look into Horne's previous postings in the Eastern Arctic, and the more they looked the more it became clear that Horne had sexually abused his students in all the Eastern Arctic communities he'd been in, with the possible exception of Grise Fiord.

Social workers reached out to experts in the south for assistance in dealing with the crisis. The experts focused on Lake Harbour in the beginning, Cape Dorset and the other communities less so. This lack of attention to the other communities, and the complex feelings people had about speaking out against Horne, would have grave consequences. The silence prolonged and worsened the suffering of victims. Horrific tales of what Horne did to the boys, especially those from Sanikiluaq, the tiny island settlement far to the south in Hudson Bay, would remain untold for years.

According to Bryon Doherty, Horne was shockingly crude when he heard about the rape of the little girl. Doherty remembers that, instead of expressing any sympathy for the victim, Horne was really "worked up" about the young girl and the fact that one of his own students was being charged with the attack. Doherty had no way of knowing at the time that the boy was himself a Horne victim. He remembers Horne referring to the girl at one point as a "fucking slut."[5] Horne would later refute this.

Some school staff felt that Horne began acting more irrationally at about this time, perhaps desperately even, perhaps ready to flee the community. Near the end of Horne's time in Lake Harbour, Doherty found men's underwear, Horne's passport, and other personal items in the school, and it seemed to him that Horne was sleeping in the school's attic crawl space. Doherty contacted the board office in Frobisher Bay to speak to a supervisor about Horne's fitness to be principal, and his concern was met with the same reply he and his wife had heard before — Brian Menton told him that they were lucky to have Horne working in their community, and that was that.

Menton, the education official most responsible for overseeing Horne in Lake Harbour, never once visited Horne while he was working there, Horne said. "I think it's a fair inference that he may have been reluctant to go to Lake Harbour because he was afraid of what he would see and find out." Did Horne suspect that Menton and perhaps others knew of the abuses that he was responsible for, but found it easier to ignore them? Eventually another official, Peter Grimm — coincidentally a close friend of Horne — did visit, but he ignored the complaints of the staff and reported that all was well with Horne's leadership.

Horne, like all teachers in the N.W.T., was subject to semi-annual reviews of his performance.

Grimm visited Lake Harbour and assessed Horne's work in the classroom in the 1984–85 school year. He wrote the following report after his visit:

> Edward Horne has created an unusually rich learning environment: morale is excellent. Students are being challenged and are being taught to enjoy learning. Effective use is made of computer assisted instruction. The absence of a Language Arts Curriculum and of suitable English readers has obliged Edward to develop his daily letter to the class as an effective device.[6]

The boxes for the administration were ticked. There was nothing below a B on Horne's report. Horne was still one of the shining stars of the department.

• • •

After his first year in Lake Harbour, Horne had written a letter to Eric Colbourne saying he planned to stay in the community for two years and then apply to become principal at Cape Dorset. This plan — to return for a third stint in Dorset — may even have been green-lighted if social workers hadn't alerted government officials to what they knew of Horne's predations. Unfortunately, and amazingly, the government officials who most needed to know what was going on — those in education — were not in the information loop.

Horne's hopes for Cape Dorset were advanced when Terry Hobday resigned the principalship there partway through the 1984–85 school year. Horne contacted Colbourne again; he wanted the job and he wanted it now. Colbourne wrote back saying he'd run the plan by the Cape Dorset education committee for further review. Colbourne believed strongly in increasing community and parental involvement in school staffing and operations, and local education committees were the vehicle he used to accomplish this goal.

Horne was invited to Cape Dorset for meetings with the school committee, and an hour-long meeting with staff whose tone Horne found "unfriendly."

Horne's work record was a concern. He had moved around a lot. Staff felt that they had already experienced a revolving-door principalship in Dorset. Horne's pattern of spending only one or two years in a community, a pattern apparent ever since he had left Sanikiluaq, was not reassuring.

"It was not outright hostile," Horne said, "but they were decidedly cool. And they did not raise any suspicions of sexual impropriety or any concerns about my teaching."

Colbourne, a writer and researcher, now retired and living in his home province of Newfoundland and Labrador, recalled that the first time he suspected there may have been a problem with Horne was when Horne applied to return to Cape Dorset to take over the principalship.

After Horne's interview in Cape Dorset, at which Colbourne was not present, the chair of the education committee came to Iqaluit for meetings. Colbourne knew they were seeking a principal, and they perused the applications that the regional office had received. One was from Horne.

"I remember the chair saying immediately, 'There is no way that man is going to be the principal in Cape Dorset.' I was taken aback. And the reason I was taken aback was I thought Edward had a good reputation in Cape Dorset."

Like everyone else, Colbourne believed Horne was bilingual in Inuktitut and English and appeared to be on good terms with everybody in Cape Dorset. "I was surprised at that outburst, but I didn't think anything of it beyond that. We had given the community the authority to decide who the principal was going to be, so I left it at that."

Back in Frobisher Bay, Colbourne soon received a message from the community — they wanted another applicant, the present vice-principal Mike Rokeby, as principal, but would accept Horne as vice-principal. The conversations that went on behind closed doors among committee members in Cape Dorset are not a matter of record. But that community was also in crisis — a number of Horne's victims had already taken their own lives, and violence was increasing. Some parents in Cape Dorset were suspicious about Horne, a few openly complaining about the amount of time he spent with boys in the evening at the school. But the chasm between the Inuit community and qallunaat officialdom was as vast as it had ever been. That gap — the two solitudes, to borrow a term used decades earlier to describe the inability of English and French Canada to communicate effectively — apparently ensured that nobody told education officials in Frobisher Bay about Horne's predations, and no one in those offices thought Horne might be responsible for abuses, despite complaints from teachers like the Dohertys in Lake Harbour. And so the power structure in education concurred with the local recommendation — they were still willing to move Horne back to Cape Dorset in a position of authority, although not the principalship.

Horne believed Bert Rose was still firmly in his corner and that he was disappointed that Horne didn't get the principalship in Cape Dorset. But Horne was offended at being passed over for the top job and declined the offer to return to Cape Dorset as vice-principal. He was, however, determined to leave Lake Harbour. So he applied for a transfer to the position of principal and teacher in Nanook School, the small school at Apex, a bedroom suburb of Frobisher Bay, about five kilometers south of the community that would soon be renamed Iqaluit. The request was granted.

"If I knew what that son of a bitch was doing — and maybe I should have picked up on some of that, you know, maybe I should have — but there is no way I knew," Colbourne told me. "There is no doubt that Edward Horne was a talented man. He was intelligent, and at a time when we were looking for those types of skills for development of Inuktitut learning materials — there is no doubt he was useful. But if I knew that bastard was under criminal investigation, then he would not have been in Iqaluit or Apex."

Amazingly, the government's stance was that while the social services department actively investigated reports of Horne's predations against boys in Lake Harbour (liasing with the RCMP who were pursuing their own investigation), no one informed officials in the education office of their concerns over Horne. While that seems astounding and may be difficult to accept, the bureaucrats would also ask you to believe that social services officials did not alert Ken MacRury, regional director of the government of the N.W.T. for the Baffin Region, to the fact that Horne was possibly a pedophile and had been abusing northern children for years, citing privacy concerns.

• • •

Shortly before he left Lake Harbour in 1985, Horne sent a letter to an old friend who had lived in Sanikiluaq for a time when Horne was there. He wrote casually about people they knew, gave a broad update on life in the North, and seemed impressed by his friend's time spent in China, a country he claimed to know well.

About China and Beijing in particular he wrote of his own experience: "I was happy there, perhaps too happy. I'm deliberately not going back there this year. It's too easy to become too settled in Beijing, too comfortable, leading the privileged life of a foreigner. I had a bicycle, and rode downtown many times. I had supper at the Youyi Hotel almost every night (better than Language Institute food!) Another of my favorite bike trips was to the Summer Palace."

He lamented not learning much Chinese in the six-week course he took there and admitted that he would like to return but Jeannie was afraid to make the trek to the Far East with him. "Convinced that there is constant war in that area. I don't know how she would cope there," he wrote.[7]

There was no hint in the letter that Horne's time was almost up, or that he suspected that the authorities were on to him. In writing of people from the North whom he and his friend both knew well, he even speculated matter-of-factly at one point about what might have happened to the missing boy in Sanikiluaq all those years ago. "Alec Inuktaluk disappeared in 1977 and was never found. He probably committed suicide by walking off the ice," he wrote. He did not mention having been a suspect in the boy's disappearance.

Putting forth the idea that he might be ready to leave the North, he was "more than ready for a break," he said, but said it was "a poor time to be job-hunting in southern Canada. For a teacher, most of B.C. is dead."

It sounded as if his summer was shaping up just the way he liked it — full of exotic travel. While Jeannie and the kids were to spend the summer with her family at Great Whale River, Horne was planning to spend three weeks in the Philippines — "I've been there before," he wrote, "and find it complex and fascinating, warm-hearted people," adding, "From there I'll go to Bangkok and either settle down for six weeks, or strike out by train across Burma and India. I'd love to stop off in Vancouver, but it's expensive." He made no mention of the son he had in the Philippines.

He said he'd applied for a transfer back to Frobisher Bay. "I love my work here," he wrote, adding, "Local politics can be nasty, but the kids are great."

. . .

After Horne's holiday in Asia during the summer of 1985, during which time Jeannie and the children visited relatives in Great Whale River, the Hornes arrived in Apex in late August to settle into yet another community and begin Horne's new assignment. Six weeks later he was arrested in Apex.

. . .

Horne often complained of his inability to get along with his mother. But nonetheless, his mother, Muriel, went north to visit him and his family in 1984. She went to Great Whale River, Jeannie's hometown, to which the Hornes sometimes returned on summer vacation. Muriel suffered from diabetes and was unused to Inuit country food, but she went along with what she was served while she was visiting, including trying *maqtaq*, or whale skin with blubber. On her return south, she stopped in Montreal to visit friends. Relieved to have access to some of her favourite foods again after her northern culinary adventure, she indulged in cookies and other baked goods she wasn't supposed to be eating. Muriel fell into a diabetic coma from which she never recovered. She died at the Royal Victoria Hospital in Montreal on July 16, 1984. She never lived to see her eldest son charged with child sexual abuse.

The Arrest

ED HORNE CLAIMED THERE WERE NO VICTIMS AT APEX. "I FELT I
had cleaned up my act much beforehand, but then I was scared," he told a
lawyer. "I did not face up to my cumulative record, to all I had done, but I
knew that I had been doing something that was wrong and that I wasn't going to do it anymore. I mean, that was my mindset when I went into Apex."[1]

Horne claimed he left Lake Harbour because he was asked to by the
regional education office in Iqaluit, mainly to be involved in developing
curriculum.

"It had been clear for years that they were desperate to get some material
development going," Horne explained. "And I was the only person who was
very active in that area."

Eric Colbourne and the South Baffin supervisor Brian Menton were the
officials Horne remembers dealing with at the time, as well as Bert Rose.

Horne said none of these men expressed concerns about his performance
in Lake Harbour. In fact, based on Horne's classroom attendance statistics
(typically 90 percent of his students attended regularly where 50 to 70 percent was the norm in other schools at the time) those education officials
admired him.

"I think this is part of the reason why regional office failed to realize
that there was a problem," Horne later reflected, "that things on the surface

appeared to be going very well. This is by consultants and supervisors. I don't like to brag about all the good things that people said about me, but the fact is that I ... to put it bluntly, I fooled them into thinking that things were going great."

. . .

Nanook School, in Apex, had experienced a serious staffing problem when a teaching couple had abandoned their post to run a restaurant in Frobisher Bay. Horne's move to Apex was approved by Eric Colbourne in consultation with Bert Rose. Colbourne was about to leave to attend McGill University in Montreal, and his position was being taken over by Rose. Although Rose didn't officially take on his new responsibilities until August 1, it was known earlier in the spring that he would be assuming the role, and so naturally he was involved in the staffing decision. But Rose told me that he was unaware of the investigation into Horne's crimes when Horne arrived in Apex in the fall.

But another teaching colleague was all too aware of the investigation. Shortly after Horne arrived in Apex, he got a call from his friend Mike Rokeby, who had beat him out for the principalship in Cape Dorset. Rokeby had arrived in Sanikiluaq as a teacher the year Horne left that community, and he had been in Cape Dorset since 1980, first as teacher then as vice-principal before getting the top job there. Rokeby had been contacted by the RCMP. He wasted no time filling Horne in on what he knew — he tipped Horne off that the police were investigating him for sexual abuse against boys. Horne could have fled at that point, but he didn't. His reaction was unusual, considering the severity of the allegations. Horne wasn't flustered because, he claims, by that point he was completely delusional.

"I felt awfully sad, but I didn't think anything would come of it," he later said of the investigation.[2]

. . .

Ann Meekitjuk Hanson is a well-known Inuit resident of Apex, a broadcaster, writer, actor — credited under the pseudonyn Pilitak, she is one of the stars of the film *The White Dawn* — and former commissioner of Nunavut. When I reached out to Hanson during the writing of this book, she acknowledged it was still a painful subject, but she generously shared her thoughts on the tragedy and her own encounter with Horne.

I learned that she'd been chair of the education committee in Apex when Ed Horne was suggested as a possible principal for the school there in 1985.

"In the Eastern Arctic, we were starting to have education committees in the early 1980s. We were just an advisory committee consisting of local people," she told me. "We had no powers, just advisory for principals and teachers. This was the beginning of learning how to have some input into our education system. It was a very exciting time for us, since we wanted to contribute and have some voice to our children's education." Hanson was to be included in interviewing a new principal and teacher, along with Bert Rose, the new superintendent of schools for the government of the Northwest Territories. "I was very excited and felt proud. I learned that the person to be interviewed was a Mr. Ed Horne."

She'd never met him and was curious, so she had prepared some questions.

"I was informed that Mr. Horne was fluent in Inuktitut and knew about computers. Computers were just beginning to appear in our village and classrooms. This was very important to us."

She recalled that Horne and Rose spoke a lot during the meeting, and she was the last to ask questions.

"After the interviews, [Rose] told me that Mr. Horne was the one and would be hired. I told him that I didn't want to hire Mr. Horne because he would not look at me at all. He would not look at me in the eye and I found this to be very strange and that I could not trust a person who does not look at me when I spoke."

Shortly after this experience, Hanson had a most disturbing exchange with her young daughter, who came home from school one day and said that Mr. Horne was making little boys take off their pants in his office.

"My daughter looked scared and was nearly crying. I comforted her and told her 'Do not talk like that.' I said those things because we were brought up not to talk about adults like that, that was our upbringing with our people. At the same time, I was horrified and wondered maybe he was going to spank them! I didn't do anything because I didn't know what to do."

When Horne was arrested, Rose, who had been so supportive of Horne, called Hanson to his office and told her what Horne had been doing with the boys.

"I just cried and cried. I could not speak. I was too horrified and thought about my daughter's words. I just wept until I could not cry anymore. I am weeping once again. Many of Mr. Horne's victims have killed themselves, a lot are addicted to substances, some are homeless, some are just surviving, some are just going back and forth to jails and Corrections. So very sad."

. . .

The Horne case showed early on how difficult it was for Arctic RCMP detachments to communicate with each other and coordinate investigations. The geography, language barriers, and the fact the crimes covered a span of years dating back to 1971 complicated the Horne case from the start.

Then, as now, there were no roads connecting the communities in the Eastern Arctic. In those days before email, officers trying to collect information from other communities when the Horne case ramped up communicated by what the RCMP called "memos" sent to the places Horne lived and worked. It wasn't a perfect system, but that's the way it was.

"You'd call down and say, 'There's a memo on the way,'" Brian Morrison told me. "That would initiate a file on their end. You'd do the same thing in Cape Dorset and so on. One of the problems was a lot of times, when it's an old file, and it's not in their community, you don't get a whole lot of enthusiastic enquiries. A lot of the times I'd ask to have someone interviewed, and the response would be 'No one wants to talk about it.'"

Many of the Horne files were considered "old" because Horne had lived and worked in the territory so long and had moved around more than most government employees. In 1985, when the police were building a substantial case against him, he had taught in some of the most far-flung Inuit communities.

By the time Morrison and his colleagues had amassed many charges against Horne, they knew it was only the tip of the iceberg. Morrison, who had been working closely with lead social workers since he arrived in the North, was aware there were at least one hundred boys in different communities who had suffered at the hands of Horne, but the RCMP had difficulty getting people to talk on the record. Shame, embarrassment, fear of retraumatizing the children, and a sense of stories getting lost in translation between English and Inuktitut kept most victims and their families quiet.

Horne didn't appear to be feeling any shame in the fall of 1985 when he began attending fitness classes in the evening in Frobisher Bay. The class was primarily made up of moms and their babies. Donna Morrison, Constable Morrison's wife, was there, trying to get back into shape after the birth of her second child. Few men ever participated in the class, but one most certainly stood out. Donna remembered a man who was "a little stout" (a description Horne would probably not like) and seemed older than the average age of participants, which was about twenty-five years old. The man was Horne, but Donna didn't know his name at the time.

She remembers it was a typical aerobics class from "back in the day — Jane Fonda style," but with one big difference — the instructor was an RCMP officer, one of her husband's colleagues.

The man she now knows was Horne came across as "a little eccentric," she said. "Back in the eighties when we were doing aerobics we were all wearing Reeboks and leg warmers and he did his class with bare feet. That stood out. I'd never seen anybody do that."

• • •

Horne sometimes appeared to be flaunting his criminal behaviour, daring the authorities to catch him and eluding them constantly. The gift to an RCMP officer of the piano with the film inside may have been plain sloppiness on his part. But it was still a bold gesture. The coolness, verging on hostility, shown him during his interview for the principalship in Cape Dorset should have caused a more rational person to cease their predations when back in Lake Harbour, but he continued to offend. And the amount of time he spent with the boys, in situations where he was up close to them, bathing them or wrestling with them in exercise classes, could be seen as taunting parents, daring the authorities to question him. Some have suggested that deep down inside, Horne wanted to be caught. But Morrison doesn't believe it for a moment. He doesn't think Horne hoped to be caught or was daring the authorities.

"He did think he was the smartest person in the room all the time," Morrison told me. "He might have been. But no, he didn't want to be caught. I remember him being upset when the jail door locked. He was not happy."

• • •

Const. Brian Morrison/RCMP report, dated October 7, 1985:

> I spoke to [Const. Jim] Raeburn and he says that he is in the process of an investigation. He has nothing concrete. Things are up in the air and both Dorset and Lake Harbour are in the process of taking statements from the young boys involved.... Apparently, Horne [keeps] the school gym open late at night and encourages the young boys to attend to play with the computer and run around in gym shorts. The school board is apparently aware of this activity and Horne's sexual preference but have not taken action as there has been no formal complaint and apparently Horne is quite the man with computers and they don't want to lose him, if it's avoidable.[3]

• • •

In the spring of 1985, Ken MacRury was aware that social worker Val Haas and her co-worker were investigating sexual assaults in Lake Harbour and Cape Dorset, but he did not know the details or that they involved Horne until shortly before Horne's arrest. MacRury, a Nova Scotian, had moved north to Frobisher Bay with his wife, Sheila, in 1971; they were among the first teaching staff of the newly opened Gordon Robertson Education Centre. After that he worked in smaller communities for a few years before returning to Frobisher Bay. By 1985 he had attained the role of regional director after working with communities in developing the institutions of local government like settlement and hamlet councils. He remembered, "We communicated quite readily. Social Services was directly across the hall from the executive office, so I would see them regularly. They would sort of keep me informed of some of the things that were going on. I would have to say in the back of my mind I do have a recollection of them talking to me about investigating a teacher in Kimmirut [Lake Harbour]. But I don't remember a name. They are pretty delicate about releasing too much information in case they might be wrong."

The role of regional director was a balancing act. Employed by and reporting to the Department of the Executive headquartered in Yellowknife, the director coordinated the affairs of all the government's departments in the vast Baffin Region, which stretched from Sanikiluaq in southern Hudson Bay to Grise Fiord on Ellesmere Island and theoretically to the North Pole. Each department had its own regional superintendent who reported to a director (later called a deputy minister) of that department in Yellowknife, but who also reported to the regional director in Frobisher Bay. The reporting to the regional director was usually administrative in nature, rather than dealing with professional matters.

MacRury remembered calling Bert Rose's house that October night in 1985:

"Being regional director in those days was delicate, I had some authority, but not total authority — so I advised Bert that his best process would be to immediately suspend Ed Horne without pay, just get him off the payroll as soon as possible. Then, on Monday morning [the arrest happened on a weekend], I called Bert into my office, and I asked him if he had suspended Ed Horne and he told me, 'No, he's one of our best teachers.' He was defending him. And I said, 'No, that's unacceptable.'"

By this time MacRury had spoken to Val Haas, the lead social worker on the case, and to RCMP constable Brian Morrison, and there was no doubt in MacRury's mind: Horne had to go. But Rose, much to MacRury's frustration, was standing by Horne. Even though Horne had blurted out from the confines of his jail cell on that Saturday night, "It's all true," Rose stubbornly believed that Horne could be salvaged, that the department could not afford to lose such an innovative, results-oriented teacher.

MacRury continued, "I met with Bert and I asked him if Horne had been suspended. And he started to give me the song and dance that he didn't want to do that because he's a wonderful teacher and we don't want to ruin his reputation. And I told him, 'Bert, either you suspend him right now, which you have the authority to do, or I'm going to call your deputy minister and between us we will suspend you.'"

Joe Handley was the deputy minister of education at that time. Handley, a Métis from Saskatchewan, was new to the Northwest Territories, having only just moved to Yellowknife that year to assume his position in the department. He subsequently held deputy minister responsibilities in a number of departments before running for elected office and eventually becoming premier. Earlier, in or around 1979, he had been engaged as a consultant by the government of the N.W.T. to work for a special committee struck by the legislative assembly to prepare a portion of a report titled *Learning: Tradition and Change in the Northwest Territories* that dealt with the administrative structure of education in the territory. From 1979 to 1985 he was employed with the Frontier School Division in Manitoba. He had just accepted his role as deputy minister when the Horne story broke.

MacRury admired Handley and had quickly established a solid working relationship with him; he had phoned him and told him about Horne as soon as he knew of the case. He didn't hear more from Handley after that, understanding that Handley was handling the Horne case internally within the department.

MacRury remembered that Val Haas was the one who first alerted him to the investigation into Horne, that she and another social worker had contacted the RCMP by September, and that Constable Morrison had started doing interviews and collecting information about Horne. The social workers told MacRury they liked working with Morrison. That was fortunate because the picture emerging from Horne's time in the North was getting more disturbing each day. The social workers realized this was becoming a sexual assault case of a size and scope they didn't anticipate, one that could possibly stretch their resources to the breaking point.

"Val told me the more they looked into it, and they started going back to Kimmirut and back to Dorset and Sanikiluaq, it just seemed to snow-ball," MacRury said. "It just kept getting bigger and bigger. That wherever Horne was there was a problem. There had been complaints. From what I could recollect, there had been complaints that were never dealt with. In both communities — Cape Dorset and Kimmirut. They weren't handled by the social worker, if there was one — many communities didn't have a social worker — or it didn't go to the RCMP, or they didn't deal with it, but it wasn't something brand new that nobody had ever heard of before. There was a history people swept under the rug, or they ignored it, or it was, 'Oh don't mind those kids, they don't know [what] they're talking about.' That sort of thing. We were quite concerned that government staff had not dealt with it."

One of the social workers who was deeply involved in the Horne case from the beginning, Deb,* remembers education officials just didn't be-lieve Horne could have abused all those boys. The overwhelming evidence obtained that led to Horne's arrest indicated Horne was a pedophile, but immediately after his arrest, Deb recalls, the education establishment — she wouldn't say who — kept saying Horne was innocent, openly criticized lead social workers for their "witch-hunt" against the man, and even went as far as to suggest that all the kids — over one hundred — were lying. It got so bad that the RCMP, with whom she had been working tirelessly, at one point had to warn the education officials that they were coming very close to obstruction of justice.

Brian Morrison got along well with the social workers on the Horne case. He doesn't recall outright denials from education officials but said the optics of Horne's constant transfers from community to community still look suspicious to him.

MacRury distanced himself from the case after Horne was arrested. As far as he knew, the Horne matter was being handled within the Department of Education. It was out of his hands.

But the question of how Horne got away with his crimes against children lingered.

"That's the question," MacRury admits. "He shouldn't have gotten away with it. In retrospect there were indicators that this was happening. There were children who were making complaints to social workers or other teachers, and people didn't deal with it. They just turned a blind eye. It should have been dealt with much earlier. For certain in Cape Dorset and Sanikiluaq. All of it was going down. Why didn't somebody jump on it and work on it? I don't know."

Around the time Horne was arrested, Dennis Patterson,[4] now a retired senator who represented Nunavut in the Parliament of Canada, was the minister of education in the Northwest Territories, and was living in Apex and commuting to Yellowknife. When charges were laid against Horne, Patterson felt the shock waves. Just a month before he'd praised Horne to an education official from Alberta as an example of everything that was going right in the classrooms of the Eastern Arctic.

Patterson was a close colleague of the Alberta minister David King, whom he knew from his University of Alberta days. When King became the president of the Council of Ministers of Education, Canada (CMEC), King and Patterson agreed that in addition to hosting a meeting in Edmonton, Patterson would arrange for the ministers to visit the Northwest Territories. The group included senior officials and deputy ministers and was intended to show off the N.W.T.'s education system — quite appropriate because at the time the N.W.T. used Alberta's school curriculum and their grade 9 and grade 12 departmental exams. In conjunction with that visit Patterson invited King to Frobisher Bay and Apex. Patterson was eager to present to King what, in his estimation, was a "model school," complete with Inuktitut language and programming. Horne's classroom in Nanook School in Apex is where he took him.

"We went to his classroom and we spent time with him and the kids. It wasn't a long visit. But it was like, okay, here is some of the great stuff we're doing here," said Patterson. Horne was considered by many to be fluent in Inuktitut — an illusion fuelled by wishful thinking on the part of education administrators, in Horne's own later opinion — and admired (in this case deservedly) for having developed the syllabics font for the Macintosh computer. "I'm wondering now what I would have seen if I had a sharper eye.

But it seemed to be a classroom full of engaged, happy kids with a teacher who was exemplary with how he was running the school. I didn't see anything untoward at all."

Patterson admits to having heard about a choking incident involving Horne and a student. Like other officials before him, Patterson did not discipline Horne or see to it that Horne was reprimanded. Patterson believes the story came to him from his deputy minister, Brian Lewis. In the schoolyard's playground, Horne had a physical encounter with a male student that left the student temporarily unconscious. Whether Horne choked him or put him in a wrestling-type hold like a half nelson, Patterson wasn't sure. But the force was enough that the boy passed out briefly. Patterson dealt directly with his deputy, staying out of operational matters so he could focus on policy and legislation for the most part. But he admits that there was no excuse for not doing more to look into what may have been going on between Horne and his male students.

The deputy minister arranged, with Patterson's concurrence, for someone to go into Dorset and investigate. "This was not routine. We didn't have corporal punishment or anything like that in the schools. And we were dealing with a cross-cultural environment," Patterson said. "This sounded really serious to me." The assistant superintendent sent in Peter Grimm to investigate. When Patterson followed up with Grimm, the verbal report was essentially "No cause for alarm, nothing to worry about."

The North is small, and people talk, so Patterson eventually got the lowdown on what really occurred when Grimm showed up in the community. It turned out Grimm was "partying with the school principal," which Patterson suspected included drinking alcohol. "And I thought, 'Well, shit.' The principal would have been responsible for something like that happening on his watch in his school on his playground, right? I was minister. What could I actually do? But I didn't do anything. I am so ashamed, this should have been a red flag."

The consensus among most education officials at the time, Patterson said, was that Horne was "dedicated, brilliant, maybe a little eccentric." Patterson was pressured at one point by the education establishment in the Baffin Region after Horne was arrested to believe that Horne was innocent and that the boys were lying or exaggerating about Horne's predations. Early Horne supporter and Nunavut Arctic College instructor David Wilman approached Patterson shortly after Horne was arrested and asked if Patterson would give Horne a contract to do Inuktitut curriculum work if Horne was able to work in the N.W.T. in the future. Patterson rejected the request.

"By then Horne had allegedly been criminally abusive to scores of students and emerged as having been a pedophile. I had learned at the time of his arrest that a piano was moved for some reason in Kimmirut in the school. And in the soundboard were pornographic pictures. And it implicated him in abuse of students. I knew that at the time [of his arrest]. I was horrified."

The big pedestal onto which Patterson had elevated Horne, inviting the chairman of the CMEC to spend time in Horne's classroom, toppled when Patterson heard of the charges and the volume of complaints. "I remember thinking he had been very careful about intimidating these poor kids into not telling anybody, which I think is what happened. They were terrified of him."

. . .

On October 12, 1985, Horne arrived at the RCMP detachment in Frobisher and was put in a cell for the night. Morrison remembers that the schoolteacher was subdued, but arrogant.

"I remember he wore these black horn-rimmed glasses," Morrison said. "He was very cocky, very self-assured. He was the greatest person that ever came to the North, and all you had to do was ask him and he would give you all of the opinions, very strong opinions. Very intelligent. Extremely bright. He had a strong sense of superiority, like he was the smartest person in the room. All the time."

Horne told the police he was a First Nations person from a reserve in B.C., but other than that, he divulged nothing about his family background.

Morrison remembered: "I kinda got him talking. He might be deep in thought, but if you spoke to him he was kind of like 'Why are you doing this?' And 'This is not right,' until we actually sat down in the interview room. I said something like 'How long have you had these deviations from normal sexual desires?' Something along that line, and he took offence to it; he questioned the terminology. So I changed the terms, the wording, and that's what made it so difficult, because if I asked him a question I had to ask him five different ways before he would answer. But he did indicate to me in the form of a positive response that he did abuse the kids. But he wouldn't elaborate on what he did."

Horne's wife was questioned too. She was co-operative, but her answers seemed a bit out in left field to the investigating officer. But one thing she said stood out for Morrison that night: "I do remember her saying, 'I wondered why he had that jelly that men use with men.' I thought that was odd."

I asked Horne to tell me what he remembered from the night he was arrested. He said, "I had fallen asleep on the floor watching a football game on television. I was groggy and not surprised. I had been warned a few days before. You seem to be looking for me to be devastated by a terrible anguish. That's not how it was."

Shortly after his arrest, there was a question put to Horne, one whose answer would set in motion years of confusion and, later, more sexual assault charges. The question: Are there any other victims? Horne replied: "I have to speak to my lawyer."

. . .

Joe Bovard said he remembers the Horne arrest "like it was last week." The Major League Baseball conference finals were on television, and Horne and Bovard had decided to meet at Bovard's home that afternoon to watch the Toronto Blue Jays take on the Kansas City Royals. This would be easy for them to do as they lived next door to each other, sharing the old nursing station in Apex, which had been renovated into a cozy duplex. Bovard was in his kitchen getting the popcorn and the chips ready, wondering where Horne was, thinking "Gee, hurry up, bud," when his phone rang. It was the RCMP.

"They said we just arrested somebody that wants to talk to you. And I said 'OK, put him on.' And it was Ed! Ed says, 'Joe, I need you.' I said

'What's wrong? Get over here, the game's gonna start!' And he said, 'No, I'm serious. I need you. I'm in trouble. I've been arrested.' I didn't believe it. I said, 'Ed, come on, stop screwing around. Get over here. The game's gonna start.' Honestly, it took him about a minute to convince me. And then I said, 'OK, don't say anything more right now. I don't even want to know what you're arrested for. I'll be right there.'"

Bovard, a lawyer, went to the RCMP station, where he was briefed on Horne's situation. His reaction was "Are you kidding me? And we had a lot of charges strewn over many communities. Historical charges, and new charges. I looked at this and I thought, *Ed Horne?* So then I went to talk to him. And he told me he wanted to retain me. And we had a really long talk. That's when I started representing Ed."

The Kansas City Royals would defeat the Blue Jays that night two nothing, and the Royals would go on to win the World Series. Horne would watch some of that series later that month from inside a remand centre in Edmonton.

Bovard represented Horne through the leadup to his first criminal trial. He told me at one point, "Everybody loved him.... He was this supersmart guy."

Bovard moved north to Frobisher Bay in February 1982. He was hired as the director of the Frobisher Bay–based legal aid centre called Maliganik Tukisiniakvik (known locally simply as Maliganik) — "the place to understand laws" — taking over from Dennis Patterson, its founding director. Bovard was at the time the only practising lawyer in the Eastern Arctic. After practising in Toronto for a couple of years, he responded to an ad in *Ontario Reports* for a lawyer to run Maliganik. His job, like most lawyers who went North to work in those days, was to be a legal jack of all trades. Although he did do some civil work — uncontested divorces, helping in the sales and purchases of small businesses — criminal cases comprised the bulk of his work. Unfortunately, crime was rampant throughout the region. Training paralegal workers in all the communities as well as training justices of the peace was high on Bovard's list of priorities at the time.

Maliganik was overseen by a board, and Bovard was impressed by its Inuit members. He worked with the board and with Elders in each community to select Inuit to act as local court workers — liaisons between the RCMP, himself, and Maliganik. Bovard went out of his way to maintain good relations with the police, whose co-operation he felt was essential in developing a better understanding of the criminal justice system at the community level.

The court of the time was a travelling court. Every month or so when the court party would come over from Yellowknife, Maliganik representatives would attend court sessions in Frobisher Bay, as well as travel to several communities that were on the schedule for that court circuit. The local court worker would meet with Bovard as soon as he got off the plane, and he or she would have all the files on those charged with an offence. They would have interviewed everyone they could and would sit down and discuss the cases with Bovard. The court worker would tell Bovard about the interviews and what people were saying about each case. Bovard would then meet with the accused, with the court worker present, because the court worker would often have to do double duty and serve as interpreter. Real pressure developed on the court workers over time because many local people thought they had a lot of power — that they could, for example, get unsavoury charges withdrawn. It was clear more community education was needed if Maliganik wanted to avoid uncomfortable exchanges between court staff and their friends and family in the future.

In recalling the training he did with local court workers, Bovard says, "To this day I am so impressed with the quality of their work, their intelligence, their imagination, their hard work, and their dedication to their community."

It didn't take long for someone working in the Eastern Arctic to feel somewhat alienated from Yellowknife. It was common for people in Frobisher Bay, and anywhere else on Baffin Island, to feel that government headquarters, located so far away, wasn't sensitive or knowledgeable about what was going on in the region — it was two different worlds. Bovard said that when he first arrived in the North, the level of representation in the criminal cases for the Inuit was very low. In other words, the lawyers were qallunaat, as were the judges. "The lawyers that would come over were great," he says, "but they worked in Yellowknife, so they weren't really connected to the Baffin in any meaningful way." These facts made Bovard even more determined to do his job well.

The court party used to go to Cape Dorset quite often in those days. It was during one of those court sessions that Bovard first met Horne. Horne used to bring his class to court as an educational experience. Bovard wanted to know who this teacher was and struck up a conversation with him. A friendship grew over a shared fascination with languages, particularly Spanish, Bovard's mother tongue. Horne would show Bovard books he bought in Spanish, and they'd talk about the challenges of attaining fluency. Bovard believed, as many people did then, that Horne was fluent in Inuktitut. The fact that Horne was married to an Inuk, had Inuit kids, and had lived all over the North also impressed him, as did stories about Horne's attempt at re-translating the New Testament into a more modern version of Inuktitut.

Subsequently, every time Bovard went to Cape Dorset in the early 1980s, he visited Horne, his erudite friend. In the fall of 1985, when Horne arrived in Apex to begin teaching, he moved in next door to Bovard in the revamped nursing station. Bovard thought this was a fortuitous arrangement as the two men enjoyed watching baseball on television, discussing language, and were both raising young families. Horne even babysat for Bovard's kids a couple of times.

Now a retired Ontario court judge, Bovard reflected on Horne, saying, "He did a lot of good things. He was also convicted of having done a lot of bad things. Sexual assault, pedophilia, that kind of sexual assault, is something that has profound lasting effects on the victims, which in turn affects their relationships with others and their communities. In these cases that kind of ripple effect is quite extensive. It would be horrible enough if it had just happened in one community. But it happened in so many different communities; it increases the magnitude of the effects this behaviour had. I have no way of knowing this, but as a judge, wherever there are these types of sexual assaults, oftentimes there are recriminations among the people that should have known, could have known."

. . .

Horne resigned from his job when he was arrested. But Bert Rose, still in disbelief about Horne's guilt, instructed headquarters to treat his resignation letter as merely an intention to resign, which would have entitled Horne to severance pay, worth fifty-five hundred dollars. Rose had once again gone out on a limb for Horne. According to Horne, it wouldn't be the last time. When Horne was on bail and living in Toronto in April 1986, he claimed that Rose contacted him by telephone asking if he would be interested in doing a translation of *Jonathan Livingston Seagull* into Inuktitut. Horne said he turned the offer down, sensing a coldness in Rose's tone, as if Rose was making the call reluctantly.

Rose denied offering this work to Horne, who had become "poison" in his mind by then. "By 1986 I was swamped at Baffin Divisional Board of Education and I greatly doubt I would have suggested anything involving Ed," Rose said.

"Faked Bad"

ED HORNE WAS REMANDED BY THE NORTHWEST TERRITORIES Territorial Court in Frobisher Bay to the Forensic Services Unit of the Alberta Hospital Edmonton for psychiatric assessment on October 22, 1985.[1] Once there, after drinking a coffee and eating a sandwich, Horne signed a form concerning the various articles he kept in his possession, including a gold-coloured wedding band that could not be removed from his finger. Horne was scheduled for a number of procedures, including hematology, psychological testing, a brain scan, and an erotic preference test. No questions were to be asked about his offences — the reason given being they were before the court.

From the start, Horne was concerned about bail. He told intake staff that because the people in the North "are not particularly sophisticated," if he was seen "walking the streets" after his arrest the population might have thought he was, in effect, "free." He then appeared almost apologetic about the fact he was unable to discuss the events leading to his arrest. He stated, however, that what he really wanted help for was what he described as "depression" — the doctor used quotes around the term in a letter. Horne told Dr. Herbert Pascoe that he sometimes had periods of depression so profound he could barely function. He would become withdrawn, solitary, and "afraid" — of what, he had no idea. There were occasional highs too, he said. He said only his wife and oldest son were aware of his troubled state.

When he first arrived, he was seen walking around the facility appearing anxious and nervous. In the next few hours he was busy writing letters and appeared more relaxed. He watched a baseball game, something he hadn't been able to do with his friend and lawyer Joe Bovard ten days earlier, and he told staff he would like some refined literature — "classics" — to read. He was eating well and made a special request that there be no organ meat in his diet.

Hospital intake staff received a version of his life story. He told them he was born on a reserve and that his parents were North American Indian. His father was a shy man and there was no relationship between them. He described his late mother as "an extremely inadequate withdrawn individual" who had had trouble "coping with life," so much so that he had had no strong relationship with either parent and had been on his own since a very early age. He expressed concern over the well-being of his wife and children, but said his father and his brother should not be contacted about his being kept at the centre.

His teaching career had been stellar — he had not received many, if any, negative reports as a teaching professional. But he was getting sick of teaching and wanted a change. Depression, he said, was a constant problem. In his teaching career, Horne said he was "in the public eye for four or five hours a day" and that he was able to hold himself together for that time. But it was a struggle. He explained the techniques he used to try and escape his despair: running hard outdoors until exhausted in the freezing cold, or jumping on a snowmobile and getting "lost" for a while out on the land.

He spoke of the suicide attempt when he was a university student, standing alone on the Lions Gate Bridge in Vancouver at midnight. He said he never sought psychiatric help while working in the North because he was afraid it would reflect badly on him and harm his career — something the doctor Horne was speaking to at the hospital assured him would not have been the case. The depression Horne felt on and off "tended to remove me from the world," he said, "made me more solitary, made me feel that there was something wrong with myself, and one of the usual things that I would do would be head for the couch, lie down and go to sleep." He told staff he had had no psychiatric intervention in his lifetime. He said he had felt suicidal in the past twenty years, and besides the Lions Gate Bridge incident, had taken unnecessary risks to "test death." As examples, he said he used firearms carelessly, kicked the Berlin Wall, stole hubcaps from police cars in East Berlin, and took forbidden pictures of Soviet defence equipment.

He told them about his early jobs in northern British Columbia and his Arctic teaching. When asked why he had moved so many times in the Eastern Arctic, he tried to put responsibility on others, saying he was asked to transfer because "the area was troubled" and a person with his skill and competence was required in a new community. In spite of his excellent teaching record, he claimed he wanted to move on to a future career in computers or the travel industry, and the languages he claimed competence in were Spanish, Portuguese, German, Danish, Russian, Chinese, Latin, Greek, and Inuktitut.

It was noted that during his life Horne never used drugs and rarely alcohol. "I never had the time," he said, referring specifically to drinking. While being interviewed, the issue of sex, particularly same-sex involvement, was thought to be an important topic, but questions were limited because of direction from Horne's lawyer.

The day after his arrival at the hospital, he was seen again pacing restlessly, telling staff he was "worried" and unable to fall asleep. He was given chloral hydrate (a non-benzodiazepine sleeping pill) or Valium (diazepam, a benzodiazepine tranquilizer), as he would be throughout his time there. He also met with legal aid staff. Later he verbalized to staff his displeasure with the way he was being treated at the centre, complaining of having to go to bed at 10 p.m., like a child. However, explanations of rules and routines seemed to put him at ease.

In the following days he started loosening up a bit and played a game of pool with one of the staff members. He was still writing letters and could be rather sulky. He began asking for books about computers and the law and provided a list of books he wanted from the public library. He also requested to see the chaplain, Rev. William Archer, from whom he wished to obtain a New Testament Bible, saying, "I like to translate the Bible into simple

English so that people up North can understand better." Later he appeared quiet and slow, watchful of staff, pacing back and forth.

The next day he checked the roster to see who his nurse would be. He socialized minimally with other patients. He requested Valium for sleep again. In the next few days, he began engaging with others and was seen playing ping-pong with another patient, even sitting down for a game of Trivial Pursuit — no doubt taking great pride in scoring points.

A week later, Horne was observed working on shorthand. It is unclear why he was insistent on practising this writing skill, but perhaps he was anticipating taking notes in court. His poor eye contact when speaking was noted by staff. Again he was seen playing ping-pong with a patient, but this time he had begun to sound like an instructor with the player, "like a teacher to a student," it was noted. Once a teacher, always a teacher.

He was quick to complain. He told staff he hadn't been outside in weeks, and he didn't like being locked up. He said he'd lived in the North his "whole life," where he spent a great deal of time outdoors. Staff noted he seemed attention-seeking at times, frequently asking to have his pencil sharpened — "you can't work on shorthand with a dull pencil" — even though his pencil didn't appear to need sharpening.

His shorthand practice continued and so did the games of ping-pong. A week into his stay, a staff member noted Horne was "superficially pleasant." More testing was done, including the erotic preference test, during which he was described as "very anxious." Penile circumference responses (PCRs) were recorded while he viewed slides with and without sexual content. Horne co-operated fully with the testing but had little reaction — described as small PCRs — to most of the sexual material he was shown, making it impossible for the doctor to ascertain whether Horne preferred children or adults. Ultimately, the doctor was unable to confirm or rule out pedophilia. All that was clear that day was that Horne showed a preference for females compared to males.

Back on the psych ward, Horne played more ping-pong and, for the first time, was heard talking about the North in a relaxed way. He appeared at ease but it was noted — as it was throughout his life — "at times avoids eye contact." Again, he stressed he wanted no organ meat in his diet, apparently to control his polycythemia, a blood disorder identified in his youth where a patient's blood is thicker than normal.

He had been writing letters to Jeannie but had not received any responses. He told staff he couldn't talk to her on the telephone because she was hearing-impaired. Later he was heard complimenting the therapeutic environment at the centre. He also received a money order and a Visa card. He sent a blank personal cheque to his lawyer, Joe Bovard.

More testing was done. His EEG showed a slight abnormality correlating with an epileptic disorder, but it was considered minor. Throughout his EEG testing he was hyperventilating.

As time went on, he was sleeping better on the ward. His major concern was having to go back to Frobisher Bay and wait for trial. His other concern was that he get some form of counselling for his depression. He was told to talk to his lawyer about that.

During the following days, Horne submitted to the Wechsler Adult Intelligence Scale, the Bender Gestalt test, and the Minnesota Multiphasic Personality Inventory. His intellectual assessment revealed that he operated at a "superior level of intelligence." His Verbal IQ was 137 (very superior), Performance IQ was 107 (average), and his Full Scale IQ was 128 (superior). His highest scores were in tests of memory, practical judgment, and verbal fluency. His low scores were in tests involving visual alertness and perceptual organization. Anxiety and tension were blamed for the marked difference between the verbal and performance scores.

On his personality assessment test, he was described as "exaggerating his symptoms in order to gain some advantage." The doctor also reported that "he likely shows intellectualizing and obsessive-compulsive tendencies." In a summary written later on the ward, his 128 IQ was a point of interest, but he was described as having "faked bad" on his personality test.

In early November, Ed spoke to Jeannie on the telephone and this seemed to cheer him up. She had returned to Great Whale River with the children. He said she couldn't hear him very well, but nonetheless she allayed his concerns about their children by explaining they were being cared for with help from her extended family and friends. But in the days following this call, Horne became glum again, complaining to staff he wasn't "accomplishing anything" by being there and that he wanted some help for his problems. Jeannie told him she would wait for him "no matter what," and this put his mind at ease somewhat, but he told staff he had days where he felt as if he was "losing control" and this worried him.

He was grumpy for several days, complaining about the environment — a room was too warm for him one day, too cold the next. He complained bitterly after staff used a flashlight one night to check on him. When he learned that a group of patients had gone to the swimming pool without him, he became angry. "I've the right to participate in all activities because there is not enough to do around here anyway," he said, before storming away from the office and throwing the book he'd been reading against the wall. This incident was described by staff as "extremely childish." He was later seen walking by, glaring at the office in a "sulky and angry manner."

During his stay, his short fuse with people he considered less mentally robust than himself was evident. He called one woman, who was mentally ill, a "bitch" because she supposedly stole his cigarettes — a charge she denied. He later told staff he regretted using that "terrible swear word."

Still unhappy about the book situation, he asked staff if they could use his charge card to order books from a local bookstore for him. When told he would have to consult with the unit supervisor, he exploded, saying he'd already "wasted two weeks" of his life in the ward "doing nothing useful." Calming down a bit, he said, "I'm not mad at you. But you've just delivered me a real blow."

Things looked up the next day, however, when Reverend Archer arrived with a copy of the Greek New Testament. Horne was pleased, telling staff that "translating this will keep me busy for six months!"

Trouble sleeping began again, so more Valium was administered in the evening. He pulled a muscle playing ping-pong one day, which sent him to the nurse requesting pain medication. He threw temper tantrums when he didn't get his way. He told one patient to "shut the fuck up," then later apologized to staff, blaming the outburst on the Valium, saying, "It must be getting to me."

The reading material he'd received after all his complaints was helping him relax. By the middle of November, he had a visitor from Iqaluit, a government employee named Peter Baril. And he told staff that the photographs of his children that arrived in the mail were giving him "the strength he needs to carry on."

By the middle of November, Horne was better at controlling his temper. He didn't need Valium much anymore for sleep, and he finally had enough books to read. He wanted to stay at the hospital for as long as he could before the bail hearing. He said it was more comfortable than a jail cell, which was undoubtedly true.

During his stay, Horne called other patients "crazies." But shortly before he was released in early December, he was observed spending more time with his fellow patients. However, a nurse noted: "He is selective as to who he associates with — those whose manner suggests superior attitude and are here for 'treatment.' Intolerant of psychotic patients. Moody man, who displays childish temper tantrums if he does not have everything to his liking." Apparently, he was visibly upset after losing a pool game and refused to play bingo when he was unable to have the cards he always played with. "Has no difficulty making his needs known," a nurse reported.

Horne was also overheard complaining about the centre with an equally disgruntled patient, denying the charges against him, and saying he was only there for treatment and counselling.

As the day of his release drew near, Horne complained of a backache and was given Valium. He was again watching staff closely, harping about a book order, asking if a taxi service could help by driving downtown to pick up the book for him. When the nurse pointed out that the bookstore might not be open on Sunday, he angrily shot back, "Well if that fucking lazy slob of a teacher had done his job properly I would have had my book weeks ago. This hospital seems to hire nothing but incompetents." It is unclear who the "teacher" in question was. He calmed down but paced outside the office door as he had done after a previous complaint, glaring at staff.

Horne was discharged from the hospital on December 9, 1985. After speaking to his lawyer, he requested bail so he could spend Christmas with his family. He also said he didn't need further treatment as he was "now functioning with a full deck."

• • •

A mental health co-ordinator involved in the case wrote a letter to RCMP constable Brian Morrison:

> Last October 1985 I was requested by Social Services to make a special trip to Lake Harbour. I interviewed male youngsters and found very saddened, angry, frustrated boys between the ages of 10 and 16 years of age. Completing the interviews meant spending some time with the school authorities at which time I found a number of aggressive outbursts and a high degree of anxiety experienced by the children which alarmed and concerned me. Of note, one of the older youngsters had attempted suicide previous to my coming into the settlement.
>
> I found the victim children generally very anxious, questioning, fearful, depressed and angry. I also found the same with the parents after a meeting with them. Added to this was the same general feelings felt by the teachers and other caregiving people in Lake Harbour. Something of this magnitude must be addressed and I trust that some of my findings and observations will assist you in your endeavours.[2]

Another social worker's report to Constable Morrison in October 1985 outlined the gravity of the situation with heartbreaking clarity:

> Mr. Horne's behaviour has had ramifications for the entire community. As he held possibly the most prestigious position in the communities and attended the Catholic Church (in Frobisher Bay) regularly, people are struggling to understand how and why he abused his position and the trust of the boys.

She went on to report:

> All the teachers are under attack. Some of the children refused to go to school and one of the victims attempted suicide a week ago. We are happy [Horne] was caught at this time as he had just approached the priest about teaching catechism to young boys — this may have even done far more damage. At the present, I can't tell you how many victims are involved — but Mr. Horne has used force with these boys — he forced himself upon a number to have anal intercourse and when the boys refused to strip, Mr. Horne stripped them.

. . .

John F. Thornton, assistant professor of psychiatry at the University of Toronto and a member of the Clarke Institute consultation team, visited Lake Harbour November 13–15, 1985, and wrote a report detailing what he heard and saw there, having been invited by a nurse to assess the impact that Horne's — at the time — "alleged pedophilia" would have on the community. During his time there, Thornton met with a social worker for a couple of hours, then with the education committee; he attended a parents' meeting that lasted three and half hours and a teachers' meeting for one hour. He also conducted individual interviews with parents of three of the children involved in the sexual attack on the young girl that uncovered Horne's crimes. Only two of the children were seen, but at least one parent of every child involved attended the meetings. Thornton encountered a community that was "clearly devastated" by what had happened, beaten down further by guilt and shame. People openly wondered how it all could have been prevented. All the parents felt their children were adversely affected by the unveiling of "the secret." But their major concern was that no further harm should be done by unnecessarily reviewing what had taken place, either during Thornton's visit or at some point in the future in court.

Particularly with regard to court, they wanted to keep their children out of any legal proceedings as much as possible. Parents were deeply worried about how Horne might plead. No one outside the community, or even inside the community, knew all the names of the child victims, and they wanted to keep it that way to avoid any teasing, name calling, embarrassment, or shame at the hands of other children. The parents were also distraught about the effects the sex acts Horne forced upon their children would have on the children's health. They asked for guidance on how to discuss what happened with their children, especially those who were scared and reluctant to open up. The situation made parents even more wary of people in positions of authority in general, and teachers in particular. They also let it be known that they weren't keen on psychiatrists meeting with their children without consulting them first.

Thornton concluded his report by saying Horne's predations had a "major and significant" impact on the children directly involved, their parents, and the community as a whole:

> There is information from all the children's parents that the children were adversely affected before, during and after the unveiling of the secret. The experience to which they were exposed is clearly not a normal part of one's sexual development, though it is difficult to assess precisely the ongoing impact this will have in the future for the children involved. The parents have been burdened with a sense of guilt and shame, feeling that they have let their children down, in that they have not protected them adequately, and this had led to many of them doubting their ability as parents. The community as a whole has been devastated, as have the individuals involved, that such a thing could happen virtually under their noses while they did not realize it was happening.[3]

He did mention signs of hope. A number of people said since Horne left town things were improving at the school. A few people explicitly said it was not good that the parents "should feel hatred all the way" and hopefully they could learn to forgive. Thornton noted this sentiment did not mean the people were soft on Horne. But they did desperately want to move on.

The experts who descended on Lake Harbour in the wake of the Horne crisis were not just in the medical field. On November 24, 1985, Joe Handley, deputy minister of education, contacted Manitoba-based education consultant Kevin Van Camp regarding the reports of sexual abuse in the community. Handley asked Van Camp to visit the North to interview "as many adults as possible" and report his findings directly to Handley. Van Camp spent December 6, 7, and 8 interviewing people in Frobisher Bay and Lake Harbour. He was not reinvestigating the case, nor was he expected to provide conclusive evidence of wrongdoing by anyone. Ideally, the report would provide an objective viewpoint on a difficult situation and make recommendations for action.

Submitted to the government in December 1985, the Van Camp report identified a number of factors that allowed Horne to maintain control over children for so long. The report was viewed favourably in the hope that it could spark change.

Van Camp found that many, if not most, of the children apparently did not realize Horne's actions were wrong, or were coerced to put their concerns aside. Administrative supervision of the school and its staff by "long-distance" was found to be a factor, given the prohibitive cost of flying senior staff to communities for in-person visits.[4] The very positive view of Horne held by many in the senior levels of education had also been a major impediment to investigating suspicions at an earlier stage. Horne, despite often portraying himself as a renegade outsider, was in fact one of the "old boys" of the system and, as such, enjoyed a great deal of trust.[5]

In Lake Harbour, the Community Education Council was relatively new and, as such, didn't have the confidence to challenge views held by their overseers in Frobisher Bay.

Horne's knowledge of the language was also a strong factor. Although he generally shunned the company of adults, he nonetheless managed to appear to outsiders to have his finger on the pulse of the community. Being an advocate for the use of the local language in education was incorrectly equated with being an advocate for local authority, and it enabled him to control what education officials saw and heard coming out of the community.

Various government departments had mandates, written or implied, to foster the well-being of children. But the flip side of fostering well-being — preventing abuse — was seldom contemplated and therefore seldom addressed. The departments that were expected to collaborate in the nurturing of child welfare — mainly Education, Social Services, Health, and Justice — did not have positive enough working relationships, and so the children, as well as Horne the predator, fell through enormous cracks in the system. The bottom line, Van Camp discovered, was that people in the community saw government as unresponsive. The problems they faced as a result of so many children being victimized were a result of power imbalances, poor communication, and fear.

"Government is seen as remote," Van Camp wrote, "and that it would not keep concerns, suspicions, etc. confidential." Therefore, many voices were quiet, too quiet, in the leadup to Horne's arrest. "They knew something was wrong," Van Camp wrote, "but did not feel they had the expertise to be sure, and consequently did not have the confidence to proceed."[6]

Horne's position as a trusted principal allowed him to control the situation. Parents and other community members knew the principal and suspected that he was a problem, but they did not know his superiors in Frobisher Bay, who seldom visited the community, or how to contact them. The community was small, home to less than a dozen non-Inuit; Horne was the only one who had taken the time to learn Inuktitut. Parents in Lake Harbour were reluctant to complain and couldn't fathom the sexual activity going on. They had seen sexual deviancy before. Incest was not unheard of in small, northern communities. But such actions were not committed by people wielding the kind of authority Horne had.

Van Camp went on, "Nothing in their experience led them to imagine something of the nature of what was happening. They did not know what to look for from the children or how to interpret what they saw."

As principal, Horne was the one responsible for evaluating the school's operations for administrators in Yellowknife and Frobisher Bay. Lake Harbour's isolation allowed Horne "to exercise an extraordinary level of control."[7]

Van Camp addressed the issue of the choking incident at the school that Horne himself had reported. He was under the impression that Brian Menton had attempted to investigate the incident but that the local education committee didn't want to proceed because they were absorbed in the dismissal of a classroom assistant at the time. In fact, Menton had not investigated the report, had not visited Lake Harbour when Horne was there, and met the complaints against Horne from Bryon and Maureen Doherty with suggestions that they should be thankful to have a principal as dedicated and competent as Horne. Van Camp wrote: "No one is clear of the exact nature of the choking incident. In that Horne himself reported it, something happened and as such it certainly was a clue. Whether he was showing youngsters a game or attempting to coerce someone is immaterial. There was not, in my view, a proper investigation."[8]

He recommended that a policy and board bylaws be put in place to ensure thorough investigation and written reports on every incidence of physical violence toward children.

Other than Frobisher Bay, where he interviewed education officials, Van Camp visited only Lake Harbour, and his report only discussed the situation there, but his comments could just as easily describe the situation in all the communities in which Horne had taught.

Out on Bail

ON DECEMBER 20, 1985, THE COURT IN FROBISHER BAY RE-
ceived a letter from Dr. Herbert Pascoe of the Alberta Hospital Remand
Centre with a detailed summary about Horne's mental health. Dr. Pascoe
had seen how manipulative Horne could be and made sure the court
was aware of this. Horne was "extremely attention seeking," he wrote,
and "highly complaintive — unjustifiably so" and "sarcastic with nursing staff," though he would always try to put on his best face when
being interviewed by staff "in an attempt to make the best possible
impression."[1]

A show cause hearing — commonly known as a bail hearing — was held
before the Honourable T. B. Davis in Frobisher Bay on Friday, December
20, 1985. Ms. N. Boillat was the counsel for the Crown, and Joe Bovard
served for the defence.

There were a total of fifteen counts before the court, stemming from
eleven incidents. The Crown began to read the allegations against Horne.
At that time, Horne had no criminal record, his wife and children were
in Great Whale River, and he was jobless. The other communities Horne
worked in were brought up, with Gjoa Haven incorrectly listed as one of
them — sloppy work on the part of the court. The charges were coming out
of two communities only: Cape Dorset and Lake Harbour.

The court heard that an investigation by the RCMP had revealed that Ed Horne had performed numerous sexual acts on boys ranging from twelve to sixteen years of age. The boys were students at elementary schools in the two communities. Everything at this point was alleged. Horne had not made a plea one way or another.

No children were present in the court. The Crown's case was the transcript of testimony of the boys in question, in addition to a statement given by Horne concerning two of the offences. The Crown then began detailing the accusations against Horne. One might expect this would be the first time that the public would have an opportunity to learn the nature of the charges against him, a high-profile, well-known, and generally respected teacher, whose arrest had spurred, if not outrage, at least curiosity. But Joe Bovard's first act, once court was in session, was to ask for a ban on publication.

The first witness called at the hearing was Patrick Lorand, the local Catholic priest, who said he had known Horne for about a year. He confirmed that a place called Catholic Family Services of Toronto was aware of Horne's case and that they were prepared to offer him psychological or psychiatric services if he were granted bail, and if he needed a place to live or a job, they could suggest organizations to help him if he went to Toronto. When questions were asked about the specific structure of these mental health services, Lorand said he wasn't sure.

Lorand, who believed Horne's claim of Indigeneity, also mentioned a Father Jack Davis who was involved with the chaplaincy to the Native people in Toronto who could help Horne when he arrived, as well as a Brother Albert Robertson who had worked in Thunder Bay with convicts, many of them Indigenous. The priest also confirmed that Horne would be allowed to stay at the Catholic Mission in Frobisher Bay for a short time if the court released Horne to travel south.

David Wilman, principal of the Teacher Education Program in Frobisher Bay, was the next witness. He said he'd known Horne for seven years, during his time working on curriculum projects and "as a friend." Wilman explained that the program trained Inuit teachers for jobs in the schools of the Eastern Arctic, and that curriculum development integrating Inuktitut into the classrooms was a valuable program that Horne could easily be a part of — even if he were found guilty of the charges before the court. This type of curriculum development would not involve Horne ever being in a classroom with children — Wilman said that he would have "severe reservations" about Horne returning to a classroom. Wilman described Horne as "one of the few recognized experts in [curriculum development]," saying that Horne had "independently produced material that has been in use in the schools for 12 years …" Wilman added, "I certainly think we can't afford to waste the talents of someone like Ed Horne." Wilman said that he had discussed the possibility of a role for Horne in curriculum development with the superintendent of education, Bert Rose, and he believed that Rose was in agreement. Under cross-examination, however, Wilman admitted that he was not in a position to decide whether or not Horne would be rehired if convicted — that would be up to the executive branch of the government.

. . .

Horne himself — then forty-two years of age — was called as a witness. He was asked by his defence lawyer, Joe Bovard, what his ancestry was. Horne replied: "My ancestry is Métis — part Algonquin, part English." Confirming he had been in the N.W.T. for fifteen years he said, "This is my home, sir."

Bovard told me he does not know why he asked Horne to state his ethnicity. But there may be good reasons why a manipulative accused like Horne would put forth a claim of Indigeneity. Although the *Gladue* rights used today in Canadian courts — which require the court to give special consideration to the background and circumstances of an Indigenous person when setting bail or imposing a sentence — were not in existence in 1985, the seeds for it had been planted and had been germinating for years within the system.

Horne had made previous claims of Indigeneity while living in the North. Dennis Patterson, the lawyer Bovard took over the legal aid centre from years before, recently offered a possible explanation for Horne's claim: "I think it might have been an effort to elicit sympathy from the judge. It was not uncommon, even in 1985, to emphasize the cultural clash that could be a factor."

In any case, Horne's assertion of Métis identity was accepted by the court and a plan was set in motion for Horne to volunteer at an organization called the Association for Native Development in the Performing and Visual Arts, located in Toronto, if he were granted bail.

Horne told the court he had no close relatives in the Northwest Territories or Toronto, and that he wouldn't return to his home province for work because the economy there was "depressed." Toronto had better options for him, he said.

Horne's finances were reviewed. He said he had cash resources of about eighty thousand dollars. He was amenable to the help Catholic Family Services could provide and to volunteering with the Native film organization. Educational opportunities in Toronto appealed to him, and he said he'd been looking in a Toronto newspaper for an apartment.

Horne elected to be tried by a judge, rather than a judge and jury. The lawyers discussed and settled on Frobisher Bay as the trial location, ruling out Lake Harbour for logistical reasons. Dates for a preliminary inquiry needed to be set, and because lead RCMP investigator Const. Brian Morrison would be in Newfoundland for parts of February and March, the inquiry was set for April 8, 9, and 10, 1986.

The judge was satisfied Horne would appear in court when called and would behave in the interim, but he was concerned about the public perception of Horne being out on bail. Although there was a ban on publication of the case at the time, many people still knew Horne had been arrested and charged with terrible crimes against children, so it was important that restrictions be placed on him. It was agreed he would have no contact with children and would report every Friday to the RCMP at O Division, 225 Jarvis Street, Toronto. The Crown also asked Horne to hand over his passport to the RCMP in Frobisher Bay.

The court set bail at two thousand dollars. Horne pointed out that would be easy to arrange since his bank account was at the Royal Bank of Canada's branch located in the very building the bail hearing was being held in, the Arnakallak Building, close to the beach.

Despite the order prohibiting access to children, there seems to have been no concern over the continued contact Horne would have with his own three young sons as his family was set to join him for Christmas. Horne was granted bail and moved to Toronto where he took a volunteer position with the film association and the opportunity to get therapy for his problems.

Horne and his family spent 1986 in Toronto. Horne recalled walking his son, John Paul Akavak, to public school a few blocks away on the first day of classes.

In the fall of 1986 Horne enrolled Akavak in a Catholic school where there were many boys in his class with his name, John Paul, since when Pope John Paul II was chosen in 1979, many boys were named after him. Jimmy attended the same school, and Horne registered him in an Italian-language kindergarten.

• • •

In the North, the RCMP and social services had ramped up their investigation into the criminal acts Horne may have committed. An exhaustive investigation unearthed many indignities. By April of 1986 the RCMP had compiled a long list of charges against Horne. The allegations involved eleven boys and twenty-three incidents of sexual assault.

Horne waived a preliminary inquiry and consented to trial in the Supreme Court of the N.W.T. On May 13, 1986, he was ordered to stand trial on ten counts. There were now eight boys. The charges had changed from the police report. There was no mention of anal rape. Horne had agreed some things had occurred, but not others. By July 24 his lawyer was now Neil Sharkey as Joe Bovard had moved south.

An agreed statement of facts was signed on January 13, 1987. All the complainants were his students. Neil Sharkey was counsel for Ed Horne, and Brian Bruser, counsel for the Crown. In it, the entry for the crimes against Boy #1 ended, as they all would, with the words: "The sexual contact in each incident was initiated by the accused," and the boys "engaged in all the activity without resistance." These were words at odds with what the boys had told police.

. . .

Horne had abused many more boys than he admitted to abusing when he entered his guilty plea in 1987. I asked Horne — who acknowledged he'd already said "I have to speak to my lawyer" when police asked if there were more victims — why he didn't confess everything about his predations when he was arrested that first time.

His answer implies that he was trying to protect the victims rather than himself: "Because I would have been 'outing' individuals who, as far as I knew at the time, didn't want to be 'outed' as victims." He added a comment relevant to the later second criminal case: "The new wave of accusations came up in the late 1990s when word got around that there were huge cash payments for those who accused me. I was ashamed that some of these new allegations were true, and I agreed to plead guilty."

. . .

On January 20, 1986, Joe Handley, deputy minister of education, sent a letter to Bert Rose, by then regional superintendent of education, excoriating him for his handling of the Horne case and blasting the old boy's network of friends who had come up through the system together, who seemed to rally around each other when times were tough rather than protecting the schoolchildren in their care.[2]

There were other serious personnel issues broached in the letter to Rose that, taken together with the Horne crisis, made Handley question Rose's judgment and leadership abilities.

Harsh words were levelled at the "superficial" attempts made by Brian Menton and Rose to investigate allegations of child abuse in Lake Harbour in 1985. Social services ended up picking up the pieces after revelations about Horne were unearthed, and that made administrators, especially Rose, "appear to not be sensitive to community feelings" or even more seriously, to be willing to "let die or cover-up a very serious charge," Handley wrote. He acknowledged the Horne story went back further than the time during which Rose had been superintendent, but he said he was troubled the system allowed Horne's crimes to go on for so many years.

The old boy's network he unambiguously described Rose operating in "did much in discouraging those who might have suspected what was going on to not report primarily because they did not believe such a report would result in action," or, if action were taken, it might well backfire on the one reporting the issue.

The Handley letter became one of the cornerstones of the plaintiffs' case in the second civil case, launched in 2004. Until that date, it was not even known to exist outside the knowledge of a select few individuals in the Department of Education, including, of course, Rose himself. Years later, after leaving the department, Rose claimed to have destroyed his copy. When its existence became known, it became somewhat of a Holy Grail item that every northern journalist wanted to read and report on. But the department was not about to make copies available. It was believed — as it turned out, correctly — to contain an admonition as to how Rose and other senior officials in the Baffin Region had reacted to the charges against and the investigation into Horne. But no journalist was ever able to access the letter until *Nunatsiaq News* finally got a copy through a freedom of information request. That copy, however, had been redacted to the point of being useless.

The Nunavut Court of Justice issued a broad sealing order in 2008 on all matters related to the civil actions involving Horne victims. A publication ban was ordered as well.

In the summer of 2009, the Canadian Broadcasting Corporation fought vigorously to unseal the file that included the Handley letter as well as the Van Camp report. But the same judge who had issued the broad sealing order denied the CBC's request.

The sealing order continued to protect the government bureaucrats who had been negligent in their supervision of and investigation into Edward Horne.

There may also have been a feeling that Handley had overstated the point he wanted to make and that the letter could be used to weaken the government's position in the civil case — that, in fact, Handley had put in writing that education officials knew or should have known that all was not right in their supervision of Ed Horne.

PART THREE

Her Majesty The Queen Vs. Edward Horne

WITH THE TEMPERATURE HOVERING AROUND -27°C AND BLOW-
ing snow forming ice crystals on the courthouse windows, the judgment
against Edward Horne was rendered in Iqaluit on February 16, 1987.

Since Horne had pleaded guilty, there was no courtroom drama of the
sort felt in criminal trials when an accused is battling it out to avoid serious
jail time. Horne knew he would go to jail. It was the amount of time and
reasons for it that needed to be determined.

There was no crowd of curious onlookers to greet Horne and the lawyers
as they made their way to the courtroom. The bone-chilling Arctic weather
was to blame for that. But also, the reality was that everyone who knew
about the case just wanted it to end as soon as possible.

The editor of *Nunatsiaq News*, Jim Bell, reported on the Horne
cases as they unfolded, from 1985 onward. Bell recalled defence lawyer Neil Sharkey[1] mentioning his client's impressive IQ during the sentencing submission and that Horne came from a mixed First Nations
Euro-Canadian background.[2] Sharkey also noted, for anyone who was
unaware at that point, that Horne knew multiple languages, including
Inuktitut, and mentioned Horne's work developing a syllabic font for
the Macintosh computer. The myth of Ed Horne was alive and well
with reports like these trickling out from the courtroom. But virtually

nothing about the actual crimes or the victims and what they felt was ever revealed to the public.

. . .

The Honourable Justice T. David Marshall was presiding. Marshall had the kind of life that could easily inspire awe in anyone who took the time to look into his past. He was a doctor *and* a lawyer from Haldimand County, Ontario, a rural area on the Niagara Peninsula, on the north shore of Lake Erie. Marshall had skills that made him rather well suited to Arctic life — one very striking one being that he could fly an airplane. He had become a qualified pilot when he was sixteen, and while serving as a judge in the N.W.T. he was known to sometimes fly much-needed medical supplies into communities he visited. Appointed justice of the Supreme Court of the N.W.T. in 1982 (the same year he was made honorary Chief of the Six Nations), he became an Ontario court judge ten years later.

When Horne's sentencing began that day in 1987, the expectation was that Justice Marshall would not mince words. He did not disappoint and delivered an eloquent judgment. Given the sordid nature of the offences, though, it was a painful case on which to rule, and his words were undoubtedly delivered with the heaviest of hearts.

Justice Marshall called Horne a teacher of "high repute,"[3] whose reputation was entirely shattered by his own actions. In various and repugnant ways Horne had assaulted eight boys over an extended period of time. Marshall wondered aloud how such conduct as Horne admitted to could have gone on undetected for so long. In part answering his own question, he opined that fear and shame had kept the boys from revealing Horne's crimes. He also spoke of the nature of Inuit communities, a topic he said he would revisit in more detail later.[4]

He noted that the facts leading to Horne's exposure and arrest were revealed in an unusual and "sadly ironic"[5] way, speaking of the shocking photos of boys that were found stashed inside a school's piano. He also spoke about the initially unrelated case of three young people who were investigated for sexual assault in Lake Harbour in the spring of 1985, two of whom later admitted to being victims of Ed Horne. Further investigation of similar claims by other boys led to the matters at hand, the judge confirmed.

He reviewed Horne's teaching record, his talents as a linguist, and especially his impressive reported ability in Inuktitut. He uncritically acknowledged Horne's claims of Indigeneity. And he noted that while he realized Horne had a wife and three boys to care for, he could not let those facts sway his judgment. He spoke of the numerous witnesses who testified that the people of these remote northern communities felt an enormous wrong had been done to them by the government in sending a person such as Horne into their midst. "There is no doubt that that is so," Marshall said.[6]

Judge Marshall accepted Dr. Herbert Pascoe's diagnosis and stated that he was fully satisfied from all the evidence that Horne was a pedophile. He then spoke of the condition of pedophilia. He believed Horne could be rehabilitated, that with the right treatment, Horne's desire for children could be controlled.

He talked about strong prison sentences as a deterrent to the menace of pedophilia and felt they sent a message to society that this type of behaviour was unacceptable. But he showed compassion, too, in stressing that courts must not be vengeful in difficult cases "where there is a tendency to great social revulsion." These cases, he said, more than others, "require our utmost in judicial equanimity."[7]

Marshall was more qualified than most judges to speak on complex medical issues, and he understood that pedophilia was a disorder that could not be cured, only managed. He showed a touching empathy for the accused and the sadness of the reality that his condition had doomed him to live with when he said, "Indeed I am sure that the accused sorely wishes his appetite for young boys did not exist. It is a curse to him to have it, and if he could I am sure he would have shed it — but he cannot."[8]

Marshall seemed to understand the lifetimes of pain that were to follow these crimes. Before sending Horne to jail that very first time, Marshall offered his heartbreaking and eloquent views on what had happened:

> I want now to relate the problem of pedophilia to the
> North. Clearly, the problem for all society is a serious

one, but it is, I think, even more serious in the Canadian Arctic. Our communities are remote and problematic in this regard. The non-Native presence in our Northern communities consists of the mounted police officers, the nurses and teachers. These people, though a minority, represent and speak the language of power — and indeed they wield power — controlling law enforcement, health and education, not to mention housing, welfare, and other services, though this is changing as Native people take on these roles.

He went on:

The local people are, of course, accustomed to accepting this authority, so often in the hands of the small white community. Because the language and culture of the people are not the language and culture of the authorities, they are much less inclined to question that authority. By reason of the governmental authority in the communities, these people may be much more vulnerable to sexual predatory activity, be that in the form of homosexual, pedophilic or heterosexual aggression than is the usual Canadian child in a setting in southern Canada. Governments and courts must be cognizant of this greater vulnerability.

To put it another way, he said, "Pedophiles, just as they may seek out organizations catering to depressed and fatherless boys to satisfy their sexual appetites, we may expect will prey on Native children in the villages of our North because of the natural innocence of the people here as regards these unnatural sexual perversions."[9]

He said there were two more problems making this situation even worse. First, the serious "problems of language" between Inuit and non-Inuit in the North, and second, there was usually no access to counselling or medical care for the family or the child victim of such a crime:

"There is not a single psychiatrist in the Northwest Territories and limited counselling possibilities exist, and certainly there is little help for these Native boys in remote Arctic communities."[10] In any other part of Canada, he said, from Corner Brook to Vancouver, help for victims like these was easier to get. The insidious, covert, and concealed nature of these crimes added to their horror and level of destruction. Therefore, governments and the courts must be all the more "careful and vigilant in these cases," he said.[11]

Horne was sentenced to six years in a federal penitentiary, the court's decision filed in the N.W.T. on February 17, 1987. Horne served the sentence at Bowden Institution, in Innisfail, Alberta.

This was supposed to be the end of Ed Horne in the North. But as forceful and apparently final as this judgment was, much more was to follow. In fact, Horne said years later, "even after the arrest, therapy, the elapse of about 10 years between my prison sentence and my next arrest, I still, at the time of my second arrest, had not absorbed the enormity of the crimes I had committed."[12]

Prison and Release

EIGHT MONTHS INTO HIS SENTENCE AT BOWDEN INSTITUTION, Horne requested psychiatric treatment and was admitted to the Regional Psychiatric Centre (RPC) in Saskatoon on November 12, 1987. Initially, he found the RPC environment "a positive carnival of sexual excess," he later told his lawyer. Horne said that while there he was propositioned by a young male patient.

Horne was examined by doctors at the RPC. He also made use of the library, supposedly reading anything he could find about sexual disorders in order to shed light on his pedophilia. Horne also reportedly translated the biblical book of Ruth into Inuktitut during his time in the institution. This story was told to me by a number of sources. However, when I asked Horne about this in 2021, he replied, "Total fabrication. Ruth is the book most often studied because it is short and [written] in simple Hebrew. Can't remember why I was looking at Ruth, I can only say that I never translated any part of the Bible into Inuktitut."

Eventually, Horne "accepted full responsibility for what he had done and he admitted his offenses," his lawyer said, and in the words of the reports from the RPC he showed "great empathy" toward his victims. He was discharged on July 7, 1988. But whatever gains he made through treatment were short-lived and tenuous because it was reported that he soon attempted suicide. A later defence lawyer would describe the prison as a "place where you have to look people in the eye and growl just to be understood and taken seriously."

Robin McGrath, author of the highly regarded collection of Inuit writing titled *Paper Stays Put*, met Horne in the 1980s in Frobisher Bay and never felt any reason to dislike him. In fact, she recalls being impressed with how warmly the student hockey players visiting from Cape Dorset greeted Horne when they saw him during a home game against the Frobisher Bay team.

In 1989, while he was in prison, McGrath paid Horne a visit. She knew his wife and sons were in Alberta, getting support from a local church while Horne remained incarcerated. McGrath's feeling was that if his wife was still standing by him, she had no trouble also offering her support.

During a long and intense talk, McGrath said Horne told her something that astonished her: he'd been diagnosed with multiple personality disorder — a condition not mentioned by any of the professionals who treated him over the years and that he had been unaware he was suffering from. He told McGrath that he'd been videotaped on numerous occasions when he went into an altered state and that six or seven alternate personalities or identities emerged. "He said he saw the tapes and could not deny what he saw, but that he had no conscious awareness of these other personalities," she said. He also told McGrath that he pleaded guilty to the charges against him because if what he saw on the tapes was possible, "anything else he might have done while in these states was also possible, and that he could not put any child through the process of testifying under those circumstances."

Other than a bilingual Hebrew-English Torah and a few brief notes, he got little from her except that one prison visit. She knows Horne could be very manipulative, but she didn't feel like he was trying to get anything from her.

• • •

Horne was paroled in 1990 and granted final release in February 1993. Horne was no longer eligible to teach in Canada, so he became a taxi dispatcher in Red Deer, Alberta. Jeannie was still with him, as were their boys, now numbering four, as Jeannie and Ed had adopted a boy named Jordan in 1992, whom the family called Bungee.

Horne's taxi job consisted of three twelve-hour shifts a week, enough to live on, he said, and for the most part the family did well. But the oldest boy, Akavak, was sneaking out at night to smoke pot and was skipping school; Jimmy, whom Horne called the "brightest boy I ever knew" was underachieving; and Danny, whom Horne claimed "had been viciously maltreated by his mother" had come to realize that he was Horne's favourite child.

Life in Red Deer was tough for Jeannie, though, as she had no extended family or friends, there was no Inuit community there, and her hearing impairment made day-to-day life difficult. In March 1995, she moved back to her home community of Great Whale River with Jordan, their youngest. The three older boys stayed with their father for the next few months.

Horne was broke and unable to offer his family what he felt they deserved, so he set his sights on Mexico for a fresh start. He wanted his boys to accompany him and tried to convince Jeannie to let them go. But the boys spent the summer of 1995 at Great Whale River with Jeannie. By September she had decided that the kids would not be moving to Mexico with her husband; they would remain with her. Jimmy and Danny wouldn't take sides. The oldest, Akavak, then sixteen, returned to Red Deer.

Akavak planned to join Horne in Mexico City once Horne secured a job and a home. But Akavak changed his mind and decided to stay in Red Deer. Horne was crushed and had no contact with Akavak or the rest of his family for the next four years.[1]

Once in Mexico, Horne began teaching adult education classes and met a local woman he wished to marry.

Another Criminal Case

IN 1997, AN INUK INMATE SERVING TIME INSIDE THE PENITEN-
tiary in Prince Albert, Saskatchewan, began talking during group therapy
sessions about a former teacher, Ed Horne, telling the group that he was a
victim too, and that there were many more men like him still suffering in the
North, especially in his home community of Sanikiluaq. This inmate's claim
of victimization by Horne was later discredited. But his information about
other victims got the attention of the RCMP in the Arctic and a new investigation was launched. The second criminal case against Horne had begun.

• • •

They were men now, some with their own families. Most of them lived in
the same communities where the abuse had taken place. Many of them were
related to each other. They could not escape the memories of the abuse they
had suffered, but they never talked about it.

Betty,* a former schoolteacher and resident of Sanikiluaq who knew
many Horne victims, said it took years before she realized the extent of the
damage Horne had done.

"I worked with a fellow, he was almost a recluse," she said of a man she
got to know over the years when she worked at Nuiyak School. "As [his

story] came out, he was in tears. And I realized I was talking to someone who was six years old, emotionally. He was going through so much." This man ended up laying charges against Horne during the second criminal case, launched in 1999, a case in which dozens of men finally came forward about their abuse.

Betty remembered this reclusive man's bravery at finally speaking out, but his fear at the possibility of having to face Horne again.

"He would look around and say, 'Did I do the right thing? Is he going to get me? Can he tell what I'm doing? He told me not to say.'"

The man would be one of many to make the heavy-hearted journey to Iqaluit to give testimony to a lawyer in a preliminary inquiry in Horne's second criminal case. Airplanes chartered by the RCMP arrived in Sanikiluaq from Iqaluit, and a certain number of men at a time would travel up to give statements there. There were so many victims they couldn't all go at once. Betty recalled, "People were used to going to the airport to greet and to say goodbye to family members. And a woman I worked with at the school was up there saying goodbye to her brother, who was one of the victims who was going up for a deposition. And she saw her brother-in-law and she didn't understand. She shook his hands and thought, *Oh my God.* All these years she has known him, she didn't know. She knew he had troubles. A lot of the men were like that. You didn't know. Everyone in the town realized: we're all related. We all know someone who has gone through this."

. . .

Horne had been living in Mexico as the police built their case against him. Canada tried to extradite him and found that it could not. Instead, Canadian authorities joined forces with Mexico to withdraw Horne's work visa and jail him on March 21, 1999. Horne was held by federal authorities in Mexico until he was released to Air Canada for a flight back to Canada a week later.

Horne told me he disputes a report he heard in the media at the time that said he was arrested at the Toronto airport as the result of a tip.

"I was arrested in my office in Mexico City, and held for a week in a Mexican jail. From there I was escorted back to Canada by RCMP officers who had flown down to deliver me. I believe the lie fed to the media reflects unease over the illegality of what the RCMP had done. I did not have the resources to contest this in court, and did not want the headlines that would have been the result. There was no real option but to face the music, and cooperate."

Horne must have realized that he had no grounds for joy, or even complacency, when, on the plane, he recognized a fellow passenger. He was an RCMP officer who had served in Cape Dorset when Horne taught there, travelling in plain clothes. The officer had flown to Mexico solely to travel back on the same flight as Horne so he could positively identify the man. Horne was arrested on his arrival at Pearson International Airport in Toronto. This time the sexual assault charges against him involving more northern boys went back decades, to his earliest days in the N.W.T.

• • •

The day of his return, March 29, 1999, was a momentous day for Horne. He thought that he had paid his price to society for the crimes he admitted to having committed and that once that price was paid he would be a free man for the rest of his life. Well read, he understood the concept of double jeopardy — that one cannot be prosecuted twice for the same crime. Until his imprisonment in Mexico before his removal to Canada, it may never have dawned on him that one can, however, be charged for a different crime against the same person, or for the same crime against a different person.

Three days later was a momentous day for the people of Nunavut as well. On that day the map of Canada changed with the split of the Northwest Territories into two territories, the largely Inuit territory of Nunavut in the east, extending west along most of the Arctic coast, and the remnant Northwest Territories in the west. Nunavut was touted as a territory that would allow Inuit to shake off the restrictions of an outdated colonialism and flourish under Inuit leaders and decision-makers. Reams have been written, and more will yet be written, about the results of what some call "the

Nunavut experiment." For the purposes of this book, it is necessary to note only that Nunavut adopted a unified court system. All other jurisdictions in Canada have two levels of trial court. The first level is a provincial or territorial court. The second is a superior or supreme court, or Court of King's Bench. Nunavut is different. Because of its immense size — one-fifth the land mass of Canada — it was thought wise that all judges should have the ability to hear any kind of case. Thus, the Nunavut Court of Justice was created as Canada's first and only single-level court. And within that system, Nunavut does have a court of appeal.

. . .

The RCMP had built another substantial case against Horne in Nunavut. There were many more victims than in the previous criminal case. There were also charges from Great Whale River,[1] stemming from his brief time there in the 1970s.[2]

On Monday, November 1, 1999, Horne had a bail hearing in Iqaluit. Justice Robert Kilpatrick presided. Crown counsel was Debra Robinson, and defence was James Brydon.

Horne was charged with sixty-six counts of sexual offences said to have occurred between 1971 and 1985. There were forty-four male complainants. The ages of the victims at the time of the assaults ranged between five and seventeen years. There were eight counts of "buggery," eleven counts of gross indecency by way of fellatio. There were a further three counts alleging acts of gross indecency ranging from fondling to digital penetration. All the communities Horne taught in were on the docket this time. The people of Sanikiluaq, in particular, were finally being seen and heard among the other victims in the massive Horne tragedy.

In 1985, the first time he had faced a judge in a bail hearing, Horne was a highly respected teacher with eighty thousand dollars in the bank and a number of high-profile friends rushing to defend his character. That was all gone. The Crown argued against bail on a number of grounds. Horne was a flight risk — a man who had travelled the world, claimed he could speak many languages, had eighteen hundred in American dollars available to him, had no fixed address in Canada and no job. The defence argued that Horne had no history of breaching orders, had successfully complied with mandatory supervision before his release in 1990, and could live in Yellowknife until his court appearance where "the state can bear the expense of his transportation" back to Iqaluit when the time came. The defence did acknowledge, though, that Horne had no address and no apparent connection to Yellowknife.

Judge Kilpatrick ultimately refused bail, saying that the sheer number of victims, the number of communities affected, and the span of years related to Horne's alleged crimes justified incarceration until his court dates.

"It is alleged that the accused as a teacher systematically abused his position of trust and authority to violate personal integrity of the very students he was there to help," Kilpatrick said, echoing the sentiments expressed about Horne years earlier. "It is alleged that these acts were not impulsive or random but the result of planned and persistent conduct over an extended period of time. This court is satisfied that … the charges involved here are of such magnitude and are so numerous that to release this accused would undermine public confidence in the administration of justice. Judgement accordingly."

Horne was told not to have contact or communication with any of the complainants named in the information before the court. He was then sent back to the Yellowknife Correctional Centre, where he had been held.

A preliminary inquiry was set for January 24, 2000, to determine what charges would proceed to trial. Crown prosecutors Richard Meredith and Debra Robinson devoted themselves exclusively to the Horne case for the next several months. Horne was still incarcerated at the Yellowknife Correctional Centre, after having been shuffled between the Baffin Correctional Centre and the RCMP cells in Iqaluit since the end of March 1999.

When Horne was locked in a Yellowknife jail cell awaiting trial, his infamy preceded him, and he was taunted, and inmates threw food at him. His only visitors were lawyers and the Rev. Brian Mee, a United Church clergyman who provided spiritual support. Horne, who was then a Catholic, accepted the sacraments, or Holy Communion, from Mee, apparently the only man available to offer such a service to him at the time. He ordered books from the public library, including Charles Dickens's novels *Bleak House* and *Martin Chuzzlewit*. He also requested a copy of the Hebrew Bible that was eventually provided to him on disc.

During the preliminary inquiry, Horne's lawyer filed a motion saying the RCMP cells, in particular, had been abysmal for his client's health while he awaited hearings — depriving him of sleep, exercise, and a healthy diet. An affidavit was filed with the motion adding that Horne had been subjected to verbal and physical abuse at the Yellowknife Correctional Centre and received death threats at the Baffin Correctional Centre. The hearing to look at these conditions was delayed due to a lack of lawyers to deal with it.

Justice Mary Hetherington said that while she appreciated the matter was urgent, the Nunavut Department of Justice simply didn't have adequate staff. She set the next hearing about Horne's situation for February 8, while the Crown lawyers said they hoped their preliminary inquiry would wrap up a day before that. Meanwhile, security was ramped up at the courthouse after a witness lunged at Horne during a hearing, turning over a table, sending papers and water glasses flying. The agitated witness was wrestled to the ground by three bystanders.[3]

. . .

Wearing an old pair of track shoes and a tight-fitting grey suit stretched over a bulky piece of body armour, Horne entered Iqaluit's courthouse on Tuesday, September 5, 2000. But the security measures weren't really needed — few people other than journalists showed up to observe Horne's sentencing hearing.

The RCMP had compiled sixty-six charges against Horne involving forty-six male victims. Eight men said Horne anally raped them, among other assaults. Four of them reported Horne attempted anal intercourse with them, and one said Horne used a finger to penetrate him. Most of the charges were for indecent assault.

Horne eventually entered a guilty plea, and an agreed statement of facts was tabled with the court. It reflected an obvious compromise between what was reported to police and what Horne was willing to agree to. The rape of the boy in the shower at Nakasuk School from 1981 was there — the only anal rape Horne ever admitted to carrying out in the North — an attack that alone carried a possible fourteen-year jail term at the time.

Of his own accord, Horne gave the Crown the names of four other men who had not come forward, one of whom was dead.

Horne ultimately admitted to sexually assaulting twenty-three boys ranging in age from seven to sixteen years, from 1971 to 1983, in Sanikiluaq, Cape Dorset, Lake Harbour, and Iqaluit.

Justice Virginia Schuler presided over the sentencing.[4] Horne's lawyer demanded a light sentence for the following reasons: Horne had provided the name of a victim who had since died, Horne hadn't been convicted of any crimes since 1985, and he had received psychiatric treatment. His lawyer also told the court that Horne had effectively "picked himself up off the economic carpet"[5] after he was released from prison last time and was set to marry a woman in Mexico, although there was no indication that he was divorced from Jeannie. Brydon also pointed out that Horne was fifty-seven years old, had spent enough time in jail, and had done a lot of rehabilitation to cure himself of pedophilia. He conveniently ignored the fact that pedophilia cannot be cured, only managed.

"The system asked us to take into consideration a number of things. Reformation. Well, how are we going to reform Mr. Horne? He's already done it," Brydon said. "If we really hammer somebody, what's the net effect? People are going to say, 'Let's just break him.'" With all of that considered, Horne's sentence should be two years plus a day, he said. The Crown called for five years.[6]

In final submissions, Crown prosecutor Richard Meredith spoke of the victims' relief at not having to testify against Horne after he pleaded guilty. The preliminary hearings were agonizing enough for many of them. But Meredith made it clear that the horrors of the Horne case were so extensive that a tough sentence was required. In such cases, he argued, often the guilty parties are "challenged intellectually, or have other limited resources, that even though it doesn't explain or excuse the behaviour, might be considered circumstances attenuating in view of the particular nature of the person. Here, [that] is not the situation."

The extent of Horne's violation of his position of trust in the communities, the number of boys he molested, the locations where he abused them, the number of years the offences had gone on, and the age of the children were all discussed as legitimate reasons to lock Horne up for the Crown's requested five years. Threats were used toward the boys, Meredith noted, but with children this young, "outward threats or force isn't necessary to coerce a child into acts, especially with a person of trust and authority. Even in mid-adolescence a child is different, bolder perhaps, able to say no more easily. But that was not the case here."

The Crown viewed Horne as becoming more violent and brazen as time went on. The attack on the boy at Nakasuk School in 1981 showed how reckless he could be, anally raping his victim in a public place where people could — and, did, in fact — come in and could have witnessed the act.

"There were no boundaries to his conduct," Meredith told the court, "except to make sure that he didn't get caught." He called Horne's actions predatory and spoke of the consequences to the victims. By this time, the court had received almost all the victim impact statements and they were scathing, full of anguish over lost educational opportunities, failed relationships, and illnesses.

"I was terrified before the victim impact statements were read," Horne later told me. While at first, they sounded to him like statements compiled from items ticked off on a checklist, there were touches, he said, that sounded real, like Stephen,* who felt bad driving by his old school, "remembering what happened to him there."

The victims' statements made it clear that generations to come would feel the impact of Horne's predations. This has, sadly, turned out to be the case.

Once again, Horne was not designated a "dangerous offender" in Canada. Such a designation has to be requested by the Crown. Such a request was never made.

• • •

When it was Horne's lawyer's time to speak to the judge, he brought the myth of Horne front and centre.

"One of the significant aspects of this case is that of mythology," Brydon began. "A myth frequently stems from truth, but takes on certain aspects of exaggeration, gossip, aggrandizement. And if one can traditionally in all cultures make one's enemies significantly brave, significantly terrible, or significantly threatening, then one's standing within that culture rises. Edward Horne is a myth. There is truth to the fact that Edward Horne exists. There is truth to the fact that Edward Horne did many bad things in his past, but those things have been elevated to the level of the terrible and the fantastic and they have been elevated for many cultural reasons."[7]

The judge cut him off.[8]

"Well, Mr. Brydon, Mr. Horne has admitted the facts that were put before me."

"I realize that," Brydon said.

The judge continued: "Whatever else there may be out there, what people may be saying, that's not obviously my concern. My concern is to sentence him for what he's admitted having done."

Brydon paused, then responded, "With the greatest respect, My Lady, this is the first time that Mr. Horne has been able to answer these charges at all. We have had for the last 15 years, a public display of scapegoating that attaches to the name, and with the greatest respect I think Mr. Horne is entitled not only to make his submissions to this court, but also in the sense to make these submissions to the public at large."

Brydon proceeded to tell Horne's life story as he knew it.

"He came from a home where 'dysfunctionally' is probably somewhat of a watch word," he said, describing Horne's parents' suffering from lingering mental illnesses, his father's death from Alzheimer's, and his long estrangement from his brother.[9] The story about Horne running away from home and sleeping in the cow barn emerged, along with tales of scrounging for pennies, and growing his own food to survive. He touted Horne's IQ as 190, which was an exaggeration. He briefly mentioned Horne's marriage to Jeannie, and their sons. Pointing to the academic success of Horne's children, all of whom were Inuit, Brydon insinuated the victims' stories didn't ring true.

"Both Mr. Horne's sons have graduated from grade 12," Brydon told the court. "We have heard, or we have read in the victim impact statements about how many of these people would have graduated from high school had Mr. Horne not done what he did. I suggest to you that this is strong wishful thinking. Mr. Horne's children are a posit to that strong wishful thinking."[10]

(Brydon's argument did not hold up over time. A few years after the second trial ended, two of Horne's boys would take their own lives.)

He went on to detail Horne's battle with depression and seasonal affective disorder, conditions made worse by living in the Arctic, where the cold is unrelenting and the period of darkness, depending on the latitude of the community, may last from November to February, when the days get lighter again. He went so far as to suggest seasonal affective disorder and depression led Horne to abuse the boys.

He went on: "His self-imposed isolation was enhanced by a geographic and cultural isolation and at that point in many ways he lost touch with certain realities, not the least of which is his reality as to morality." He insisted that in most of Horne's "relationships with children" little or no extrinsic violence was used, although Horne as a boy was subjected to "overt violence," raising the spectre of Horne's allegedly abusive home life again.[11]

A heavy sentence would "break him," he said. "You scapegoat everything onto Ed Horne and we ignore the dysfunctionality of our own society," he added, coming close to overtly suggesting that it was Nunavut's communities that were dysfunctional, not the disgraced teacher. He also stressed the positivity of the prison rehabilitation programs that Horne had access to and claimed to have benefitted from.

Brydon disputed each aggravating factor. The children were abused at Horne's home? At school? Well, there are only so many places to commit these offences, he said. And the children went to the house voluntarily, he added, attempting to place some of the culpability on the victims themselves.

He disputed the idea that the crimes got worse as time went on, instead describing a "logical progression" to Horne's predations.

Then he highlighted Horne's teaching record and his work in Inuktitut. In doing so, he embroidered the myth of Horne, a myth he had decried earlier in the hearing:

"It is ironic that Ed Horne, out of a sense of community loyalty, created a database allowing the translation into syllabics of the Bible and of the Anglican hymn book."[12]

For sentencing, Brydon stuck by his request for two years plus a day.

When the Crown returned, they attacked arguments about Horne's rehabilitation and suggested that the idea Horne was completely rehabilitated was absurd.

They went on to point out that there were many charges in the first criminal case in 1987 that Horne and his lawyer didn't agree to and that this showed Horne did not take full responsibility for his actions. In fact, he had wilfully ignored many of his past crimes in the hope that no one would ask him about them or come out of the woodwork in the future to complain.

"Back in 1987, there was a specific sentencing factual scenario that was before the court that in no way can be compared to what we find out many years later was the actual scenario," the Crown argued.[13]

They took issue with Horne's statement that being in jail was tantamount to torture for him, pointing out that conditions in jail were not ideal, but "torture" was overstating it. As for Horne's weight loss in jail, he was offered food, they said; he just chose not to eat it.

The Crown vigorously disputed assertions made by the defence that the RCMP had been guilty of negligence in 1985 when an officer asked Horne, "Are there any others?" Brydon had suggested that the failure of the police to follow up on that question at the time was negligent, even though Horne had not answered the question. Brydon was tacitly suggesting that if an act of abuse had not been discovered by the time of the first criminal case, it should not be admissible in the second case.

"That same question could be asked now," Meredith countered.

Meredith had no time for Brydon's implication that Horne was somehow a victim himself, saying, "Mr. Horne may have had difficult moments in his life, but he's not the victim. The victims are those young children that were victimized by him, a person, an extremely intelligent person, who for not just 10, 12 years but even more than that was committing offenses of this nature. And not once during over a decade did he seek out the treatment realizing something was morally wrong in his behaviour. Obviously nothing was done to try to correct that."[14]

The judge asked Horne if there was anything he wished to say. Horne stood up in court.[15]

He said Brydon had covered most of what he would have said but there were some details he'd like to fill in: "I returned voluntarily from Mexico, the deportation was illegal, I could have resisted it. My legal advice was that I could be denied a work visa but I couldn't legally be handed over to the RCMP. However, I had enough sense to know that I'd be a fugitive for the rest of my life if I didn't come back to Canada and face these charges. I'm glad I did."

He said the Crown's submissions were fair, honest, and rational.

> But today I'm afraid things have gotten a bit out of hand on both sides and some things have been said that aren't true. There wasn't a 14-year period of abuse. The charges that I faced in 1987 were for a four-year period. The therapy I received, particularly at the Regional Psychiatric Centre, didn't relate to any particular time period, to any particular community. In fact, to a distressing degree, it failed to address the questions of sexual abuse. It was largely a life skills program dealing with anger management, self-esteem, balancing a chequebook, and so on. And I had access to the staff medical library and I found there was literally nothing. Research on sexual offenses, what are the risk factors, what are the odds, what are the treatment considerations, there was nothing, and I suspect that even now, 13 years later, that's probably still true. Where I felt I could, where I felt the biggest impetus in me to straighten out my life, the question that there must never, never be any more victims, and I'm going to speak about that shortly. But I could look at my fellow prisoners in this program, I could see them sitting in the morning watching *Sesame Street*, I could hear their talk out in the yard about "In

Europe this is a mental health problem, the Ancient Greeks did it all the time!" I didn't hear contrition, I didn't hear "I hate what I did and I'm never going to do it again." I didn't hear that. And one time a staff member said to me, "Don't think you're better than anybody else around here." And I said, "You don't want me to be better than that? No. That's not me." I've decided that's not me.

Horne spoke of Reverend Mee's friendship and how much it meant to him.

But I think it's unfortunate that he said I feel I've already paid for my crime. Because as I said to the RCMP, "You cannot pay for a crime." You can pay for a chocolate bar, a magazine, a lot of ground maybe, but you can't pay for a crime. It's a false analogy. Once a crime is committed there's no paying for it. I could spend a hundred thousand years in jail without undoing one bit of the damage I did. As for my feelings about the crimes I committed, it's difficult to carry on in the face of such knowledge that everybody I loved, everybody I cared for from 1975 probably right up to the present, I blighted their lives. This includes the direct victims, and everybody's an indirect victim … My son, a police officer, who has to pick up a newspaper and read these stories about his dad, I did that to him. I feel keenly the anger, the confusion, the hurt of the people who laid these charges. Questions about why — when they were laid, why they weren't laid sooner, why some people didn't tell the truth, that's not my dominion. My dominion is that I did a terrible, terrible wrong. The immutability of the past is the saddest fact of a human condition. I can do virtually nothing. What I can do, and I'll talk to social services, the police suggested to me that I write letters of apology. At the time it was, as my lawyer pointed out, a ruse to get written confessions, but the idea I think has merit. I'm nervous enough about it that I would only do this through social services. I will approach social services and ask them for guidance. Any letter that I wrote to a victim would not go to the victim but to social services to decide whether or not that letter was appropriate because, God help me, I'm not going to do anymore harm and I'm not going to write a letter to a person that's going to make things worse. If there's anything I can do to make things better I will. At this point I don't know what more I could have done at any stage. I don't know what more I can do now. Thank you for your attention, Your Honour.

The judge adjourned around noon and delivered the sentence the next day, September 7, 2000, at 9:30 a.m.

. . .

In his plea deal, Horne admitted to abusing twenty-three young boys, from seven to sixteen years of age; most were seven to eleven years old when the offences occurred, and for that reason Justice Schuler said she would refer to them as young boys. She used the 1971–1983 range for the years of offences, noting that the time frame is not precise because, in light of their ages, the victims were not all able to specify exactly when they were abused.

"The fear or embarrassment or confusion which the child feels as a result of the offense may be counted on by the offender to ensure silence," she said. "Nothing — not his own intelligence, not his own difficulties as a child, not his own conscience — stopped Mr. Horne from pursuing what he wanted to do."[16]

All of the acts were extremely intrusive, she said. They were significant invasions and violations of the personal and sexual integrity of the victims. There was violence in these crimes, she said. "When committed against children the violence is both physical and profoundly psychological."[17] She denounced the "coercive and exploitative conduct" representing the use of compulsion against someone who is defenseless. The victim impact statements described lives ruined by Horne's abuses, school dreams abandoned out of fear, anger problems, and suicidal thoughts.

"While no one can say with certainty whether or how their lives might have been different had Mr. Horne not abused them, the psychological harm caused by child sexual abuse is well recognized and some of what the victims refer to in this case is similar to what victims in other cases I have sat on have written."[18]

She didn't bow to the defence's call to a short sentence. She made it clear she was not sentencing Horne as a scapegoat, the unfortunate word used by defence counsel. Horne was a teacher, she said, someone to whom parents, students, and the community looked to encourage and protect children, as well as to educate them. The extreme breach of that trust, the location of many of the offences, the age and number of the victims, all underlined the severity of the crimes. There was irony in Horne's admission that school had been one of his favourite places as a child, a place he considered a refuge. She also harshly denounced Horne for turning innocent activities like bath time into opportunities to abuse children.

She credited the seventeen months he had spent detained as three years, and issued a total sentence of five years.

"Mr. Horne, would you stand up please." He stood.

Justice Schuler read him his sentence and also outlined the conditions that prohibited him from possessing firearms, ammunition, and explosives starting that day and expiring five years from the date he was released from prison.

"Mr. Horne, I just want to say that I sincerely hope that this is the last time that you will be before the court and I say that so that the victims can get on with the healing process and not be reminded of you and your offenses, and also so that you can continue in your efforts at rehabilitation. And I hope that with this a tragic chapter in the history of this region will have closed."[19]

. . .

The people of Sanikiluaq were not satisfied with the verdict. They were angry. They felt the sentence was too lenient and expressed their frustrations in a statement released to the public through northern news outlets six days later. "The five-year sentence is not enough," the statement read.

The community had circulated a petition appealing to the Nunavut Department of Justice to reconsider the sentence.[20] Mayor Annie Amitook, who drafted the statement, said the punishment should have been much harsher, and there was a feeling throughout her community that Horne got off easy because he was a white man. (The people of Sanikiluaq clearly didn't buy Horne's claim of Indigeneity.)

The petition to have his sentence reviewed was signed by sixty-six people in the village and was sent to Sanikiluaq's member in the Legislative Assembly, Peter Kattuk, demanding Horne be jailed for "a lot more years."

The Crown responded. "We're not going to be appealing the decision. We're happy with it," said Pam Clarke, Nunavut's chief Crown prosecutor.[21] Clarke explained that the sentence handed down by Justice Schuler was in line with what the prosecution had requested and was appropriate.

But the statement from Sanikiluaq blasted the court for letting Horne off easy and accused the system of being racist, pointing to criminal cases in which Inuit offenders were given far longer jail sentences than Horne for similar sex crimes. In the statement, Amitook also said that the sentencing did not take into account how Horne's crimes had spurred a cycle of violence and self-destruction that was still plaguing her community.

"The victims of Mr. Horne continue to do the same thing as far as molesting boys in our community," she said.

Amitook also said that many victims of childhood sexual abuse end up killing themselves. "We had a suicide a month ago," she said. "He was a victim of one of Mr. Horne's victims."

Many of the men Horne violated when they were children do not seem to take charge of their lives, Amitook said. "A lot of the victims of Mr. Horne are good people in our community, but they don't seem to want to stand up and work for themselves. They depend on their parents and their families." While many of the men had availed themselves of healing programs since Horne's arrest in 1999, Amitook said the light sentence had shaken people, hurting them all over again. Amitook also placed little faith in Horne's assertion that he had not molested any children since 1985. "I can't believe that," she said.

Horne would later make a statement about his crimes that indicated he had reflected on his terrible legacy: "It was a fledgling school system that was struggling to establish its credibility, particularly in the newer communities like Sanikiluaq.... I delivered a devastating blow to an evolving school system."[22]

After sentencing in 2000, the defence launched an appeal, claiming Horne's time in prison should be lessened — the main arguments being that the judge did not take Horne's rehabilitation efforts into account and that the sentence was much too harsh. This appeal was dismissed on May 23, 2002.

Horne served his sentence at Bath Institution, east of Bath, Ontario, and at Pittsburgh Institution (now part of Joyceville Institution), the nearby minimum-security jail near Kingston, Ontario.

"Staff at both institutions told me the second sentence was unnecessary and they worked to get me out early," Horne told me in December 2021, still bitter about his second run in jail.

Uncle

IN 2005, I WAS ON ASSIGNMENT IN SANIKILUAQ, WRITING ART-
icles about programs at Nuiyak School, when I unexpectedly learned more
about the Horne tragedy.

Lunching alone at the local hotel, Amaulik Inns North, with Arctic
spring sunshine pouring through the windows, I was approached by a silver-
haired man who looked vaguely like Mr. Miyagi from the Karate Kid films.
He held out his hand and said quietly, "I am your uncle." For a split second,
I actually believed him.

As the man who called himself Uncle and I spoke briefly, twenty or so
men wearing lumberjack-style jackets over hoodies gathered around the coffee urn at the other side of the restaurant, drinking coffee and refilling their
mugs. I didn't know it then, but these men were Ed Horne victims, heading
out onto the land with Uncle where they would talk, shed tears, and listen
to Uncle play an Inuit drum — a *qilaut* — in a healing circle.

Uncle is Jens Lyberth, a Greenlander of Inuit heritage who speaks
Kalaallisut, the Greenlandic dialect of the Inuit language, as his first language. But he has called Canada home since the early 1970s. When I met
him, he'd been coming to Sanikiluaq, as well as Cape Dorset, Kimmirut,
and Iqaluit,[1] since 2002, providing mental health support for any man impacted by Ed Horne's abuse. A number of the men would say Uncle helped

them cope with their childhood sexual trauma more than any non-Inuit mental health professional from the south ever did. It was Uncle's sensitivity to their struggles, and understanding of their culture and language, that set him apart from other social workers.

Uncle said that from the moment he set foot in Canada he felt an affinity with the Inuit; he could relate to their sense of having been mistreated and misunderstood by the French and English authorities through the ages. In Iqaluit in the 1970s, Uncle discovered he could recreate his childhood lifestyle through the pleasures of hunting and camping, one of the many reasons he stayed rooted to the territory for so many years. Another reason was a job that kept him busy — working for the housing authority in what might seem like a thankless job, as a rent collector.

It didn't take long for Uncle to identify problems with housing in the fast-growing settlement of Frobisher Bay. By law, a person in public housing only had to pay twenty-four dollars a month for rent in those days, but the reality was that many people had difficulty even coming up with that amount, he said. Moreover, maintenance on the housing units was sub-standard and many of them had been poorly constructed, often with inadequate insulation.

In later years, until 1993, Uncle's home often became a refuge for women and children fleeing abusive relationships in troubled towns. One day he and his wife came home to find thirty-six children sleeping in his house. It was the weekend.

Spurred on by the obvious needs all around them, Uncle and his wife, who were devout members of the Baha'i faith at the time, began hosting potluck suppers whenever they could. Women would cook and bring food to their house and everyone who showed up would get a meal every weekend.

Uncle first heard about Horne's abuse of kids in Sanikiluaq in the late 1970s. He knew because he heard people talking, saying things like "That man is really bad." Parents and Elders also told him, "The children were not normal. They were acting violently, aggressively." He would later hear this in Iqaluit, Kimmirut, and other villages when he travelled for work.

"When I travel, I go to the Elders, I greet them, I eat with them. We tell stories. And it became very evident there was a difficulty in coping with children who were antisocial. And you realize there are psychological issues in those kids from the abuse. So, once it becomes clear, you cannot erase it from your system. With my upbringing, I wanted to help as much as I could."

This was the beginning of Uncle's move into social work and healing. He would eventually be contacted by lawyers for the plaintiffs after the first civil case was successfully settled to lead healing workshops in the North under the banner of the Society for Northern Renewal.

He explained his healing philosophy to me this way: "If you are not in balance you just live physically, you don't really think, you don't really feel, you just exist. And that's what happens when you are abused … all of a sudden you will see things, smell things, taste things, that will trigger that experience. And when that is triggered, many bad things can happen. And so many bad things have happened to these beautiful people, because of the abuse. In the healing, there's a balancing of the person. That is why we go out on the land."

Uncle was not the first to realize the value of on-the-land experiences to troubled Inuit. Early on, most schools incorporated land activities into their cultural programs led by experienced hunters and Elders, so that students could learn the hunting and life skills that many were not learning from their families in town. When the regional correctional facility, Baffin Correctional Centre, was built, it was filled with troubled young men. But farsighted administrators organized on-the-land programs taught by competent local men who took the inmates on hunting expeditions — probably the first experience in Canada, perhaps the world, where the prisoners were required to be armed to carry out their duties. Uncle knew of these initiatives and followed their positive example. He realized that the land was an effective healer. When he worked with Horne victims, he took them out on the land a lot. It was a cornerstone of his approach.

Uncle no longer counsels Ed Horne survivors professionally. He has run a healing and cultural tourism business called Ice Wisdom. He lives in Ottawa, a place where thousands of Inuit from the Eastern Canadian Arctic live today; he will sometimes run into men on the street or while shopping that he once counselled. There are usually no words during these meetings, he said. "It is so interesting where they will get hold of me and just hold me in their arms. There is no need for words anyways. This is how I feel their gratitude."

Some of the men had received mental health help from professionals before Uncle worked with them. He doesn't want to denigrate the work of those professionals who, he thinks, did the best they could. But Uncle believes they didn't have a sufficient understanding of the cultural heritage of the men and that, therefore, their efforts were somewhat ineffective.

Psychiatrists are people who "learn through books," Uncle said. "There is a big difference between learning through books and actually doing work. You have to understand the language, the cultural heritage, how that person was impacted."

Uncle's recollection of Horne's ability in the Inuktitut language differs from the recollections of others and even from those of Horne himself. He said that Horne "was one of the most well-spoken people in our language, Inuktitut." Uncle had just moved to Canada and was impressed by this man who clearly had a handle on the local language. "His Inuktitut was absolutely fluent. He understood the grammatical background of our language." Uncle believed in Horne's Inuktitut ability. Was he impressed because he was new to the dialect himself? Or was his encounter only a fleeting one?

Uncle said Horne got away with abusing boys in the communities for so long because the teacher was "a professional. A true professional abuser. Well planned. Well executed, exactly the way he wanted."

Criminal Case #3

ON MAY 2, 2005, HORNE WAS BACK IN AN IQALUIT COURTROOM. His head was down, hands clasped in front of him, his eyes just slightly lifted. He wasn't wearing a bulletproof vest as he'd done on a previous occasion when attending court there. He had close-cropped, sandy-grey hair, and he was wearing baggy, light blue jeans. Judge Beverley Browne was presiding over a case that would drag on and would later be presided over by Judge Robert Kilpatrick.

Four men who had not been plaintiffs in the previous two criminal cases had accused Horne of sexually assaulting them when they were boys. A hearing would be held two years later, from October 15–17, 2007, also in Iqaluit.

The following January the defence pleaded its case, and Horne would speak in court in his own defence for the first time. Judy Chan was Crown counsel, and Tom Boyd served as Horne's defence lawyer. The bulk of the case would be heard by Judge Kilpatrick.

Prior to going to trial, the Crown sought to have "similar fact evidence" made admissible in a voir dire hearing. A voir dire is often described as a mini-hearing or a trial within a trial. It occurs before or during a criminal trial, when a judge considers a question raised during the proceedings, usually about the admissibility of evidence. If the judge so rules, the evidence that resulted in the mini-hearing can be admitted as evidence in the case under trial.

In this case, the Crown sought to introduce similar fact evidence, despite such evidence usually being inadmissible because it relates to the accused's character or propensity to commit a crime. Accordingly, the Crown required permission from Kilpatrick before introducing such evidence.

Horne had chosen to plead not guilty in this case, unlike his approach in his first two criminal trials. Therefore Kilpatrick was asked to adjudicate on whether similar fact evidence could be used as evidence against Horne's credibility. Outside the statements of the four men, the Crown lacked any corroborating evidence to support the men's allegations. To bolster their case, the Crown tried to suggest that the facts presented in this case were identical to those of the previous cases in which Horne had pleaded guilty, attempting to imply that he was guilty this time as well. Kilpatrick decided not to allow the admission of similar fact evidence due to its prejudicial effect. The testimony of the four men would alone serve as the basis of Horne's prosecution.[1]

The paucity of corroborating evidence left little possibility for a robust prosecution. The Crown had perhaps relied too much on the possibility of the similar fact evidence being allowed and had done little to investigate the charges. In effect, this case would rely on "he said/he said" testimony.[2]

It is obvious why the Crown wanted propensity evidence allowed. All the crimes Horne admitted to in the past were very similar to what the men in the current case were alleging, only now it was the men themselves speaking out in court about the abuses they had suffered. This had never happened in the history of the Horne cases. The public had never seen Horne's victims before or heard their voices in open court because Horne's previous guilty pleas had obviated the need for the victims' public testimony. There was a publication ban protecting the names of the men, but there they were, on the stand for the first time, accusing Horne of sex crimes. There were moments of high emotion as the men told their stories. In the end, though, that is all it would be — moments of drama and the possibility that Horne might crack. But he didn't.

With carefully chosen words, Judge Kilpatrick prepared everyone for a case where the passage of time would be a problem: "Forensic inquiries do not readily penetrate time's darker recesses. As months turn into years, as years turn into decades, the process of distilling historical truth from fiction becomes increasingly difficult," he said. "It is into this place of shadow and uncertainty that the court must now travel."[3]

The first man, Peter,* said that when he was between the ages of ten and twelve Ed Horne sexually abused him many times in Cape Dorset, in the shower at the school and in Horne's home. Peter described baths at Horne's home where a number of boys were molested and said that Horne showed them pornographic films on his television. He also described being dressed up in a costume — a wedding dress, complete with high heels — and made to pose for pictures.

Horne testified that none of this occurred. The presence of costumes or the dressing up of boys would have caused a commotion in the school, Horne said. He especially took issue with the suggestion that his wife wasn't at home during some of these alleged attacks because Horne had asked her to leave. "Any suggestion that an Inuit woman would be ordered out of her house with one or two small children in an Arctic blizzard ... that wouldn't happen," Horne said.[4]

The men were grilled about why they had waited so long to go to the police and report Horne's alleged abuse. One man explained that he had gone to police about Horne, but when the RCMP came to his house his mother was drunk and his complaint was not taken seriously. Another man said, when asked why he had laid a complaint, "I got kicked out from school and I couldn't go back to school because I was misbehaving a lot after the incident and because of these things ... I couldn't go further with my education. My behaviour was turning very negative and I was ending up in court a lot with my behaviour and I wanted to go ahead and try and make corrections with myself."[5]

The Crown asked, "I'm still not sure why you are making these allegations against Ed Horne. Could you explain it a little bit more?"

The man replied, "I don't understand your question." It was left at that.[6]

When the men were cross-examined, they crumbled. Time and again their answers were "I can't remember," or "It was too long ago."

There was so little solid evidence, and the passage of time was so great, one wonders why this case ever went to court. One theory is that the

Crown may have brought the case forward to give the community a sense of what kind of evidence would be necessary in future cases of a similar nature. The Crown could have refused to prosecute based on the paucity of evidence provided to support the allegations. Perhaps knowing the case would fail based on the four first-hand accounts from close to thirty years prior, yet also knowing that the community was angry and there might be more people who would try to exploit this situation for compensation, the Crown may have prosecuted the case just to set a precedent. Instead of refusing to bring the case, the Crown tried to deploy all reasonable arguments in an attempt to provide closure. At a later date, if someone else reported that Horne had sexually assaulted them decades earlier, the Crown could respectfully refuse to prosecute without drawing the ire of the community, citing this case as an example. If this theory were true, then the Crown was using these four accusers as guinea pigs and their uncorroborated testimony as an antidote to any future trials in the long Horne saga.

The judge stated why the case was so problematic when he presented his final decision:

"All the essential ingredients for a fabricated account could be fashioned from the well-publicized details of Mr. Horne's earlier behaviour and the circumstances under which these [earlier admitted] offences were committed," Kilpatrick said, adding that the passage of time and the age of the complainants when the alleged incidents occurred could be used "as a convenient excuse" for the lack of contextual detail accompanying the disclosures.[7]

"These same excuses could serve as a cover for fraud and readily defeat any attempt to uncover the truth through cross-examination. The claim of having no memory of particular details would be a complete answer to probing questions by the defence."

Horne was acquitted.

One of the complainants told me that despite losing his case, his impression of Horne was that he "seemed beaten, vulnerable" during the trial, yet "he was still wearing that same mask. He had a lawyer who knew what to say. I was there by myself on the stand and he was grilling me. I was telling everybody my story. And just the way the lawyer was grinning at me … he won that case, and said, 'Yup, he's a liar.'"[8]

Horne quickly left the North, and would live in Nicaragua for several years.

Civil Cases

ALTHOUGH HORNE NEVER HAD A FORMAL INTERVIEW WITH A journalist, and no intimate details about his sex crimes were ever published, the enormity of what Horne was accused of and the scope of what he had already served time for — the sheer scale of his alleged predations in the second criminal case — had attracted the attention of a bright and aggressive lawyer, Geoff Budden, and his colleague Stuart Morris, in St. John's, Newfoundland.[1]

Budden and his team had successfully fought for and secured massive compensation for victims of physical and sexual abuse at Mount Cashel Orphanage in St. John's.

The orphanage, operating since 1898, was run by the Congregation of Christian Brothers, a lay order within the Roman Catholic church. Allegations of abuse were first brought to the attention of provincial social workers in 1974 and to the Royal Newfoundland Constabulary — Newfoundland's urban police force — the following year. The investigation was hampered by senior officers in the Constabulary and in the provincial Department of Justice, and the investigation was ordered closed in 1977. But reports of abuse persisted, and the dogged work of journalists ensured that the stories made it into the public consciousness; fourteen years after abuse was first reported to them, the Royal Newfoundland Constabulary was ordered to reopen its investigation. Almost concurrently, the government announced a public inquiry into the mishandling of the earlier reports and the coverups by police, social services, and the Justice Department. In 1990, the orphanage closed, and two years later it was demolished. The Christian Brothers were ordered to pay millions of dollars in compensation to the more than one hundred victims of abuse at the hands of members of the Roman Catholic lay order. The Mount Cashel scandal is generally credited with exposing sexual abuse within the Catholic Church throughout Canada and the United States.

Budden and his team successfully prosecuted the civil cases that exposed how coverups by the authorities worked to silence victims and help child molesters cloaked as pious believers get away with their crimes. They secured judgments in the tens of millions of dollars as compensation for the victims.

After securing recompense for victims of Mount Cashel in 1999, Budden, along with a team from Newfoundland and an American lawyer, considered the pros and cons of fighting for another group of wronged Canadian boys: the victims of Edward Horne. The lawyers would soon learn of some of the most shocking child sex crimes imaginable, only this time, unlike the Mount Cashel scandal, it was not under any church affiliation — it was just one man who had allegedly abused all the boys.

Budden and colleague Stuart Morris spearheaded civil actions on behalf of Ed Horne's victims.

About eighty-five plaintiffs, all boys when Horne lived and taught school in their communities, participated in what would be the first civil action launched against the government that had hired Horne — a government that had become two governments after Nunavut was established in 1999.

Budden filed a statement of claim on behalf of the men in 2000. When that case was settled out of court in 2002, awarding $21.5 million to Horne's victims, Budden told *Nunatsiaq News* that it was the largest damage award he knew of in Canada related to sexual abuse by a single perpetrator.[2]

By 2002, the government of the Northwest Territories and the government of Nunavut had already paid out $4.2 million to the victims to cover legal and research fees, and to provide therapy for the victims who wanted it. The rest of the money was said to be divided into individual awards for each of the men and for the estates of three men who had died. But many more than those three plaintiffs had died. A social worker told me in 2005 that, according to her sources, about 20 percent of all Horne victims had died by suicide.

Budden worked with U.S. lawyer Stephen Rubino on the first civil case.[3] In their statement of claim, it was alleged that territorial government officials failed to protect the boys against Horne's sexual abuse by not providing proper supervision over their teacher, and failed to provide the victims with adequate care and counselling afterward. After a fairly short deliberation, both sides agreed to use an "alternative dispute" method and settle the matter out of court. In the press, Budden praised the territorial governments for how they behaved during the negotiations.

"I think part of the reason this worked is that the government approached it with a realistic sense of their exposure and a sincere desire to resolve the issue through good-faith negotiations. I think the way the government handled this is a lesson other governments could learn from," Budden said, adding that most of the men would accept their compensation in "structured settlements." The amount of money each victim received varied according to personal circumstances, but the average payout was $240,000.

Instead of taking their money in a lump sum, some of the men chose to have some or all of it put into investment funds and then paid out regularly over a period of years — the "structured settlements" that Budden referred to. But others took the lump sum. One victim would spend $125,000 in two weeks at his local co-op store. He would not be the only Horne victim to spend all his compensation money quickly.

Cape Dorset experienced a severe gas shortage in the summer of 2003. Strangely, it was linked to the Horne settlement money. The mayor of Cape Dorset, Matthew Jaw, suggested to *News/North* that a big reason for the shortage of gas was the proliferation of snowmobiles in the community following the huge cash settlement people there received after the settling of the first civil case involving Horne. Although Cape Dorset had five hundred thousand litres of fuel brought in on the annual sealift the previous summer, an emergency airlift from Rankin Inlet was necessary in June to supply the community with an additional eighty thousand litres of gasoline. An operations manager for the Petroleum Products Division in Nunavut told *News/North* that the demand for fuel was growing faster than the tank farms were.

"The compensation did nothing to help the victims," a former teacher who worked with Horne told me, voicing concern my book would retraumatize victims.

It was clear from the early stages of writing this book that compensation really only had a superficial impact on victims' lives.

There are plenty of stories similar to this one: a victim who fought his demons hard enough to become a skilled interpreter-translator in the North, went south to Ottawa in 2002 with his compensation money, abused drugs and alcohol, and was soon broke. He ended up homeless and injured, clinging to life with the kindness of strangers and groups like Tungasuvvingat Inuit supporting him.[4] But victims also used the money to buy food, clothing, and furniture for their families, and to supply much-needed gas for their vehicles to go hunting. The money also led to the creation of the Society for Northern Renewal, a group that provided mental health support for Horne victims for a few years.

In 2004, a second group of litigants launched a second civil case, led again by Budden and Morris, who represented about sixty-nine men and one woman. It might have begun very much like the first civil action, where victims told their stories to lawyers, were assessed by mental health workers, and governments once again conceded wrongdoing and paid out a settlement. But it didn't go that way. The two governments decided to fight back. Their biggest, and most shocking, defence was that many of the plaintiffs had consented to sex with Horne, or were fourteen years of age or older — fourteen being the age of consent in Canada before it was raised to sixteen on May 1, 2008 — and, therefore, were not eligible for compensation.

The second civil case was problematic from the outset because of the greater possibility that some of the claims of abuse would be fraudulent. At that point, the public knew more about Horne's crimes than ever before, and it would not have been difficult for a student who was around when Horne was teaching, but was not molested by him, to claim he had been abused and provide details based on what brothers or friends who were legitimate victims had told him. In essence, it was more likely that the plaintiffs in the second civil action had greater motivation from money than truth.

In any case, shocking new revelations were unearthed during the second civil action. Government failures to oversee Horne — and other teachers — were investigated in a way they hadn't been before. Previously unheard legitimate victims, who had been in jail or too nervous to speak out during the other cases, finally came forward. And notably, Horne was interviewed at length about his life and career for five days in Toronto in 2007. That had never happened before.

. . .

Joe Handley eventually left the bureaucracy and sought elected office. By the time the second civil suit was launched, he was premier of the Northwest Territories.[5] His comments casting doubt over some of the victims' claims were printed in a Canadian Press story that was published on September 21, 2006. Sounding very much as if he was blaming the victims, Handley's comments were a stunning departure from the strong stance he had taken in his earlier role as deputy minister of education when he wrote his scathing letter to Bert Rose, lambasting him for his poor oversight of Horne. This time he supported the government's hardball defence strategy against the victims, believing there was merit in fighting the possibility of another multimillion-dollar payout to victims.[6] Inuit to this day are still incensed that Handley would suggest any claimants consented to sex with Horne. But Handley was voicing one of the key arguments in the government's defence strategy during the second civil lawsuit. His position as premier guaranteed that his suggestions would receive prominent press coverage.

Handley later apologized for what he said to the Canadian Press reporter, saying he thought he was speaking off the record with his personal views. This is hard to credit coming from a seasoned politician, more so because he later made similar comments to CBC North — essentially putting forward the same argument — about the veracity of the Horne victims' claims.

Once word of Handley's comments to the Canadian Press were publicized, the legislature erupted and voted to censure him — a serious reprimand, just one level below demanding a resignation.

"This has been a very difficult motion to bring forward," said Inuvik Twin Lakes MLA Robert McLeod, "because the premier is well liked across the territories and on this side of the floor. I know this whole episode has bothered Mr. Handley but you take that and multiply it tenfold and that doesn't even come close to what (the victims) had to go through."[7]

Faced with a stern challenge by the government, Budden and Morris dug deep into the government's past for damning information. In the grand scheme of things, the entire formal education system run by government in the North was quite new, having really begun around the time Horne started teaching in the Arctic in 1971. However, despite this relatively short time period, the second civil case did not go smoothly. Many files were missing or destroyed. There was a level of disorganization in various government departments that meant that vital information about Horne and the people overseeing him was frustratingly unavailable to the plaintiffs' lawyers and, later, any journalist seeking details.

Lawyers for the victims nonetheless uncovered stunning information about the inner workings of government that bolstered their claim. They hunted down everything they could find about the NWT Teachers' Association and what they knew of teachers who had allegedly abused students. Budden's team homed in on a supposed "de facto policy of consultation" within that association that kicked in when a teacher was accused of sexual misconduct with students. To that end, Budden wanted the teachers' association, in which Ed Horne had served an executive role at one point, to produce certain relevant documents supposedly about policies regarding sexual misconduct with students. The association apparently was responsible for regulating the ethical standards of teachers and for disciplining teachers who were in breach of those standards, including Horne.

In confidential government correspondence obtained by the lawyers, it was revealed that the government had covered up for at least two schoolteachers, both male, both working at schools in the Baffin Region in the 1970s, who had been accused of having sex or pursuing sexual contact with underage female students — activity that should have been reported to the police but wasn't.

In the case of one teacher who encouraged underage female students to clean his apartment and have sex with him, the problem was simply passed on to another region; the teacher was moved from Baffin Island to a school in the central N.W.T.

In the other case, a male teacher who was in the habit of phoning girls at home and spending all hours at the school seeking relationships with girls was told to resign and did. But more detailed correspondence about these cases and how they were handled by the Department of Education had been destroyed.

In their quest for truth in the second civil case, lawyers requested that claimants provide a staggering amount of personal detail, as well as hand-drawn reproductions of where they lived, where Horne lived, and to their best of their ability, describe the buildings and rooms in which the alleged abuse took place. The lawyers required the same of Horne.

During their investigation, the most damning discoveries the plaintiffs' lawyers made were complaints against Horne when he was teaching that had been ignored by officials. During their investigations, the lawyers also tracked down former Sanikiluaq school principal Allan Clovis — retired and living in Tobago — who had a good memory for a painful subject. Clovis revealed he'd told regional education superintendent Gerard Mulders that he'd heard Horne had molested a boy in Sanikiluaq in 1972. The government looked very bad in the Clovis report, and they could find no way to deny the terrible picture that emerged. The officials overseeing Horne in those days had failed in their duty to protect the students in their care.

Because of the number of plaintiffs, the process took years to inch its way through the court system, but eventually the defence requested a sample of twenty men, later reduced to twelve, whose entire lives, including psychological profiles, would be examined in detail. The victims in the second civil case represented all the communities Horne taught in: Sanikiluaq, Cape Dorset, Grise Fiord, Lake Harbour, and Frobisher Bay.

What investigators didn't find was solid evidence that Horne had been intentionally moved during any one of his transfers from one Arctic community to the next. Those moves had always looked suspicious to any-one with even a passing interest in the Horne case, but the records were sparse. The only Horne transfer that appeared to be properly documented was in 1985 when education official Eric Colbourne approved the final move to Apex from Lake Harbour.[8]

When this exhausting case was finally settled, sixty-six plaintiffs received cash compensation plus access to counselling and treatment paid for by a fund set up under the agreement. The case had been gearing up to go to trial, but in the end, as was the case with the first civil trial, a deal was reached through an alternative dispute resolution process. Victims were, therefore, spared the agony of testifying in court. But they had been through the ring-er. Some didn't even fully understand the process. One victim asked during an interview with a lawyer "What's a lawsuit?" It is important to note that throughout the Horne tragedy, except for one or two men, the victims' first language was Inuktitut. There were language barriers, although translators were always present during testimony.

Horne has strong views about what was alleged in the civil cases. "Two lawyers went around Sanikiluaq with clipboards and recruited victims. I don't know what proportion of the resulting accusations was valid," Horne told me. "It seems to me blindingly obvious that when hundreds of thou-sands of dollars were offered for totally unsubstantiated accusations, that the narrative should be viewed with caution. My guilt is overwhelming. But that does not justify a tsunami of accusations that were not and could not possibly have been true."

· · ·

"Almost any sensible person would be relieved that something has been set-tled through negotiation rather than having to go into open court and tell your story," Geoff Budden was quoted as saying in a *Nunatsiaq News* story on January 25, 2011.[9]

Norman Tarnow, the director of legal and constitutional law for the government of Nunavut, explained how the breakdown of division of cash between the two governments worked: Nunavut was responsible for 44.34

percent of the $15 million — nearly $6.7 million — and the Northwest Territories was on the hook for the rest. That share was based on a formula that had been established at the time of the division of the Northwest Territories into two territories, a formula that divvied up assets and any future liabilities, Tarnow told Chris Windeyer of *Nunatsiaq News*.[10]

Budden would not tell the media exactly how the $15 million would be broken down between cash payments and a fund for treatment. But he said the fund would be administered by a board similar to the one that managed a $3-million reserve that was set up as a result of the first civil case. In both civil actions, individual payouts varied according to the personal circumstances of each victim.[11]

· · ·

During questioning by lawyers in 2007, Horne made a stunning statement: "[The education officials] had every reason to believe that the class was going well, on the basis of what they saw. Particularly on the basis of attendance figures that were, for the time, astounding. I feel like I'm the one that's responsible for misleading them. I convinced them that all was well. Everything they saw, everything they could check looked good, and that's my responsibility. I don't think it's negligence on their part. I think it's simply a deceitful, out of control teacher ... myself."[12]

In 2021, I asked Horne if he had duped his colleagues in education into believing he was a great teacher.

"Duping? I wish I could say unequivocally, no," he said. But then, in a moment of introspection, he added, "But I remember one specific moment, two or three years before my arrest, when Bert Rose had visited my classroom and praised it strongly. And I thought to myself that great teachers don't do those things to their students. There were doubtless other times when I turned aside praise with the 'dark side' in mind, but we're looking back forty years, trying to retrieve what I have always tried to bury."

The "Pretendian"

WITH HIS DARK WAVY HAIR, BROWN EYES, AND TANNED COM-plexion, Ed Horne could certainly appear to be an Indigenous person to some people. During his years in the Arctic he would claim now and then that he was Native or "part" Native.

Most people who spoke to me on the record about him, having known him personally while living in the North, believed he was Indigenous, and were very surprised when I told them he was not.

Bert and Joanne Rose recall Horne telling them he understood an Indigenous tongue. They don't recall what First Nations language he claimed to speak, but when Joanne asked him "Where did you learn that?" He said, "At home." She got the impression he had intended — that he had been raised in a multilingual Indigenous environment.

More than one colleague said they believed Horne was Mohawk. Inuit I spoke to for this book did not ever think Horne was Indigenous, but a few Horne victims during civil suit proceedings believed he may have had Mohawk ancestry. A teaching acquaintance was buttonholed by Horne in a parking lot in Iqaluit in 1985, where Horne poured out a brief life story, saying his father and mother were each half-Mohawk from Quebec, and that his family had moved to British Columbia in order to deny their Indianness.

His defence lawyer Neil Sharkey said in 1987 that Horne was of mixed Euro-Canadian and Indigenous ancestry. In Sanikiluaq in the 1970s anthropologist Hugh Brody believed, based on conversations, that Horne was Athapaskan. Newspaper editor Jim Bell heard that Horne's father was Salish.

In recent years, a national mini-obsession has developed over outing "pretendians," people in the public eye, often in academia or the arts, who have claimed to be Indigenous and have built their careers on such claims, often receiving special funding for their education or artistic endeavours because of their Indigeneity. But when Horne began his identity charade, such cases were rare. Archie Belaney, who had masqueraded as Grey Owl in the 1920s and '30s, and Sylvester Clark, aka Chief Buffalo Child Long Lance, even earlier, were among the few cases that had ever come to public attention.

Before I ever met or communicated with Ed Horne, I investigated his background for this book and uncovered the fact that he definitely does not have Indigenous ancestry — a detail he would make a point of mentioning in our conversations, seemingly aware that his erroneous claim was something a journalist would seize upon.

His ancestors came from England and the east coast of Canada, including Spoon Cove, Newfoundland; Prince Edward Island; and Anticosti Island, Quebec, a large but sparsely settled island tucked into the Gulf of St. Lawrence with a population today of just 240 people. Horne's grandparents were related — they were first cousins once removed, the family trees intersecting during the time they lived on Anticosti Island.

In court in 1985, Horne's defence lawyer, Joe Bovard, asked his client to state his ethnicity. Horne said, "Métis." Today, Bovard can't explain why he even asked Horne this question.

An important legal precedent was set by the Supreme Court of Canada in 1999 when it heard a disturbing manslaughter charge against an Indigenous woman. Aware of the over-representation of aboriginal people in prisons, the court ruled that sentencing judges must pay particular attention to the circumstances of Indigenous offenders[1] in an effort to encourage judges to take a restorative approach to sentencing. Incarceration — jail time — would be a last resort. Since that date, *Gladue* principles — the accused's name in the case was Gladue — have been considered in the sentencing of Indigenous accused in Canada. Horne's first court appearance predated the *Gladue* decision by fourteen years. But that does not mean that northern courts were insensitive to the circumstances of Indigenous offenders.

For years, courts in the North had taken into consideration the life circumstances of accused brought before the courts for show cause and sentencing hearings. Indeed, some of Canada's earliest case law in which the circumstances of Indigenous life and customs were seen as mitigating factors in the commission of a crime or even in determining whether a crime had actually been committed was developed in the N.W.T., especially under the enlightened judgeships of John Sissons and his successor William Morrow. They ruled, often controversially at the time, on cases ranging from seasonal hunting rights to Indigenous adoption and even murder. Their critics accused them of unjustified leniency. But their decisions stood. And so Indigeneity already mattered in the northern courts of 1985. Horne knew this, so he played the race card and won. He prevailed at his show cause hearing in 1985 and was granted bail. Once he reached Toronto, he parlayed his faux Indigenous identity into a volunteer position with the Association for Native Development in the Performing and Visual Arts in Toronto.

During an interview in 2007, Horne was asked about his ancestry:

> **Lawyer:** Do you self-identify as an aboriginal person?
> **Horne:** No. I have only one great grandmother that was apparently pure blood Indian and there's Indian ancestry even further back on my father's side from Labrador, either Indian or Inuit. The area was overlapping populations.
> [Despite his "no," the rest of Horne's answer was an obfuscation.]
> **Lawyer:** Your social insurance number, correct me if I'm wrong, but it appears to be an aboriginal number?
> **Horne:** I was born on the reserve.
> **Lawyer:** Okay. So you ... and at different times you're identified by other people as a Métis?

Horne: I would say that's fairly accurate, considering where I grew up. Métis is largely a designation that is self-applied. The legal status of the term I don't think has ever been spelled out very clearly.

Lawyer: You've never self-identified nor have been identified as an Inuit?

Horne: No. DNA technology is coming to the point where I will be able to answer that question and I'm very interested in it, but it was mainly the fact that my grandmother was half Indian. I was very close to her throughout my childhood that … and also my other grandmother who was noticeably part Indian, that I was close to them. I felt some emotional attachment to the Indian part of my heritage. The fact that my parents were racist and very vociferous about the fact that we were white. I think out of rebellion to them … against them, I looked toward … looked at the Indian component of our family. I did join the Alberta Métis Association, but it was partly to get hunting rights for my son.

Lawyer: I think you referenced [your Native ancestry] in some of your communication …

Horne: That surprises me a little because I've never accepted any government grants or scholarships or privilege that I might be entitled to on the basis of aboriginal descent. I've been wary about exploiting that in any way. Maybe when I was trying to make myself look good in the context of an application, I may have slid that in.[2]

When I asked Horne about his Native ancestry he said, "I remember one of my friends saying after my arrest that I'd have been treated differently if I had been Native, and he was told that I am part Native. I don't know that I ever mentioned it to the people around me.

"I was raised believing the family legend that my great-grandmother was Indian, and according to my mother that was scandalous. Throughout my time in the North I believed this and it weighed on me."

He took up genealogy as a hobby in recent years and found out his great-grandmother was not Indian. She was born in Ireland of an Irish mother and an English father. It was a newly discovered fourth cousin who told Horne this.

"All doubt had to be swept aside when I got my first DNA test, which showed no trace of Native blood."

After reading a summary online about this book, Horne sent me an email on May 13, 2024:

> I never identified as indigenous. As a child I was told that a great-great-grandmother was Indian, and I had no reason to doubt it. This would have made me one sixteenth Indian — far short of claiming to be indigenous. This sliver of native ancestry, with the fact that I was born in an Indian village, Bella Bella, was part of my self identity, but only of personal significance.
>
> But here is what rankles: "He also claimed to be Indigenous — a claim that would later prove to be false." This makes me sound like Buffy Sainte-Marie.
>
> And how did you find out that I had no native ancestry? I told you.
>
> I told you that a distant cousin doing genealogy told me that my remote ancestor, Mary Jane Dawson, was Irish, not Indian. And this was established absolutely by DNA testing, about five years ago.
>
> One further matter: Glancing through our more than 20 emails, I cringe at my rudeness. It was unintentional — that was not how I felt at the time. Accordingly an apology is warranted and offered.

The Aftermath

ON THE MORNING OF APRIL 3, 2005, THE POLICE IN Kuujjuaraapik, Quebec, also known as Great Whale River, were called out to an area near the village dump to respond to an alleged assault. When they arrived, they spoke to the wife of John Paul Akavak Horne, Ed Horne's eldest son (his name was spelled Aakava in court documents). The woman claimed her husband had assaulted her, but she stopped short of pressing charges. She had been kicked and punched but no physical injuries were noted by police at the time. That is why, police would say, they did not arrest the man immediately.

A day later, the woman called police to provide further details of the alleged assault. She also explained she had hesitated pressing charges because she was concerned for her husband's well-being — he had been expressing thoughts of suicide. The man was subsequently told via telephone to return to the police station as he was under arrest. This wasn't an easy call. Akavak had been a police officer in that very police force and was friends with the officer, Jason Bennett, who called him and took his statement.

Upon arrival at the police station, Akavak was detained in police custody for eighteen hours, awaiting his initial appearance before a justice of the peace.

In the case that ended up in court on February 2, 2006, Akavak argued that his rights under section 9 of the Charter of Rights and Freedoms were violated during his detention and, therefore, the criminal trial he was facing for the alleged assault against his wife should be tossed out due to a miscarriage of justice. Akavak argued that because he was arrested thirty-six hours after the offence, none of the conditions justifying detention were satisfied, thereby making the detention unlawful under the Criminal Code.

The court agreed that the man's rights were violated during the detention, but Justice Daniel Bédard determined that this type of abuse fell within a "residual" breach of Charter freedoms, which allowed a breach to occur without automatically triggering a "stay of proceedings" if the breach did not impact trial fairness. In this case, since the alleged assault involved the wife of the accused, and he had a history of violence against her, causing broken ribs and a fractured skull, there was an overriding interest in having Akavak tried despite the minor infringement of his rights and freedoms.

Ultimately, because the case involved serious domestic violence, not proceeding with the case was seen as doing more harm to the justice system than it would to Akavak's constitutional rights.

. . .

Akavak and his wife had four children together, two boys and two girls, all living in Kuujjuaraapik. As hard as the young man and his wife may have struggled to build a happy life together, it would all end horrifically for Ed Horne's eldest son.

On the night of March 7, 2012, there was an altercation between two men in Kuujjuaraapik. The Sûreté du Québec (the provincial police), who were called in at about 11 p.m., treated the incident as a murder-suicide. Sgt. Geneviève Bruneau of the Sûreté du Québec identifed the two deceased men as Victor Sam Weetaltuk, 22, who died of the first gunshot wound, and Akavak Horne, 32, who had then turned the firearm on himself and died by suicide. Horne apparently shot Weetaltuk from outside his home through the living room window before taking his own life. Weetaltuk's family members witnessed the shooting.

"Jealousy was likely at the root of the incident," Bruneau said.[1]

No one else had been involved in the crimes, Bruneau said, and so no charges were expected to be laid in the deaths of the two men, which she called a fairly "clear situation."[2]

Jeannie had already buried their youngest son, Daniel — the same boy who had been put in a harness to keep him from running away when he was a little child in Lake Harbour. He had died by suicide in 2002, at the age of nineteen.

During the writing of this book, I asked Ed Horne if he had ever sexually abused his own sons. He said he hadn't.

"I asked at Regional Psychiatric Centre if a person with my record could possibly be a danger to his own children," he told me. "They didn't know of any research. When Jeannie and the boys moved south to be near me [in Red Deer], a nurse chided me for being distant with John, while okay, warm, and caring with Danny and Jimmy. I responded that John was the age of the victims, and being affectionate with them, as they were now suggesting I be with John, was 'how it all began.' I discussed this with John afterward."

Horne told me he was not in touch with his middle son, Jimmy. "I still write to him and he doesn't respond," Horne said.

I asked Horne to explain why he still blames Jeannie for the deaths of their sons.

"They were thriving at Red Deer," he said. "They had good schools, sports, friends, church groups, family outings, camping trips. She took them [back to Great Whale River] and held them in a rotten place; surely you know how dysfunctional a northern town can be — alcohol, drugs, crime, suicides. I told Jeannie she couldn't possibly take care of Danny. She said white people were going to help her."

Horne and Jeannie never divorced. Jeannie Cookie died from meningitis in Montreal on March 18, 2024. She was seventy-eight.

• • •

In the summer of 2007, a house Horne had once called home in Sanikiluaq burned down. The fire ravaged House 505 beyond repair, but not many tears were shed in the community over it. The unlucky occupant, a foreman at the Qulliq Energy Corporation's power plant, was on vacation at the time.

"Many former abuse victims can finally release the demons!" a Sanikiluaq resident told *Nunatsiaq News*.[3]

The blaze began sometime around 4:30 a.m. on August 11.

Local rumours were that two men broke into the house in the early morning and stole a few things before setting the fire — a fire intended to cleanse the town of Horne's legacy. Const. Ian Johnson of the Sanikiluaq RCMP cautioned that there was no evidence to link the fire to memories of Horne. The officer also downplayed the break-in rumours. But the dominant feeling in the town was relief that the house with very bad vibes was gone.

• • •

In Nunavut, in the early 2000s, a claim started to emerge more and more during criminal proceedings. Jim Bell of *Nunatsiaq News* picked up on it, calling it "the Ed Horne Excuse."[4] An accused would say that Ed Horne had molested him, ostensibly to receive leniency from the judge. In some cases, childhood sexual abuse was taken into account during sentencing, and Horne was well-known to northern courts as a convicted child abuser. But investigations into the lives of some of the accused who were making these claims revealed that Horne didn't even live in their community when the accused claimed to have suffered abuse, or the accused was simply too old at the time to have plausibly been a Horne victim.

Horne did, in fact, engage in sexual activity with a nineteen-year-old male in Sanikiluaq in the 1970s, but Horne's crimes were largely committed against children he had access to, and it was easy to prove how, when, and where he got that access.

In an editorial that put a harsh spotlight on these iffy claims, Bell, known for fearlessly taking unpopular and sometimes unorthodox positions, asked: "What's the difference between an Ed Horne victim, and any other sexual abuse victim? There are probably thousands of sexual abuse victims in Nunavut, people who have been abused by fathers, uncles, brothers, grandparents, and other family or community members. Why does being an Ed

Horne victim give you a leg up in the victimization game?"[5] Unlike most sexual abuse victims in Nunavut, Bell pointed out, Horne's victims, in fact, benefitted from financial compensation, which included healing programs. "So, if anything," Bell wrote, "being an Ed Horne victim should be deemed an aggravating, not a mitigating factor in sentencing. It should get you more, not less time in jail."

But even to this day, if a northern man says he is an Ed Horne victim there is a certain awe and a quiet sadness that accompanies this revelation, and he is at least for a moment listened to, honoured, and respected for surviving the predations of the North's most infamous pedophile.

• • •

Horne once considered a career as a journalist and has kept journals for much of his life. He has written essays, and in recent years even a novel. He has investigated his own family history, written about his parents, and chronicled day by day — mileage included — his travels by bicycle across the island of Newfoundland. He had distant relatives there he wanted to connect with, even if it just meant visiting the community they once lived in for a day or two. He did that, and was particularly impressed with Marystown on the Burin Peninsula.

In 2016, Horne published a work called *Canadian Justice: A Prisoner's View; A Novel of Life and Death in a Canadian Prison*. It is available through Amazon Kindle. Erik Nelson is his pen name. The work is dedicated cryptically to "DPH and JPAH. Loved beyond measure, missed beyond endurance."

Canadian Justice is pure fiction, Horne told me, "one exception being that the material on parole in Toronto is absolutely autobiographical, except that I was never actually sent to the Don Jail." The idea of a story told from the perspective of "a deeply flawed narrator," he said, came to him from a Brazilian classic novel, *Dom Casmurro*, by Joaquim Maria Machado de Assis.

Within the text of his novel, it is tempting to hunt for clues to the real Horne. The cloak of fiction is heavy, but Horne does give away things here and there — he can't help himself — not the least of which lies in the dedication at the start of the book to his two sons who died by suicide.

There were comments his narrator made on intelligence that mirrored Horne's life. He later admitted I was close when I pointed it out to him. The narrator says, "I've noticed when someone says I'm intelligent, it's not usually a compliment. They mean because I'm intelligent I should have known better than what I did, and that makes me twice as guilty."

Manipulation and domination are common themes, and there are plenty of references to things Horne said in court, or that are in line with his experiences: inmates watching *Sesame Street* and how he could never be one of them, struggling to access decent literature to read, running until exhausted, and quotes from Shakespeare.

During an email correspondence, I told Horne I thought his work titled *Bowden Institution* was better written and more relevant to the research I was doing than *Canadian Justice*. He responded, saying, "I was intrigued you prefer the writing in *Bowden Institution*. I thought the writing was embarrassingly bad, written nearly 30 years ago, and that *Canadian Justice*, from about 15 years ago, was an improvement. *Bowden Institution* is personal and autobiographical, but I was frustrated that memories were hard to retrieve, only two or three years after the events recorded. It's as true as I could make it."

In the opening of *Bowden Institution*, he unambiguously prepares the reader for his possible lies:

> Am I to be believed? I wish I could say categorically yes, trust me. But re-reading the raw materials that form the basis of this book, I find that styles, moods, attitudes shifted as time went by. I despaired of stitching the various components into a coherent whole. Some incidents could not possibly have happened the way I seem to remember them. I've found prison anecdotes I wrote years ago that don't tell things the way I remember them. And how can you be sincere when a large part of you has been destroyed, when you don't really know who you are and what you truly believe?[6]

• • •

People who know bits and pieces of the Horne story often ask if he was a pedophile. Horne is a pedophile. But Horne himself has had trouble coming to terms with the classic definition of this disorder and how it plays out in his life. Horne confronted aspects of his sex crimes and talked about his pedophilia in 2007. This is an edited portion of that interview:

> **Lawyer:** Would it surprise you, Mr. Horne, if I told you that the teachers in Lake Harbour very much did suspect you of abusing children, and made complaints?
>
> **Horne:** Made complaints? I would be surprised. Certainly, they made statements at my trial, that they weren't surprised when the allegations came forth and when the charges came forth.
>
> **Lawyer:** Basically, what you mean is, you are a pedophile, you were a pedophile then …
>
> **Horne:** I was, at that time, depending on the definition of a pedophile. That was argued at great length in my first sentencing hearing. But as Brian Bruser, the prosecutor said, "Who cares? The actions speak for themselves."
>
> **Lawyer:** The judge, Judge Marshall, in his decision, called you a pedophile, did he not?
>
> **Horne:** Yes, he did.
>
> **Lawyer:** He made a finding that you are a pedophile?
>
> **Horne:** He made that finding.
>
> **Lawyer:** There is Ed Horne, the pedophile, who looks to exploit every angle that Ed Horne, the good teacher, can do? Isn't that the way your mind operated?
>
> **Horne:** No, because I think … what you just said there, that I was exploiting every opportunity that came up, and that I was doing every evil thing that I could … there were months at a time when I laid this aside. I was … but the unflattering aspects of the character is that…. You have given an unflattering characterization that I think is, basically, correct.

Lawyer: That there was Ed Horne, the pedophile …
Horne: Ed Horne, the person acting as a pedophile. The reason … any objection I have to that term is that pedophilia is defined as a lifelong sexual orientation that is, basically, untreatable, and requires lifelong monitoring, and makes the person a constant danger to reoffend. And I reject that aspect of the definition. But the crimes I committed were pedophilic crimes.
Lawyer: So, you said that this started … you cannot remember the first time [you abused a child]?
Horne: I am not proud of that fact, but it's a fact.
Lawyer: Why is that? Because the first instant you crossed the line, you touched a child for sexual purposes, that should be burned in your memory.
Horne: I have raised that point myself, and the fact that it is not burned in my memory is something that troubles me, and I can understand why it would trouble you.
Lawyer: You don't want to remember, do you?
Horne: Well, in a sense, you are right.[7]

· · ·

When Horne was arrested for sex crimes in the Eastern Arctic in 1985, he was taken to the Alberta Hospital for a psychiatric assessment, but there were some frustrating realities at work during the hospital stay that prevented doctors there from doing a full diagnosis of their patient. Horne himself was frustrated that he could not get better diagnostic tests. But those were the rules at the time — Horne's lawyer, Joe Bovard, gave the hospital staff and Horne strict instructions not to divulge any details of the events leading up to Horne's arrest. Therefore, the only information the hospital received was that Horne was a school principal and had been charged with sex assault involving numerous adolescent boys — a full diagnosis of his pedophilia was not done at that time. But an erotic preference assessment did show that Horne had a preference for females compared to males.

Horne was discharged from the hospital on December 9, 1985. Under Diagnosis on Discharge, Dr. Herbert Pascoe wrote "Psychiatric: No diagnosis (Suspect homosexual pedophile)."

There was a man I spoke with for this book, Tad,* who was almost molested by Horne when he was a boy but circumvented Horne's action by getting away as fast as he could. He was notable in the Horne case because he is white. I had assumed Horne was only interested in Indigenous children. Tad told me, "I don't believe Mr. Horne would have cared either way whether you were white or Inuk. He would just test the waters. If he felt that he could take advantage of you, then I think he would. That being said, I know a lot of Inuit kids who were molested by Mr. Horne. And I don't know a lot of white kids that were. I think he scoped things out, slowly."

. . .

"You said to the police, you have blocked stuff out," a lawyer said to Horne once. "You have had to. It was 30 years, look what you are dealing with here. There are things that, you say, 'That sounds like something I could do.' Well, yes, opportunity, motive, yes, 'I could have done that one, but I don't know …' You have blocked stuff out of your mind."

Horne replied, "I think every human being on earth does that. I have a lot more to block than hardly anybody."[8]

"I didn't consider how disastrously wrong my conduct was," Horne told me. "I thought it would be really embarrassing if someone found out. Toward the end, I was starting to realize that I could end up in prison. But it was coming to me, bit by bit, by fits and starts."

I told Horne I had my own theory — that his quest for excellence over the years was his way of trying to "outrun" his pedophilia, as if he thought he could cure himself through his studies.

He replied,

> I don't see myself as fleeing from an awful truth and using
> my interests to shield myself from the truth. I just didn't

have *mens rea* [criminal intent] in the years I was committing what we now recognize as grave and criminal activity. Those were the Dark Ages. I can remember only a
few instances when I knew I'd be doing something wrong.
I thought it was silly and potentially embarrassing, and
inconsequential, and seemed to be going on all around me.
I couldn't see what I did in a few minutes a month would
outweigh what I did in long hours of hard work.

Despite the introspection that Horne has engaged in over the years,
it is troubling that he sticks tenaciously to his assertion — it is never
presented as a justification — that he didn't realize at the time that he
was doing anything wrong, that his behaviour was anything other than
embarrassing and silly.

In conversation with me in June 2022, I asked Horne about how children and their parents can protect themselves from a child predator like
him. Looking at me straight on, he told me that what he was going to say
would be controversial, but also the truth as he remembers it: "The children
were very complicit," he said. "They'd say things like 'You wanna try me?'"
Children should be taught not to make overtly sexual remarks to adults, he
said, unambiguously blaming the victims.

The Man and the Myth

MY INTERVIEWS WITH ED HORNE BEGAN IN DECEMBER 2021.[1] HE answered my questions in such a way that I found indicated not so much a reflective honesty gained over time, but more likely a profound loneliness.

At various times, Horne questioned my integrity. When I asked him about his many crimes in Cape Dorset and the fact that he was a sexual predator there, he responded, "We do not agree on what is 'many.' You said recently that 'many' ran to hundreds. This was so obviously preposterous that I lost any remaining faith that you were an objective journalist."

When I challenged his comment, explaining that the "hundreds of victims" story was part of the myth of him, not meant to be read as my personal view, he said, "I have maintained that my actions were on a scale that a confused, ignorant person could brush off in his own mind. Activities on the scale reflected in the 'myth' could not have been so dismissed in the mind of the perpetrator."

This in itself is a troubling admission. The thought that "one is too many" had apparently not crossed Horne's mind. He had convinced himself that the scale — the number — of his sexual assaults was inconsequential, apparently oblivious to the emotional damage that even one attack could cause one vulnerable victim.

. . .

Horne never shied away from the interview process; he was eager — almost too eager — to answer my questions. It did not take long for me to feel that Horne was a lonely man — estranged but not divorced from his wife, no longer on speaking terms with his only surviving sons and other relatives, living with the knowledge of the suicides of his two other sons while avoiding any responsibility for them and placing the blame on his wife.

Like his victims, Horne's personal life has been full of tragedy. He is an intelligent man. Once a celebrated teacher, with a solid education and knowledge of many languages, he was working as a bike courier in Canada's largest city when I met him. Although he told me he likes the work, this is a tough way for a senior citizen to make a living.

He told me at one point: "As a teacher, I loved acting, directing, role-playing. I did TV commercials in Mexico, and would love to audition for theatre productions in Toronto, but am afraid of being recognized."

Although he denies any acts of pedophilia in his three teaching posts in British Columbia, he sought out isolated communities where he could express those tendencies and minimize the chances of getting caught.

A narcissist who once revelled in the adulation of his superiors in the educational hierarchy, his validation now comes only from within his own mind.

His penchant for introspection must, at times, seem a curse as he mulls over the reasons for his depravity and its consequences for the Inuit communities he professed to love.

. . .

During the interview process, I asked Horne in a few different ways about how he felt about his crimes against children in the North. Here is one answer he gave me: "I had no way of knowing fully the consequences of my crimes. I was isolated from them. I still don't know the harm I did. I felt rotten from the start." In what would turn out to be the most difficult line of questioning I had with Horne, I asked him if he felt in any way responsible for the suicides of some of his victims.

"I was not ready at the time to grasp that I had damaged children," he said.

Many of the children you abused died by suicide, I responded. "Do you accept responsibility for having caused their deaths?" He dodged the question with his reply, "Your disgust is showing through. It could hinder an understanding if you do not lay it aside."

"I disagree. I'm a journalist, not a judge," I said. "Under the circumstances, it is a valid question."

He remained adamant. "It is not a valid question. I have tried to draw a clear line between delusional thinking in the past and insights I have struggled with over the years. If I have failed in this, then we are on the wrong track and I don't know what is the next step." He followed up with a simple, devastating statement: "You can add nothing to the horror I feel."

He would not delve into a discussion of suicides of his victims, allowing only this: "Suicide was rampant and remains to this day a heartbreaking tragedy." He said northerners blaming him for suicides of his victims is a "cheap shot" because "neither I nor the victims were around to contradict."

Suicide is an unfortunate reality in the Indigenous communities of Canada. In Nunavut it is a tragedy that has touched almost every family. The reasons for it are complex, and studies into those reasons are controversial. There is no agreed upon method for combatting this debilitating epidemic. Suicide is, of course, not limited to the victims of Ed Horne. But in the communities where he molested boys — which is to say all the communities in which he lived and taught — his victims are disproportionately represented in suicide statistics. He may not feel responsibility for their suicides or may not be capable of admitting such a responsibility. He may indeed feel horror at the thought. But the statistics are stark and real, as are communities' perceptions of the reasons for those tragic numbers.

Kinngait, March 2022

THE ICE WAS BREAKING UP. I COULD SEE IT CLEARLY FROM MY window on the Canadian North airplane as we began to descend into the community. I was in awe of the expanse of the Arctic landscape as the music of John Williams's "Flight to Neverland" from the film *Hook* blasted through my headphones.

I have been to all the communities in the North Horne lived in, with the exception of Grise Fiord. It was vital for me to meet everyone I talked to for this book in person whenever possible — to look into their eyes as we spoke. So it was that once the pandemic allowed, I was back in the North, reconnecting with people I first met as a young journalist, or greeting contacts I'd only spoken to on the phone or sent emails to.

The communal fire of 2003 demolished one of the town's portable school buildings. But the other one in which Horne abused students was still there. I wanted to go to that portable, walk around in it. I was convinced it would help me come full circle with the story I'd been writing for so long.

. . .

On the day that I finally set eyes on the portable remaining from Horne's tenure in the community, the sun shone impossibly brightly from an azure sky, a stark contrast to the horrors that had once taken place inside that building. The old schoolhouse was more substantial than I imagined — different from the flimsy-looking portables you see on job sites or on school grounds today.

An Inuk man in his fifties wearing the fluorescent garb of a heavy equipment operator was inside. Although the space is now filled with building supplies, the original chalkboards are still there, partially visible behind the walls. I reached out and touched the chalkboard and then noticed names written in marker on another section of the wall, names written by local children many years ago.

"My name is there," the man in the work clothes said.

Sure enough, it was.

Many Horne victims are dead — from boating accidents, natural causes, the toughness of the North wearing lives away, and from suicide. Because I'd done research on the victims who might still be alive in Kinngait, I knew who this man was, and I was aware that Horne admitted to abusing the man when he was a boy. It is always notable to me when Horne admits to having abused a specific boy, as he often denies claims of abuse.

I told the man I was writing a book about Horne and his crimes.

"A lot of memories in this place," he said. "But we survived it."

Another man, wearing mirrored sunglasses, roamed around the portable that day, curious about the book I was writing. He pointed to the old lights on the ceiling — the very same lights Horne taught beneath. The chalkboard erasers were still there too.

Over in a corner where Mr. Horne made him stand as punishment for some long-ago misbehaviour, the man removed his sunglasses and wept quietly.

Later, the man told me about the compensation money he received from one of the civil lawsuits. He bought furniture and clothes and booze with it. The money was gone pretty fast. It was a real rush to do all that shopping and partying when the compensation money arrived, but it never really felt like justice, he said.

Horne victims have coped with their trauma in different ways. Some men have found God and attend church regularly. Others carve and draw art that sells internationally. And then there is alcohol.

Drinking is his way of coping with the trauma of Horne abuse, the man who stood in the corner remembering Horne's abuse said. Horne raped him when he was ten, he said. He was a trusting student, a visitor with his friends at Horne's home as a boy. What could he do? Horne had food in his house, a television, and running water. His home at the time didn't. When Horne offered him a warm bath one day, he took it.

The man knows drinking vodka straight from the bottle these days isn't good for him. It has cost him a lot. His personal relationships and artistic career would no doubt thrive if he didn't drink. But he feels drinking hard is the only way he can "fight the system" right now — a system that he feels is greatly flawed, allowing a man like Horne to walk free.

Horne's abuse was an attack on his manhood — a manhood already in turmoil due to colonialism, having to adjust to life in a community far from the traditional Inuit way of life of his grandparents who raised him.

He hides his wounds much of the time, trying to set a good example for his kids. He has riches beyond money — mainly language and much of his culture. He speaks Inuktitut and knows how to hunt. His children are fluent in Inuktitut also.

The land is not foreign to him. He grew up here. He can look up at the stars at night and understand them in ways no southern astronomer ever could. But the sexual abuse he experienced robbed him of the peace in his heart.

Much of his pain comes from knowing he is damaged and feeling power-less to change. He wants to be a better father, a more reliable tradesperson in town, and a more confident partner to his wife, but he doesn't know how. The no-food-in-the-house type of poverty is still very much a reality for many men in Kinngait, no matter how many carvings they sell. And at $120 a bottle for bootlegged vodka, that poverty will likely continue.

I asked this man what he would say if he could speak to Horne today. He believes Horne lied about how many boys he abused and that Horne lied about what he did to the victims, including himself.

"First I'd say, 'Remember me? Remember me when I was weaker than you? Yeah. I've been through so much shit man. I've done everything in the book. Yet, here you are. You got away with a lot of stuff. Me? I never got away with nothing. What can you possibly say? Are you going to still deny? Are you still going to deny me?'"

When I left the old schoolhouse that day, I headed back to Dorset Suites — the hotel where I was staying and finishing parts of this book. The man in the mirrored sunglasses walked with me, but halfway down the road he stopped and took a deep breath. He looked at me and said it felt as if a weight, like a giant rock, had been lifted off of his chest after shedding a few tears in the corner where he'd once been a boy.

Acknowledgements

I WOULD LIKE TO THANK KWAME SCOTT FRASER AND JULIA KIM for acquiring my manuscript at Dundurn Press. It feels as though it took me a lifetime to write this book, and for years I wondered who its first official editor would be. When I found out it would be Kwame, I was extremely grateful.

I express my gratitude to the amazing freelance editor Robyn So who brought lucidity and strength to the telling of this heart-breaking story.

To everyone at Dundurn Press, especially project editor Erin Pinksen, publisher Meghan Macdonald, and art director Laura Boyle: thank you for your belief in my book, and your dedication to Canadian storytelling.

Looking back over my career as a newspaper journalist, I would like to thank the following people for their support: Bruce Valpy, Jack "Sig" Sigvaldason, Pam Frampton (an early reader of the manuscript), Travis Mealing, Christine Kay, Neils Christensen, Brent Reaney, Ted Rath, and Martin Hudson.

David Berg, Sebastian Lippa, and Hugh Brody provided crucial edits to early drafts of this book. I am especially thankful to Hugh for what turned out to be a major turning-point meeting at the British Museum in London one rainy day in March 2020. Our discussion at the museum, and our correspondence during the writing of this book, helped shape what this story could be.

I would like to thank staff at the Nunavut Court of Justice in Iqaluit and the Supreme Court of the Northwest Territories for their professionalism, especially J.P. Mercado in Yellowknife.

The following people offered encouragement and, in many instances, provided clarity to the text: my parents Nora and Dominic Lippa, my sister Eliza (who is a wonderful schoolteacher in England), Aksatungua Pitseolak Ashoona, Billy Akavak, Taylor Dignan, Patricia Bell, Susan Cooper, Bert and Joanne Rose, Brian and Donna Morrison, Ken MacRury, Eric Colbourne, Mark Cleveland, Joe Bovard, Margaret Lawrence, David Gilday, Milton Freeman, Christine Moore, the late Jim Bell, Dennis Patterson, Jim and Joanne Britton, Jens Lyberth, Robin McGrath, Gerry Oliver, Mary Flaherty, Kristiina and Timoon Alariaq, Ann and Bob Hanson, and John Jamieson.

I would also like to thank Anne Collins for being an early champion of this book and giving me a boost of confidence at a critical time.

My aunt Sheila was one of the first people I spoke to about this story when I'd moved from Iqaluit back to Toronto for a little while in 2005, and I would like to thank her for her generosity.

I'd like to thank my friends Wendy and Thi Phan for providing much-needed support through dark times.

I'd also like to thank my friend Ellen Cornell for taking care of my pug, Kippy, when I travelled North.

Due to the nature of this story, I cannot name a number of people who I either interviewed or got information from. But no matter how difficult some of the conversations I had with these contacts were — some of whom worried that my book would reopen old wounds — they all knew there were important lessons to come out of this story.

Ed Horne destroyed the lives of many people in Nunavut. But he made himself available to me for interviews and provided me with information I could not have gotten anywhere else, so for that I thank him.

And my husband Kenn — Ilisaijikutaaq — I love you with all my heart. We hold each other in the light.

Notes

Introduction

1　When I interviewed Ed Horne for this book, he confirmed that he had never done an interview with a journalist about his crimes in the North. However, on at least one occasion, a *Nunatsiaq News* journalist did reach Horne by email, but Horne replied that he wouldn't comment on the charges or the outcome of the trial.

2　Robert Kardosh, "The Object Truth: Jamasee Pitseolak's World of Stone," *Inuit Art Quarterly* 30.1 (Spring 2017), 34-39.

Frobisher Bay, October 1985

1　All interviews with Bert Rose and Joanne Rose were done by the author, either in person in Iqaluit, by email, or on the telephone starting in 2011. First formal interview with Bert Rose took place February 8, 2011, in Iqaluit, Nunavut. First and only interview with Joanne Rose took place February 20, 2011, in Iqaluit, Nunavut. Follow-up questions with Bert Rose to clarify information took place via email March 16, 2020; March 17, 2020; February 2, 2021; and February 3, 2021.

2　Report from the Alberta Hospital, Edmonton, Social Service Department. Report located in the Supreme Court, Northwest Territories, Yellowknife.

3　Information about EH's interest and background in theatre comes from a few sources. The University of British Columbia, Department of Theatre, *Henry IV, Part 1*, program, January 23–26, 1963, lists Edward Horne as one of the

"Lords, Wenches, Soldiers, etc." *The Langley Advance* newspaper had a brief note about a play he was in, noted in a later chapter. EH also confirmed his theatre interests for me in personal writing, Facebook messages, and during an in-person meeting. Later chapters will contain these details.

Sanikiluaq, 1971–74

1   *Teach in Canada's Arctic* (Northwest Territories Department of Education, 1970), 7–8.

2   I include these details because Inuit in other parts of Nunavut sometimes comment on how small and dark skinned Sanikiluaq people are compared to Inuit in other parts of Nunavut. When I was a reporter, I remember one Inuk referring to Sanikiluaq as "the Hawaii of Nunavut," due to its small islands and geographical location in relation to the rest of the territory.

3   Emikotailuk is the local spelling used by community Elders. The standard spelling would be imiqqutailaq (Inuit Tapiriit Kanatami orthography).

4   Examination for Discovery of Edward Horne (hereafter cited as DOEH), April 23–27, 2007. Geoffrey E. Budden and Stuart A. Morris for the plaintiffs, Robert A. Dewar and Brad Patzer for the defendants.

      The DOEH took place at the offices of Victory Verbatim Reporting Services, Toronto, Ontario, April 23–27, 2007. It was an important part of a civil action led by lawyers Geoffrey E. Budden and Stuart A. Morris for the plaintiffs (Ed Horne victims), and Robert Dewar and Brad Patzer for the first and second defendants (the government of the N.W.T. and the government of Nunavut). This civil action began in 2004 and was settled in 2011. The documents are located at Nunavut Court of Justice, Iqaluit, and were obtained for my research by an unsealing order.

      The unsealing order was obtained by my lawyer specifically to facilitate the writing of this book. Because of the extremely serious nature of the crimes, and the delicate information I had already obtained through interviews, the clarity provided by the DOEH was necessary. True names of victims were and continue to be protected by a publication ban.

5   DOEH, victim interview by Brad Patzer, Sanikiluaq, Nunavut, October 15, 2005.

6   The details here about Ed Horne's views on sexuality in the Sanikiluaq community come from DOEH, April 23, 2007, 172, and were later confirmed to me by Ed Horne during our lengthy correspondence.

7   DOEH, Ed Horne questioning by Geoffrey Budden, April 26, 2007, 30-40.

8   DOEH, victim interview by Faron Trippier, Sanikiluaq, Nunavut, October 13, 2005.

9   DOEH, Ed Horne interview by Robert Dewar, April 24, 2007, 93.

10   Winnipeg Art Gallery, *Belcher Islands/Sanikiluaq*, Winnipeg, MB: Winnipeg Art Gallery, 1981, 11–15. Exhibition catalogue.

Sanikiluaq, 1975–77

1   Hugh Brody, interview by the author, June 8, 2020. Christine Moore, email correspondence with the author, March 16, 2020.

2   Hugh Brody, interview with the author, March 5, 2020.

3   Civil Case announcement, Superior Court, General Division, Case No. 500-17-085536-145, *Gazette*, Montreal, Quebec, December 5, 2014. Charges were also mentioned by Ed Horne during DOEH, as told to Robert Dewar, April 23, 2007, 117.

4   DOEH, victim interview by Brad Patzer, Sanikiluaq, Nunavut, October 14, 2005.

5   DOEH, victim interview by Brad Patzer, Sanikiluaq, Nunavut, October 13, 2005.

6   DOEH, victim interview by Brad Patzer, Sanikiluaq, Nunavut, October 13, 2005.

7   DOEH, victim interview by Brad Patzer, Sanikiluaq, Nunavut, October 13, 2005.

The Disappearance of Alec Inuktaluk

1   DOEH, Ed Horne interview by Robert Dewar, Toronto, Ontario, April 22, 2007.

2   DOEH, victim interview by Faron Trippier, Sanikiluaq, Nunavut, October 16, 2005.

3   DOEH, victim interview by Brad Patzer, Sanikiluaq, Nunavut, October 13, 2005.

4   Kenn Harper, interview by the author, June 21, 2021. Harper and Olaf Christensen were government of the Northwest Territories employees in 1977 and life-long friends afterwards.

5   DOEH, victim interview by Faron Trippier, Sanikiluaq, Nunavut, October 16, 2005.

6   DOEH, victim interview by Brad Patzer, Sanikiluaq, Nunavut, October 13, 2005.

7   The area described may also be called Qikkiqtaaruapik, which is a small islet in the harbour that you can see when you get closer to Kataapik, kind of behind the landforms.

8   DOEH, Ed Horne interviewed by Brad Patzer, 138.

9   DOEH, Ed Horne interviewed by Stuart Morris, April 26, 2007, 216.

Cape Dorset, 1978–80, 1982–83

1   I'm particularly referring to *Kenojuak: Eskimo Artist*, produced by the National Film Board of Canada, 1963.

2   DOEH, Ed Horne interview by Geoff Budden, April 25, 2007, 229.

3   Rosemary, who is technically not an EH victim, is not identified in order to protect her brothers who were/are. Also, Ooleepeeka, her mother, cannot be identified as it would reveal the true identities of EH victims.

4   Anonymous source, interview by the author, June 29, 2020.

In the Portable

1   Many EH victims were incarcerated when they were interviewed by lawyers in connection with a civil case.

2   DOEH, victim interview by Faron Trippier, November 16, 2006.

3   Rosemary (pseudonym), interview by the author.

Who Was Ed Horne?

1   "Horne-Hawkins," *Langley Advance*, August 27, 1942, 1.

2   Ed Horne, interview by the author.

3   "Senate Award to Strong Tory Lady," *Langley Advance*, November 2, 1977, 29.

4   DOEH, Ed Horne, transcript from second criminal sentencing, Iqaluit, September 2000.

5   Ed Horne, interview by the author.

6   Ed Horne, "Walter and Muriel," unpublished essay, undated.

7   Ed Horne, interview by the author; Ed Horne, "Walter and Muriel," unpublished essay, undated.

8   Ed Horne, "Walter and Muriel," unpublished essay, undated.

9   He later claimed her name was Lucy MacArthur and that she died of TB in 1974.

10   "Local Scouting Activities Show off Boy Scout Week," *Quesnel Cariboo Observer*, February 24, 1966, B1.

Grise Fiord, 1980–81

1   Mary Flaherty, interview by author, Iqaluit, September 17, 2021.

Nakasuk School, 1981–82

1 Horne's abuses in Cape Dorset in both his stints in the community — 1978–80 and 1982–83 — have been dealt with together in an earlier chapter.

"He Killed My Brother"

1 Ed Horne victim, interview by author.

2 DOEH, Ed Horne, interview by Stuart A. Morris, April 26, 2007, 240.

3 This is an example of the kinds of attacks on children Ed Horne perpetrated. This information emerged from a civil case.

4 The only pornography Horne admitted to boys seeing was an old *Penthouse* magazine boys found while snooping around his house in Sanikiluaq.

5 DOEH, Bryon Doherty, interview by Stuart A. Morris, April 26, 2007, 199.

6 DOEH, Ed Horne, interview by Stuart A. Morris, April 26, 2007, 256.

7 DOEH, interview by Stuart A. Morris, with information from former teacher Peesee Pitsiulak, April 26, 2007, 256.

8 DOEH, interview by Stuart A. Morris, with information from former teacher Peesee Pitsiulak, April 26, 2007, 193.

9 DOEH, April 26, 2007, 204.

10 DOEH, Ed Horne, interview by Stuart A. Morris, April 26, 2007, 204.

11 DOEH, Ivan Gallant, statement read aloud into the record, April 26, 2007, 306.

The Piano

1 *R. v. Horne*, 1987 SCC 3734, [1987] NWTR 168 (NWT SC).

2 Jonathan (pseudonym), interview by the author, Kimmirut and Ottawa, October 14, 2004; September 24, 2020; and October 2, 2020.

3 Ed Horne, interview by the author.

4 Social Service Department report, Alberta Hospital, Edmonton, October 22, 1985. Sources of information for this report were Mick Mallon, superintendent of school division, Iqaluit; Const. Brian Morrison, arresting officer, Iqaluit; and three anonymous sources in the social work field.

5 DOEH, Bryon Doherty, interviewed by Stuart A. Morris, 206.

6 This report was obtained from the Northwest Territories Department of Education by lawyers during the second civil lawsuit launched against governments that oversaw the teaching career of Ed Horne. The report was contained in documents that I obtained through an unsealing order at the Nunavut Court of Justice, Iqaluit.

7 Ed Horne, letter to Christine Moore, 1985.

The Arrest

1   DOEH, Ed Horne, interview by Robert Dewar, April 25, 2007, 81.

2   DOEH, Ed Horne, interview by Stuart A. Morris, April 26, 2007, 302.

3   This report was contained in the medical report on Ed Horne from the Alberta Hospital in Edmonton. The report was obtained by my lawyer from the Supreme Court of the Northwest Territories, Yellowknife.

4   Dennis Patterson served as minister of education, minister of health and social services, and minister of justice, culminating in his service as premier between 1987 and 1991.

"Faked Bad"

1   The hospital records used in this chapter were obtained by my lawyer from the Supreme Court of the Northwest Territories, Yellowknife.

2   This report and the one that follows are contained in Ed Horne's medical records from the Alberta Hospital, October 1985, which my lawyer obtained from the Supreme Court of the Northwest Territories, Yellowknife.

3   John F. Thornton (assistant professor of psychiatry, Faculty of Medicine, University of Toronto, Clarke Institute Team to Baffin Island), letter to Brian Brucer (Crown attorney, Yellowknife), received January 12, 1987. The Thornton report is contained in Ed Horne's medical records, obtained from the Supreme Court of the Northwest Territories.

4   K.R. Van Camp, Ph.D., "A Report to J. L. Handley, Deputy Minister of Education, Government of the Northwest Territories on Child Abuse at Lake Harbour School and Recommended Policy and Action," December 1985, 2. Obtained through an unsealing order at the Nunavut Court of Justice.

5   Van Camp, "A Report to J. L. Handley," 3.

6   Van Camp, "A Report to J. L. Handley," 4.

7   Van Camp, "A Report to J. L. Handley," 1–2.

8   Van Camp, "A Report to J. L. Handley," 16.

Out on Bail

1   Dr. Herbert Pascoe, Alberta Hospital, Discharge Summary, December 9, 1985. Obtained by my lawyer from the Supreme Court of the Northwest Territories, Yellowknife.

2   Joseph L. Handley (deputy minister of education), confidential letter to Bert Rose (superintendent, Baffin Divisional Board of Education, Frobisher Bay), January 20, 1986. Known in the Eastern Arctic among journalists (who never saw it because files related to Horne were sealed) as "The Handley Letter,"

the letter is contained in sealed court documents related to the Ed Horne civil cases at the Nunavut Court of Justice in Iqaluit. Obtained through an unsealing order.

Her Majesty The Queen Vs. Edward Horne

1 Neil Sharkey was chief justice, Nunavut Court of Justice, Iqaluit, until his retirement in April 2024.
2 Jim Bell, interview by author, June 2020.
3 *R. v. Horne*, 1987 SCC 3734 at page 1, [1987] NWTR 168 (NWT SC). Transcript from the Northwest Territories Supreme Court.
4 All quotes from Marshall come from *R. v. Horne*, 1987 SCC 3734 at pages 1–21.
5 *R. v. Horne*, 1987 SCC 3734 at page 2, [1987] NWTR 168 (NWT SC). Transcript from the Northwest Territories Supreme Court.
6 *R. v. Horne*, 1987 SCC 3734 at page 6, [1987] NWTR 168 (NWT SC). Transcript from the Northwest Territories Supreme Court.
7 *R. v. Horne*, 1987 SCC 3734 at page 16, [1987] NWTR 168 (NWT SC). Transcript from the Northwest Territories Supreme Court.
8 *R. v. Horne*, 1987 SCC 3734 at page 16, [1987] NWTR 168 (NWT SC). Transcript from the Northwest Territories Supreme Court.
9 *R. v. Horne*, 1987 SCC 3734 at page 11, [1987] NWTR 168 (NWT SC). Transcript from the Northwest Territories Supreme Court.
10 *R. v. Horne*, 1987 SCC 3734 at page 11, [1987] NWTR 168 (NWT SC). Transcript from the Northwest Territories Supreme Court.
11 *R. v. Horne*, 1987 SCC 3734 at page 11, [1987] NWTR 168 (NWT SC). Transcript from the Northwest Territories Supreme Court.
12 DOEH, Ed Horne, interview by Stuart A. Morris, April 26, 2007, 302.

Prison and Release

1 Ed Horne, interview by the author.

Another Criminal Case

1 Civil Case announcement, Superior Court, General Division, Case No. 500-17-085536-145, *Gazette*, Montreal, Quebec, December 5, 2014. Charges were also mentioned by Ed Horne during DOEH, as told to Robert Dewar, April 23, 2007, 117.
2 Civil Case announcement, Superior Court, General Division, Case No. 500-17-085536-145, *Gazette*, Montreal, Quebec, December 5, 2014. Charges

were also mentioned by Ed Horne during DOEH, as told to Robert Dewar, April 23, 2007, 117.

3   Jim Bell, "Ed Horne's Custody Hearing Delayed," *Nunatsiaq News*, February 4, 2000.

4   *R. v. Horne*, transcript of the sentencing hearing before the Honourable Justice V. Schuler, sitting in Iqaluit, Nunavut, September 5, 6, 7, 2000, filed October 25, 2000, pages 1–170. File obtained from the Supreme Court of the Northwest Territories.

5   James Brydon, *R. v. Horne*, 2000, 101.

6   James Brydon, *R. v. Horne*, 2000, 113.

7   James Brydon, *R. v. Horne*, 2000.

8   James Brydon, *R. v. Horne*, 2000, 80.

9   James Brydon, *R. v. Horne*, 2000, 81.

10   James Brydon, *R. v. Horne*, 2000, 83.

11   James Brydon, *R. v. Horne*, 2000, 80–123.

12   Brydon's statement ignores the fact that the Bible and the hymn book in syllabics long predated Horne's arrival in the Arctic. Horne also told me he never translated any Bible into Inuktitut.

13   Richard Meredith, *R. v. Horne*, 2000, 123–43.

14   Richard Meredith, *R. v. Horne*, 2000, 123–43.

15   *R. v. Horne*, 2000, 147–52.

16   *R. v. Horne*, 2000, 160.

17   *R. v. Horne*, 2000, 156.

18   *R. v. Horne*, 2000, 156.

19   *R. v. Horne*, 2000, 171.

20   Aaron Spitzer, "Sanikiluaq Residents Feel Horne's Punishment Too Light," *Nunatsiaq News*, September 22, 2000. Although I obtained an unsealing order in order to access files relevant to the Ed Horne cases, I have not seen a copy of this petition, and I do not know where it is located.

21   Aaron Spitzer, "Sanikiluaq Residents Feel Horne's Punishment Too Light," *Nunatsiaq News*, September 22, 2000.

22   DOEH, Ed Horne, interview by Geoff Budden, April 27, 2007, 203.

Uncle

1   Frobisher Bay changed its name to Iqaluit in 1987. Lake Harbour changed its name to Kimmirut in 1996. References to these places roughly past those dates use the new names.

Criminal Case #3

1   I contacted Judy Chan in Ottawa. She claimed she did not remember the details of this case. But she acknowledged the terrible impact Horne's crimes had in the North.

2   Transcripts for this case, May 2, 2005; October 15–17, 2007; and January 24–25, 2008, were not available due to the court reporter, Michael Belsito, having destroyed his recordings for these dates, according to the Nunavut Court of Justice, Iqaluit.

3   Honourable Justice R. Kilpatrick, *R. v. Horne*, 2008 NUCJ 6 (CanLII), canlii.ca/t/1vz17.

4   Chris Windeyer, "Former teacher's third trial for sex crimes wraps up in Iqaluit," *Nunatsiaq News*, January 31, 2008.

5   *R. v. Horne*, 2008, 7–8.

6   *R. v. Horne*, 2008, 8.

7   *R. v. Horne*, 2008, 10.

8   Claimant interview with the author, March 2022.

Civil Cases

1   Budden and Associates, 5 Hallett Crescent #4, St. John's, NL A1B 4C4.

2   Jim Bell, "Horne Victims Win $21.5 Million from Territorial Governments," *Nunatsiaq News*, October 18, 2002.

3   Rubino, once an observant Catholic, lost his faith during intense work over sex abuse scandals in the church and eventually retired from law. Denise Lavoie, "Church Sex Scandal Takes Toll on Victims' Lawyers," Associated Press, March 25, 2019.

4   Tungasuvvingat Inuit is an Inuit-specific urban services provider that offers community supports for Inuit of all ages in Ottawa.

5   Acclaimed as premier of the N.W.T. on December 10, 2003, Handley served one term as premier and did not run in the election held on October 1, 2007.

6   Bob Weber, "NWT Premier Defends Tough Stand in Teacher Sex Assault Civil Suit," Canadian Press, September 21, 2006. Jason Unrau, "Victims' Lawyer Offended by Handley," Northern News Services, October 6, 2006.

7   Jason Unrau, "Premier Handley Reprimanded for Sex Abuse Comments," Northern News Services, November 3, 2006.

8   Eric Colbourne was employed by the government of the N.W.T. from August 9, 1971, to December 3, 1999, as principal, supervisor of schools, and regional superintendent.

9 Chris Windeyer, "Horne Sex Abuse Victims Get $15-Million Settlement," *Nunatsiaq News*, January 25, 2011.

10 Chris Windeyer, "Horne Sex Abuse Victims Get $15-Million Settlement," *Nunatsiaq News*, January 25, 2011.

11 There is an Ed Horne–related case currently before the courts. "The Nunavut Court of Appeal has quashed a key ruling in the lawsuit of a group of Ed Horne victims against their former lawyers, as the prolonged and convoluted lawsuit was dealt yet another twist last week. More than 100 victims are suing their former lawyers who represented them ..." Nick Murray, "Nunavut Court of Appeal Deals Another Twist in Lawsuit for Ed Horne Victims," CBC News, April 23, 2020, cbc.ca/news/canada/north /ed-horne-victims-lawsuit-third-party-court-of-appeal-1.5541462.

12 DOEH, Ed Horne, interviewed by Stuart A. Morris, April 26, 2007, 11.

The "Pretendian"

1 Research and Statistics Division, Department of Justice, Canada, "Spotlight on Gladue: Challenges, Experiences, and Possibilities in Canada's Criminal Justice System," Government of Canada, Department of Justice, justice. gc.ca/eng/rp-pr/jr/gladue/gladue.pdf.

2 DOEH, Ed Horne, interview by Geoff Budden, Nunavut Court of Justice, Iqaluit, April 25, 2007, 123.

The Aftermath

1 "Police Wrap Up Investigation in Kuujjuaraapik Murder-Suicide," *Nunatsiaq News*, March 9, 2012.

2 "Police Wrap Up Investigation in Kuujjuaraapik Murder-Suicide," *Nunatsiaq News*, March 9, 2012.

3 Jim Bell, "Ed Horne's Former Sanikiluaq Staff House Goes Up in Smoke," *Nunatsiaq News*, August 23, 2007.

4 Jim Bell, "The Ed Horne Excuse," *Nunatsiaq News*, Editorial, October 15, 2004

5 Jim Bell, "The Ed Horne Excuse," *Nunatsiaq News*, Editorial, October 15, 2004.

6 Ed Horne, "Bowden Institution," unpublished manuscript, undated.

7 DOEH, Ed Horne, interview by Stuart A. Morris, April 26, 2007, 185.

8 DOEH, Stuart Morris and Ed Horne, Nunavut Court of Justice, Iqaluit, 231.

The Man and the Myth

1   I corresponded with Ed Horne through Facebook Messenger and email at first. The only in-person meeting I ever had with Ed Horne took place on June 14, 2022, in Toronto, where I discussed this book and some of the answers he had given me.

Selected Bibliography

Adshead, Gwen, and Eileen Horne. *The Devil You Know: Stories of Human Cruelty and Compassion*. London: Faber & Faber, 2021.

Anonymous. "Flurry of Activity in Inuktitut Publishing." *Ilisarniq: Igalaaq's Education Supplement* (March 1982): 10.

Briggs, Jean L. *Utkuhikhalingmiut Eskimo Emotional Expression*. Ottawa: Northern Science Research Group, Department of Indian Affairs and Northern Development, 1968.

Brody, Hugh. *Landscapes of Silence: From Childhood to the Arctic*. London: Faber & Faber, 2022.

———. *The People's Land*. London: Penguin Books, 1975.

Cloughley, Maurice R. *The Spell of the Midnight Sun*. Victoria, BC: Horsdal & Schubart, 1995.

Eber, Dorothy Harley. *Pitseolak: Pictures Out of My Life*. Montreal/Kingston: McGill-Queen's University Press, 2003.

Elliott, Andrea. *Invisible Child: Poverty, Survival and Hope in an American City*. New York: Random House, 2021.

Emerson, David. *Trauma-Sensitive Yoga in Therapy: Bringing the Body into Treatment*. New York: W.W. Norton, 2015.

Gartner, Richard B. *Betrayed as Boys: Psychodynamic Treatment of Sexually Abused Men*. New York: The Guilford Press, 1999.

———. *Beyond Betrayal: Taking Charge of Your Life After Boyhood Sexual Abuse*. Hoboken, NJ: John Wiley and Sons, 2005.

Grygier, Pat Sandiford. *A Long Way from Home: The Tuberculosis Epidemic Among the Inuit*. Montreal/Kingston, McGill-Queen's University Press, 1994.

Harris, Michael. *Unholy Orders: Tragedy at Mount Cashel*. Toronto: Penguin, 1990.

Herman, Judith. *Trauma and Recovery: The Aftermath of Violence – From Domestic Abuse to Political Terror*. New York: Basic Books, 1997.

Holmstedt, Robert D. *Ruth: A Handbook on the Hebrew Text*. Waco, TX: Baylor University Press, 2010.

Jenkins, G. Cledwyn. *Banished: A Comprehensive Look into the Mind and Soul of the Sex Offender with Sex Offender Case Studies and the Recidivism Challenge*. Irvine, CA: Brown Walker Press, 2020.

Knott, Helen. *In My Own Moccasins: A Memoir of Resilience*. Regina, SK: University of Regina Press, 2019.

MacDonald, John. *The Arctic Sky: Inuit Astronomy, Star Lore, and Legend*. Toronto: Royal Ontario Museum, 1998.

McDonald, Mary Catherine. *Unbroken: The Trauma Response Is Never Wrong: And Other Things You Need to Know to Take Back Your Life*. Boulder, CO: Sounds True, 2023.

McGregor, Heather E. *Inuit Education and Schools in the Eastern Arctic*. Vancouver: UBC Press, 2010.

Mowat, Farley. *The People of the Deer*. Boston: Little, Brown, 1951.

Ootes, Jake. *Umingmak: Stuart Hodgson and the Birth of the Modern Arctic*. New Westminster, BC: Tidewater Press, 2020.

Pryde, Duncan. *Nunaga: Ten Years of Eskimo Life*. New York: Bantam Books, 1973.

Rasing, Willem. *Too Many People: Contact, Disorder, Change in an Inuit Society, 1822–2015*. Iqaluit, NU: Nunavut Arctic College Media, 2017.

Ryan, Leslie Boyd. *Cape Dorset Prints, A Retrospective: Fifty Years of Printmaking at the Kinngait Studios*. San Francisco: Pomegranate, 2007.

Sonkin, Daniel J. *Wounded Boys, Heroic Men*. Stamford, CT: Longmeadow Press, 1992.

Soublière, Marion. *The 1998 Nunavut Handbook: Travelling in Canada's Arctic*. Iqaluit, NU: Nortext Multimedia, 1997.

Thorsteinsson, B. *Teach in Canada's Northland: Handbook for Prospective Teachers*. Ottawa: Education Division, Northern Administration Branch, Department of Northern Affairs and National Resources, 1963.

Winnipeg Art Gallery. *Belcher Islands/Sanikiluaq*. Winnipeg, MB: Winnipeg Art Gallery, 1981.

Zabin, Amy. *Conversations with a Pedophile: In the Interest of Our Children*. Fort Lee, NJ: Barricade Books, 2003.

Index

About the Author

Photo by Billy Akavak

Kathleen Lippa is a Canadian journalist. Born to a Canadian mother and Italian father in Toronto, Kathleen grew up in St. John's, Newfoundland, and trained as a professional dancer at the Quinte Ballet School in Belleville, Ontario, and the School of Toronto Dance Theatre before embarking on a career in journalism.

She has been a reporter and copy editor at newspapers across Canada. For Northern News Services, after a short stint in Yellowknife, Kathleen served as bureau chief for *Nunavut News/North* in Iqaluit.

After spending many years in the Arctic, Kathleen now lives with her husband in Ottawa and St. John's.